Finishes

Finishes

Yvonne Dean *BA Hons (Newc), BA (Open), RIBA*

Mitchell London

© Yvonne Dean 1989
First published 1971
Second edition 1979
Reprinted 1987
Third edition 1989

Typeset by
Latimer Trend & Company Ltd, Plymouth
and printed in Great Britain by
The Bath Press, Bath
Published by The Mitchell Publishing Company Limited
an imprint of B T Batsford Limited
4 Fitzhardinge Street, London W1H 0AH

A CIP catalogue record for this book is
available from the British Library

ISBN 0 7134 5675 2

Contents

Disclaimers

All information in this book is given in good faith and is up to date at the time of going to press particularly with regard to British Standards quoted. The readers and users of this material must satisfy themselves that the information given is accurate and reasonable for its purpose in terms of current building practice. This is due to the diagnostic nature of the subject and the changing nature of materials usage.

1.01 *Peuterey Ridge and Aiguille Noir. Mont Blanc, September 1981* (photographer: Steve Keates). *The scale of exposure that our buildings have to cope with is easily forgotten, and our climatic extremes are often peaks in an undulating chart of annual variations. If we catered for the worst possible conditions, our buildings would be better equipped for survival*

Acknowledgment

The author and publishers thank all those who have helped in the preparation of this book.

The author gives special thanks to the following: Dr Ian Boustead of the Open University and to Dr Barry Pepper of Tottenham College of Technology for reading the book and making valuable comments on the content; to Rosemary Handyside who acted for a short time as my research assistant on some developmental areas of the book;

on illustrations:

to Kim Davies and Mark Edwards, and the Media Services Centre of the Polytechnic of North London for the help and preparation of photographic material: figures 2.18–2.21, 2.26, 2.33, 3.04, 3.05, 3.12, 3.16, 3.19, 3.39–3.41, 3.43, and 5.01;

to Michael Marlowe for the reproduction of his photographic material: 2.29, 3.22–3.25, and 3.35–3.36;

to Steve Keates for photographs 1.01 and 6.01 and for the conversion of all slide material to black and white photographic art work;

to Julia Dwyer for her general support and help in the preparation of figures 2.02–2.07, 2.09, 2.10, 2.22–2.24, 2.27, 3.01–3.03, 3.38, 4.01, 4.03, and 4.05; (all other photographs and drawings are by the author;)

to Derek Osbourn RIBA, Head of the Department of Environmental Design at the Polytechnic of North London for his encouragement in tackling this book, to Thelma Nye at Batsford for all her editorial guidance and enthusiasm and to Alan Everett for the retention of his comprehensive section on floorings. Lastly I acknowledge the interest and reactions given by students at PNL to my lectures which have helped shape the presentation of the text.

Y D

London 1989

British Standards
British Standards are on sale to personal callers at
  195 Pentonville Road, London N1
  Hampden House, 61 Green Street, London W1
  3 York Street, Manchester M2
Orders by post to the
  BSI Sales Department, Linford Wood,
  Milton Keynes MK14 6LE

ASTM Standards
The American Society for Testing and Materials (ASTM) standards is also mentioned in this book. Further information can be obtained direct from
  1916 Race Street, Philadelphia, Pennsylvania 19103, USA

1 GENERAL NOTES

Although this volume is concerned with 'Finishes' as a subject, a title such as The Visible Appearance of the Building Fabric' might be more appropriate, or even 'The External skin and its Behavioural Properties and Characteristics'. The use of finishes is often regarded as a separate and final application to the fabric of the building, sometimes even the last part of the building to be specified. This may mean finishes are subject to compromise in their quality by late cost control exercises. However, finishes represent the true boundary of a building, the face for immediate contact and, more critically, should be seen as the first line of defence for protection of the fundamental fabric of the building. Some finishing elements are a good deal more substantial than others, and often are part of the solid outer external skin, and distinct from further applied coverings or coatings.

It is still appropriate and convenient to think of thick and thin finishes or, to be more exact, macro and micro finishes. *Micro finishes* refer to paints, films, and other surface finishes whose substance and thickness is difficult or impossible to determine or measure accurately with the naked eye. The basic units used are $1 \, m \times 10^{-6}$ and are referred to as microns. *Macro finishes* are large-scale materials that can be seen with the naked eye and a reasonable estimation can be given of their chief characteristics and dimensions, which in the building industry will be units of millimetres and metres. Macro finishes still have a detailed microstructure that determines their properties and behaviour.

Both categories of finish are used externally and internally and there are different environments for both categories. In fact, the range of temperatures and conditions we expect materials not only to survive in, but also in which to remain stable, is extraordinary, even in the British Isles, it is recognised that human beings cannot survive for long if totally exposed.

We also rely to a great extent on our own observational experience to judge conditions and the appropriate choice of materials, but our view as designers and architects, contractors and practitioners is limited.

The internal movements of molton magma in the upper mantle, together with the shifting of tectonic plates, contribute to distort the thin outer skin of continental and oceanic crust into mountains, volcanoes and other features. The earth under the continual action of rain and wind-borne dust, would become smooth and polished like a well worn pebble on a beach, were it not for this scale of internal disruption that continually changes the profile of the crust.

Our building fabric also is exposed continually to a cyclical action of wind, rain, cold and heat which in the long term erodes naturally all physical features on earth. Chemistry, too, can rough up an outer surface by encouraging the deterioration of materials.

Deterioration, however, is an inaccurate description of a process whereby materials alter to an extent where they are chemically stable in our atmosphere and often, in a state described in thermodynamics, as one of 'low free energy'. This is not good news for complex man-made products which often have such sophisticated structures that their very existence depends on a too easily altered energy balance.

As building professionals, using a technology that is often inappropriate to deal with the very real and large-scale events that are commonplace in our environment, we construct without consideration for the effects of weather, climatic change, sunshine, or temperature. We have a large body of knowledge in physics, earth sciences, and chemistry but these disciplines have become so remote and so specialised, that the experience gained in these fields is often not easily translatable and hence not easily transferable as an education asset, therefore not often used in the low technology area of building. We also use high technology solutions to help us out of awkward situations where our building technology is seen to be inadequate or failing. In fact we are really guilty of seeking solutions that may be sophisticated in terms of their complexity, and yet are an abuse of some fundamental principles in science. This can hasten decay in buildings and also use up primary resources, not only in terms of the raw materials that are extracted and refined for construction and repair, but also in terms of the energy used in their processing and treatment to keep them in a stable state.

1.01 THE IMPORTANCE OF SPECIFICATION

The specification of finishes is vital to the compatibility, durability and appropriate use of a given material. It is also a strategy for minimising the unacceptable failure in the life or performance of a finishing material.

Most materials that we use for applied finishes to the surface of buildings fall into two major categories in materials science, ie polymers and ceramics. If the nature of these materials is understood then their correct application and use will be easier to specify. Consequently this book sets out finishes as a bulk grouping of materials into categories with similar characteristics and as normally defined by the discipline of materials science. It is unreasonable to suppose that designers can memorise all kinds of different products individually with varying properties. If there is an understanding of polymeric materials and how they behave, that knowledge will assist in the specification and use of finishes such as paint, flooring compounds, roofing compounds, and adhesives. Similarly, an understanding of the overall properties of ceramic materials, and how they fail, helps in determining their use and the design of fixings, and careful supervision in installation.

Historically, building textbooks in this subject area often tended to be the only available source of reference. They dealt with the history, practice and usage of materials and their finishes. These textbooks, usually forming part of a three or four volume set, were able to contain the total state of the art in building. They were also prescriptive, ie they were able to detail exact materials in use at the time with their limited and proven application.

In the latter part of the twentieth century we have seen a great increase in terms of the materials and products available. The system of reference to all these products is best carried out by using the material that is produced and updated annually by the *Architectural Press, Barbour Microfile, RIBA Publications Ltd*, and more recently the *Building Technical File*. These are core sources and should always act as a starting point for investigation. The *Building Centre* can be used for queries on products, the *Building Research Establishment* for advice and diagnosis on building failures and now the *Design Centre* with its new Materials Centre, for innovation in materials technology. To ensure that there are no omissions in making a specification, the *National Building Specification* provides a framework for the extensive documentation now required.

The value of textbooks today is to ensure that a broad background of principles is presented which have a scientific basis. With an understanding of materials and the mechanics of likely deterioration, a diagnostic attitude to the use of materials can be developed. This should lead to a greater sensitivity in the specification of finishes and their uses.

1.02 A STRATEGY FOR SPECIFICATION

At some point every designer, architect or contractor deals with the specification of materials. Architects and designers have very specific responsibilities under the terms of their contractual arrangements with clients which is further reinforced in standard building contracts. This responsibility cannot be delegated without agreement, and designers must be in control of the situation. It is the contractors or subcontractors responsibility to carry out the works as specified. (Clauses of current contracts in use should be very carefully checked.)

Too often a document is written based on materials compiled for a previous project. Information is repeated without checking at source, or information is copied (such as numbers for British Standards) without confirming their reference or validity, or even whether they are still available and not superseded. Instead of attempting to find a master document to imitate, it is far more useful to develop a very clear strategy about specification and to apply a simple set of parameters to each material/component, building up a base of information. Existing specifications can then be used as checklists but care should be taken. No one specification will be sufficiently exhaustive to deal with every aspect of a particular building. The quotation of a British Standard may also be too broad for a specific requirement, and even the National Building Specification, if followed slavishly, may still need clarification on particular items. If the following three parameters are followed for every component in a building, a reasonable specification can be built.

1   The nature and composition of a material/component should be specified by reference to available and current British, or other recognised standards and/or Agrément Certificates, and in conjunction with manufacturers' literature if applicable.

2   The method of fixing or placing these materials in position should be specified and the use of codes of practice and their relevant parts clearly outlined.

3   The method of protection/finish to the materials should be stated and specified together with their fixings. (This check may reveal that fixings should not have an applied finish but the nature of their alloys needs more careful specification.)

It requires being organised so as the design/decision making is carried out, information is kept perhaps in a loose-leaf binder or entered onto disc on a micro. The information gathered should be concise and simply stated. There is no need for phrasing material in a dogmatic way which has a legalistic 'ring' about it, just precision and clarity about everything to be used. If this is done systematically it will form the basis of a good specification document and the source of information for Bills of Quantities. Errors, and later failures in building, are often associated with poor specification. Often the process of specifying materials is very much a last activity in the design process. In order to expedite documentation at the end of a project, there is a period of fast decision making which ultimately commit designer and contractor to unsound detailing and predictable repercussions. A good specification is inseparable from the intentions of the original designer, backed up by technologically sound information.

1.03 HOW TO USE THIS BOOK

This book is designed to be more than a reference volume. If understanding is needed on a particular finishing material, it should first of all be identified as being either a *polymeric, ceramic, metallic* or *composite material*. The general introduction in the relevant section should be read first, as a means of understanding the fundamental behaviour of the material. Reference can then be made to individual applications of that material. There are overlaps between these areas.

To use this book as a basic text for understanding the subject area, again all the introductory sections should be read first to give a broad base for understanding. The glossary sections are expansive explanations of terms used in the relevant sections and should be treated as an information dictionary.

For those with particular needs on the precise specifi-cation of materials, direction is given to source material such as British Standards and other specification documents.

Standards are often quoted by number as being relevant without being scrutinised first by the specifier. If they were used as recognised texts of reference and were all referred to in office libraries, practitioners would find that very clear directives and advice is given in these documents but which possibly conflicts with their own clauses and therefore should be co-ordinated with their specification.

Often the names and numbers of particular standards are quoted in their entirety by practioners when only a small section is relevant.

There are British Standards and Codes of Practice updated versions of which should be on the shelves of offices for constant reference. Not only is it confusing to quote to contractors entire standards which are unnecessary and require a search for the right piece of information, but also it is more likely that the guidance given will be ignored. This misuse of reference material will also imply a lack of knowledge of the exact standard on the part of the specifier.

However, even the reference to a British Standard does not cover a specifier from certain reponsibilities. A phrase often quoted in British Standards is:

'Compliance with a British Standard does not of itself confer immunity from legal obligations.'

Photographs

All the photographs are selected to illustrate particular points. A dot, the original of which has a constant 8 mm diameter, is shown on the detail photographs to give an idea of scale.

2 POLYMERIC MATERIALS

2.01 INTRODUCTION

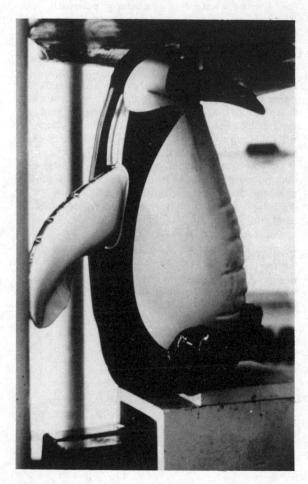

2.01 *Inflatable penguin in an Avery-Dennison testing machine. Given this stressful situation most designers would accurately predict the outcome of loading to the limit. The stresses imposed on ordinary paint films and polymeric materials may not be visually obvious, but with some additional basic knowledge designers can be aware of, and cater for, equally stressful conditions*

Polymers are a more exact description for the commonly understood field of materials referred to as *plastics*. Plastics are really a descriptive term, polymers have a definition meaning *many mers*, where one mer[1] (or monomer) would be an individual molecule, so a polymer is a joining together of many individual molecules and becomes a chain of small units with, overall, a far greater molecular mass. If some basic knowledge can be grasped of the characteristics of these long chained molecules, it can help us to understand how paints and other surface films can behave, or at the very least give us a healthy respect for their properties and usage. Many of the simpler polymers are named by adding the prefix 'poly' to the monomer.

POLYMERISATION

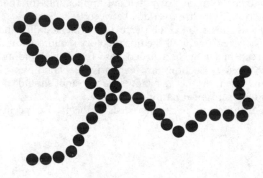

2.02 *A polymer chain. The circles represent repeating monomer units (molecules), not individual atoms*

The term *polymerisation* refers to the process by which the individual monomers can combine, and exist in a state of lower free energy. This can be engineered by bringing together compounds which may freely combine depending on conditions that are thermodynamically favourable, ie where, if the right conditions prevail, this will happen spontaneously. Often there has to be an input of energy which can be in the form of directly applied heat, ultra-violet light, exothermic reactions from other local chemical reactions or (and

[1]'Mer' is from the Greek meaning measure.

12

more rarely) from high energy bombardment by electrons or gamma-rays. Sometimes we can see this polymerisation process happening in ordinary domestic situations, eg perfume left in a bottle under the action of ultra-violet light can change from its clear liquid form to a sticky mass, from individual mers of *terpen* into a resinous mass of polymers known as *polyterpene*.

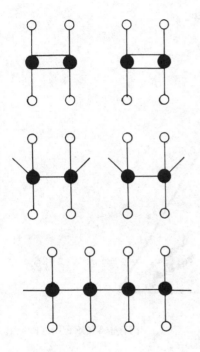

2.03 *Ethylene. An ethylene molecule with the carbon double bonds broken by an input of energy, then spontaneously linking with another altered ethylene monomer to form a polymer chain*

EXAMPLE

Ethylene is the basic building block for the polymer polyethylene, more commonly known as polythene. At the heart of the ethylene molecule is a double carbon bond which can be opened if sufficient energy is used. Chemical energy is used for this polymerisation process through the medium of a catalyst, commonly chromium oxide or peroxides which decompose quickly and attack adjacent molecules. Decomposition products are highly reactive entities known as free radicals which actively seek combination with adjacent material to attain a stable configuration. They can have the effect of altering the double bond of carbon atoms allowing

one bond to become open ended and receptive to attachment to adjacent molecules.

The length of a polymer chain can vary according to how the chain terminates. There are several ways this can be achieved or artificially engineered. The manipulation of the chemistry at this level is known as *polymer architecture* as the sense of planning and also control of these large chemical compounds has to be so exact. The length of chain is important as all sorts of behavioural properties are altered whether mechanical or chemical, affecting how the material deteriorates over time. This is particularly important with regard to the processing of synthetic rubbers, where excessive chain length can make the material highly viscous, therefore over-stiff and difficult to process, sometimes giving the finished product a characteristic roughness, which may not be desirable.

There are three fundamental categories of polymers, *thermoplastics*, *thermosets* and *elastomers*. It is important to grasp the chief characteristics of these polymers as often finishes combine polymers with characteristics across these groups giving very different properties and hence applications.

See figure 2.04 overleaf.

THERMOPLASTICS

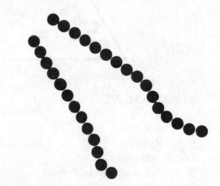

2.05 *Thermoplastics. Linear individual chains*

Thermoplastics are long chained polymers which are linear in their character but with side branches. They may have weak van der Waals' bonding (attractive forces between crystals or molecules dependent on electronic configuration) or hydrogen bonding (electrostatic link between hydrogen atoms in comparable liquid substances) between the individual polymer chains. Both forms of bonding can be further weakened

13

THERMOPLASTICS (Flexible)

Polystyrene
Polyethylene
Polypropylene
Polyvinyl chloride
Acrylics
Polyamide (Nylon)
Polycarbonate
Polymethylmethacrylate

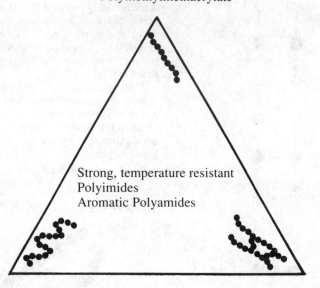

Strong, temperature resistant
Polyimides
Aromatic Polyamides

ELASTOMERS (Extensible)

Natural Rubber
Butyl Rubber
Polybutadiene
Styrene/Butadiene rubbers
Fluoro Silicone rubber
Silicone elastomer

THERMOSETS (Rigid)

Polyesters
Epoxys
Phenol Formaldehyde
Melamine Formaldehyde
Polyurethanes
Alkyds

2.04 *Common polymers and their categories*

by heating or by induced stress. Thermoplastics may be brittle (eg polystyrene) or flexible and tough (eg polyethylene), depending on the extent of molecular mobility which in turn depends upon backbone struc-ture. The flexible thermoplastics can become soft with heating, or harder after cooling. They can be repeatedly melted by heat unlike thermosets which once moulded (set) cannot subsequently be melted.

THERMOSETS

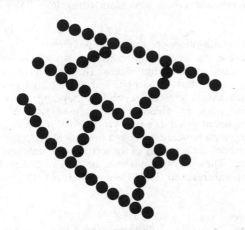

2.06 *Thermosets. Crosslinked polymers*

This group of polymers has complex structures which bond covalently (by sharing electrons) to adjacent chains, often called *crosslinking*. This is the strongest form of chemical bonding and so thermosets are rigid and resistant to deformation, whether through applied mechanical stress or heating. If the crosslinking becomes excessive (and this is where the reaction from monomer to polymer must be carefully controlled) the polymer can become embrittled and more liable to fracture. This group is also the most resistant to organic solvents.

ELASTOMERS

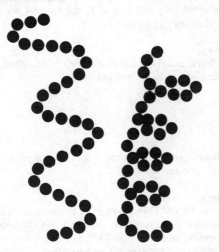

2.07 *Elastomers. Coiled chains. These are in a state of continual movement with rotation around the carbon backbone*

The chief characteristic of this group is that the polymer chains are extendable. After any imposed stress there is an element of mechanical recovery when the stress is released. Often the physical nature of these chains is such that they are recognisable as coiled chains due to the rotating arrangement of the bonds. The coiled nature of elastomeric molecules gives potential for great extension if stress is applied. The ability of the molecules to retract so dramatically after the release of stress is from an ability to recover and re-orientate themselves to their original stable position, exhibiting a form of plastic memory. This can only happen when the material is above T_g (glass transition temperature). Elastomers can be thermoplastic or thermosets, but if we want a more rigid but 'rubbery' material, a crosslinked and hence thermoset elastomer would be sought. Ordinary car tyres fall into this category and the crosslinking of rubber by sulphur is known as *vulcanisation*, and prevents viscous flow.

POLYMERS AND PAINTS

The polymers we use generally arrive in a liquid state and after application, especially in surface coatings, we would expect them to harden. We also expect this hardening mechanism to be permanent at ambient temperatures but the degree of solidity needed is dependent on the conditions of use, for example we may require the film to retain sufficient flexibility to move with the substrate. This is particularly true for timber substrates which may vary by as much as 4% extension over one season. In certain situations a film that has achieved too great a degree of hardness will be unable to flex, be less likely to resist stress, become brittle and fracture. The expectations in the performance of paint films is then reliant on the chemistry of polymers and is also temperature dependent.

2.02 GLOSSARY

Alkyds
These are a class of branched chain polyesters and form an insoluble thermosetting polymer film, formed by condensation polymerisation.

Acrylic
The full name is polymethylmethacrylate (PMMA) and is a thermoplastic. (In a glassy sheet form it is known as perspex.)

15

Amino resins
(Urea-formaldehyde, melamine formaldehyde)
These resins give good hard glossy films with good adhesion to metals. As they are insoluble in common solvents their vehicles have to be made from butanol and the higher alcohols for successful dilution. They can be converted to crosslinked thermosets either by adding acids or by being exposed to high temperatures (110–170°C). They are often combined with alkyds to improve water resistance.

Condensation polymerisation
The reaction of compounds to form long chain molecules (polymers) usually in the elimination of by-products such as water.

Co-polymers
Polymers formed from more than one individual monomer, ie two or more 'mers', can be mixed in one polymer chain giving different properties from individual polymers.

Crystalline polymers
Polymers containing localised regions in which the polymer chains are arranged regularly to give some type of order.

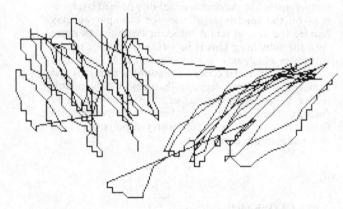

2.08 *Crystalline polymers. When individual chains of polymer align and form some order, they are said to be 'crystalline'*

Emulsion
The suspension of one liquid within another. As 'emulsion paints' carry suspended solids, ie pigment resins in a liquid medium, they may be more correctly termed scientifically as a 'latex', classified as a milky fluid with substances in suspension.

Epoxy resins
An epoxide group (epichlorhydrin) $R' - CH - CH_2$

$$\underset{O}{\diagdown \diagup}$$

reacts with phenol to form the epoxy resin.

These are very strong resins and can adhere well to many surfaces including metals. They show great stability as they start to harden, and exhibit high polarity which assists in local secondary bonding. This is a linear polymer which is always used with another component to act as a catalyst or crosslinking agent to complete a typical crosslinked thermoset structure. One drawback is that many of the secondary agents used are toxic. These compounds can be cured at very high temperatures (180–200°C) in conjuncture with phenolic resins.

Esters
These are compounds formed by a reaction of fatty acids (with R.CO.OH) components which react with alcohols. They help to crosslink polymer molecules (polyesters) when they solidify and hence fall into the category of thermosets.

Gel
The suspension of a solid within a liquid (often behaving more like a solid).

Glass transition temperature
Often expressed as T_g is the temperature at which a material changes its phase from liquid to solid. This is the definition of a glass. Most paint films do not attain glass-like qualities but stay in a phase between liquid and solid. If they fall below T_g they could become so brittle that they can crack.

Ketones
These have a carbonyl group $- CO -$ attached to two hydrocarbon radicals written as:

$$R' - \underset{\underset{O}{\|}}{C} - R'$$

Ketones are fairly reactive. The simplest one is acetone (propanone).

Lacquers
From the ASTM D16 glossary of paint terms 'a coating composition that is based on synthetic thermoplastic film forming material dissolved in organic solvent that dries primarily by solvent evaporation', (a non-convertible coating). Typical lacquers include those based on nitrocellulose, other cellulose derivatives, vinyl

resins, and acrylic resins. These films can deteriorate in the presence of household chemicals and surprisingly, of human perspiration. One major problem is that plasticisers can migrate from vinyl fabrics into lacquer films causing softening.

Micron
A unit of measurement. A millionth of a metre, ie 1×10^{-6}m. There are 1000 microns in a millimetre. Paint films are commonly of the order of being hundreds of microns in thickness, ie 1×10^{-4}m.

Microporous
This is a popular term given to some paint films today that have been engineered to give greater permeability. All materials, including paint films are able to absorb gaseous phases and to some extent liquid phases. The term originally related to fabric designed to keep out liquid phase water in its gas phase. The correct terminology for the passage of molecules is *the rate of diffusion* of materials. Pore size can be engineered but care should be taken to ensure that films have the real properties required for the situation, ie 10^{-10}m.

There are tests for determining the permeability of films, chiefly by measuring physically the transfer of water through a sealed container as in ASTM D1653 (1985). They state 'water vapour transmission rate is not necessarily a linear function of temperature and relative humidity.' ie there is not a proportional relationship between film thickness and its effectiveness.

Oils
Oils are neutral liquids (ie neither acid nor alkaline on the pH scale) and come in three classes:

1   *Fatty oils* or *fixed oils* are organic compounds from animal or vegetable sources and comprise polyglycerides or esters of fatty acids.

2   *Mineral oils* (hydrocarbons with a higher molecular weight) from petroleum and coal sources.

3   *Essential oils* which are volatile hydrocarbons, having characteristic odours and are extracted from plants.

Paints, especially traditional ones are often quoted as having a particular *oil-length*, and this relates to resin–oil ratios as below:

Resin/oil ratio	Terminology for varnish/paint
1:0.5 − 1:2	Short oil
1:2 − 1:3	Medium oil
1:4 − 1:5	Long oil

Paint
A finished coating to a material that consists of the suspension of particles in a liquid phase that subsequently hardens to form a solid film.

Plasticisers
These work by depressing the glass transition temperatures of polymers, weakening the physical bonds between individual polymer chains, making them softer at ambient temperatures and inducing a greater tendency to flow (lower viscosity). They can give polymers a higher permeability. They are not ordinary solvents (which would evaporate) although they are dissolved in the polymeric material. They can also make the polymer less durable in the long term.

Polyurethanes
These are hydroxy terminated saturated polyesters cured by polyisocyanates to produce urethane coatings. Isocyanates have high vapour pressure characteristics and can affect lungs giving asthmatic/bronchial symptoms. They form hard films in a short time with crosslinked structures characteristic of thermosets. They can be degraded by silicones which destroy adhesion by affecting surface wetting characteristics.

Resin
This is used today when describing a synthetic plastic material but more generally embraces highly polymerised acids from natural sources, and the initial compounds of polymeric materials before hard curing.

Saponification
The formation of a soap from the combination of a fat or oil with an alkali.

Shellac
This substance is made from the secretions of tiny insects (*Laccifer lacca*) which eventually cover them in a hard resinous substance making them almost twiglike. They are collected, ground down, melted and compressed into sheets. It takes 150,000 creatures to make 550 grams of shellac and this enormous wastage probably inspired Leo Bakeland to find a synthetic substitute (Bakelite the first thermoset).

Thixotropy
A substance is thixotropic when it is reduced in body and volume after the application of stress. It requires a shearing force to break down the intermolecular structure to make it flow like a liquid. This is the characteristic of paint spread from the tin without dripping. If the shearing force is removed, the paint will return to being a thixotrophic gel.

Toughness

This is a term used by the materials scientist with a specific meaning: the ability of a material to resist the propagation of crack formation, and the opposite of being brittle.

Varnishes

These clear finishes, sometimes called *lacquers*, have the same composition as paint films but lack the pigmentation. As they do not have extenders and pigments they are pure forms of normal vehicles and so will harden faster and be more highly viscous which can be a problem in application. ASTM D154 (1985): 'most varnishes are predominantly yellow but the colour of the liquid varnish is only a preliminary indicator of the dried varnish film. The initial colour may bleach or darken depending on the conditions of exposure'. The viscosity of the liquid is important to allow for satisfactory brush application. As these films harden by oxidative polymerisation a skin may form on top of the liquid in a can which is then insoluble in the rest of the liquid.

Vinyls

This term represents the simplest structure that can be obtained in a polymer chain, from monomers containing $C = C$. They can be polymerised to yield macro-molecules to a carbon backbone. A basic monomer building block ie ethylene, $CH_2 = CH_2$ would have one of the ethylene hydrogens replaced with either another atom or group. Replacement is as follows:

Cl – Vinyl chloride
F – Vinyl fluoride
C_6H_6 – Vinyl benzene or styrene
$OOC.CH_3$ – Vinyl acetate
$COOHCH_3$ – Methylmethacrylate

Vinyl is derived from the latin *vine* indicating both sides of a branch, which in this case would be the carbon backbone when the individual monomers are polymerised. Vinyl is too often used loosely as a term for sheeting, although it would, by its nature, be an indicator of a thermoplastic and so would be likely to have flexural properties.

Viscosity

This is the resistance to flow possessed by a liquid. Paint films when set should be highly viscous otherwise they will be moving. Ordinary glass (sodium silicate) is highly viscous but over time can be seen to 'creep'. If a paint film has too low a viscosity it will 'run' after hardening and be seen as defective. On hardening, paint films increase in viscosity, ultimately forming a solid film.

2.03 ADHESION

Introduction

Adhesion is an area of materials technology which has previously been left out of formal building textbooks, partly due to the comparatively recent development of the subject as a major discipline in its own right. Originally the technology of adhesion related to the correct positioning of materials so that they would not be displaced by weak forces. In timber many adhesives were used to position joints firmly although they owed their mechanical strength to the physical lapping and securing of one piece of timber to another. In the twentieth century glues have been used as integral parts of a jointing system and bring materials into the realms of **composite** technology where there is a reliance on their combined performance.

Glues have developed to a point where the adhesion strength can be as strong or now even stronger than the materials to be adhered. The mechanics of adhesion can also be calculated but require a specialised knowledge to ensure that materials to be jointed are correctly prepared and are compatible with the jointing methods used.

The nature of adhesion must now be looked at as being a result of several factors to understand how it works as a phenomenon. One of the prime concepts to explore is the erroneous notion of 'stickiness' which is not specific enough for understanding the subject. In taking the nature of adhesion as a separate topic there are mechanisms for adhesion that are just as applicable to paint technology, and also the fixing of larger scale materials such as rendering or tiles. For convenience in this volume adhesion will be regarded in two parts, relating to *organic* materials such as adhesives that are polymeric but used for jointing a wide range of materials, and *inorganic*, relating to the fixing of ceramic materials. In this section we can regard the following parameters as being essential for adhesion to take place.

FACTORS ENABLING ADHESION TO TAKE PLACE

1 Mechanical

For good mechanical adhesion, ie for one material to resist physically being pulled out by another, a surface topography that can give a dovetailing effect is ideal.

18

This profiled detail is known as *undercutting* and to be successful must be at least five degrees. In reality undercutting in surfaces rarely occurs and although the surface topography may be rough, its appearance is more likely to resemble a miniature forest landscape with a pyramidal profile that is 'overcut'.

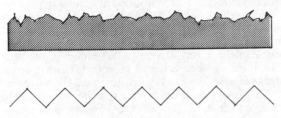

2.09(a) *Surfaces with a pyramidal profile that are 'overcut'*

Although this surface landscape is then obviously not ideal, the depth of surface roughness becomes more important and creates a more porous surface that can assist in giving greater powers of penetration for the adhesive medium. Surface roughness may not necessarily be needed and good adhesion can be obtained on perfectly smooth surfaces if other factors are adequate.

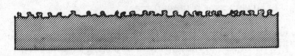

2.09(b) *Idealised topography of cold metal without surface finishing. The crystal structure gives a degree of undercutting*

2 Diffusion

In any polymeric material never underestimate the continual movement of molecules which varies to a greater or lesser degree. The notion of *migration* is becoming better understood, particularly from adhesive or sealing compounds into other materials. For example, after 100 hours, molecular segments of a polyisobutylene material travelled from one sheet to another a distance of 10 microns (A J Kinloch, *Adhesion and Adhesives* Chapman and Hall 1987). This is a small distance but in adhesion terms, if one material can diffuse even a distance of 1–2 nanometres (10^{-9}) there could be a theoretical increase by of between five to nine times in the strength of adhesion. With diffusion there can also be a more direct interaction between long chain molecules and they can 'entangle' giving a

physical meshing of material on a very small scale. This process can be accelerated by the use of liquids that are called *solvent welders*. All these compounds are really doing is accelerating the rate of diffusion of one material into another.

3 Electrical

There can be great powers of attraction from electrostatic forces which come from electron transfer. Adhesive and substrate can have very different structures which give different electronic configurations, and hence charge which can increase attraction if one becomes more positive, and the other more negative may help in initial adhesion, but not contribute to overall strength.

4 Adsorption

Genuine adsorption is different from diffusion and is the most important mechanism for adhesion. It relies on intermolecular bonding. The most common form of bonding is due to van der Waals' forces, but these are still weak **secondary bonds**. Ideally **primary bonding** should take place between the surfaces and these would cover the normal range of chemically strong bonds which include, *covalent*, *ionic* and *metallic* chemical bonding. As these are the range of basic bonds that form the internal atomic structure to materials, it follows that the adhesive used must then have a strength comparable to, or greater than, the material to be joined.

SURFACE WETTING

Apart from the adhesion mechanisms described above there are other important characteristics that the adhesive must have before any adhesion can take place. These relate to the characteristics of the viscosity of the adhesive and its ability to 'wet' the surface adequately.

Parameters for surface wetting characteristics and surface conditions

1 A liquid used for adhesion must have a *low contact angle* with the surface of the substrate. The closer a liquid drop gets to being spherical means that the contact with the surface is tangential and gives a high contact angle. This principle is used to produce surfaces that are deliberately only slightly 'sticky', and a good example is the peel off strips on message pads which have a surface that shows miniature spheroids with a limited contact.

See figure 2.10 overleaf.

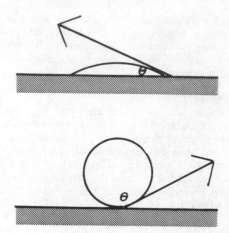

2.10 *Adhesion and surface wetting. Good adhesion requires good surface wetting characteristics achieved by a low contact angle (theta). A high contact angle will give low adhesion and peel off characteristics as exploited in re-usable spray mount or yellow message stickers*

2   The liquid used for adhesion must have a *low contact angle* for *surface wetting* to take place. This means that the liquid should have a greater ability to flow which may mean that polymeric compounds used should have a low molecular weight.

3   All *air must be eliminated* completely from the contact surfaces to be joined. There is a direct relationship between porosity and strength. Sometimes vacuum methods are used to eliminate all air from the material. In an experiment measuring the aluminium/ epoxy joints, the increase in strength was approximately 30%. (Bascom and Cottington.[1])

4   The *cleanliness of surfaces* to be joined is critical. Impurities can absorb water vapour and contaminants can affect surface spreading and interfacial contact.

Surface tension characteristics and surface wetting
There are forces present in an adhesive situation which are calculable and which result from the movement of molecules within the adhesive film. One of the problems in fully understanding these films is that often the adhesive mechanism is a dynamic one, and various molecules are in motion. A liquid that appears to have a surface 'skin' has the molecules in the outer layer under tension. Molecules are displaced from the outer

[1] Bascom, W D and Cottington, R L, 'Adhesion' (4) p. 193, 1942.

layers, being attracted to the body of the liquid. This rate of movement normally slows down as full adhesion develops. The actual rate of movement is partly due to the power of attraction by molecules within the body of the materials to the surface layer. This force of attraction is due to van der Waals' forces, and the force of attraction is sufficient to displace molecules to the side, and as well as surface tension this movement will give *surface free energy*. As molecules are displaced and travel a discrete distance they do work and work can be calculable in terms of energy. Whenever phenomena like these can be evaluated in energy terms **thermodynamic equations** can be used to model the situation.

Thermodynamics can explain when materials start to change their state. They change from one **state** or one **phase** to another, ie from liquid to solid to gaseous. Although adhesion requires surface wetting to take place, surface wetting also depends on the state of the surface free energy values of these different phase states. For spontaneous wetting to occur, there must be a reduction in surface free energy. This is more likely to happen with a lower surface tension as the cohesive forces will then be less strong. Conversely it is more difficult to wet a surface if there are high cohesive forces as the greater the surface tension. Wetting behaviour is a balance between these forces.

As the condition of the surface is critical for surface wetting to take place, there is an advantage for surface pre-treatment of the substrate to be carried out, involving the use of material that is then carrying out a similar function to use of primers in paint coatings. The function of these primers is to modify the surface of the substrate and to:

1   remove weak boundary layers, ie oil and grease or even plasticisers which might have migrated to the surface and become contaminants;

2   maximise molecular contact by increasing the surface free energy;

3   introduce strong primary bonds. It may be possible to introduce a primary layer that has dual compatibility with two or three materials, ie adhesive and substrates, whereas the adhesive might have an optimum strength with only one material, ie the primer;

Opposite
2.11, 2.12 and 2.13 *Embrittlement of vinyl (thermoplastic) tiling. The plasticiser migrates into the flooring, keeping it 'sticky' years after the initial laying. Figure 2.09 shows the high reflectance from the still 'wet' surface, figure 2.10 shows the pattern of embrittlement and 2.11 indicates the edge nature of the brittle cracking, with crack diversion around particulate material*

2.11

2.13

◄ **2.12**

4 generate and change the nature of the surface topography. This could mean the controlled erosion of the surface to create a deeper topography, greater porosity and hence greater depth of penetration;

5 assist in hardening (possibly by initiating a reaction with the atmosphere that provides a more stable coating, inhibiting migration of compounds from the substrate);

6 protect the substrate prior to bonding.

Although the knowledge needed for predicting accurately adhesive behaviour is far beyond that required by a practising architect or designer, it is important that an appreciation of the complexity of the subject is grasped, so that careful and informed decisions can be made on all materials and components that require a bonding specification.

Some concepts of the theory are difficult to grasp but made easier by the following examples.

FLOORING CASE STUDY

Thermoplastic tiles had been laid directly on boarding using an unknown adhesive. In taking up the flooring it was noticed that the tile material was in fact very brittle and fractured easily, with cleavage around boundary surfaces of large-scale particles in the flooring material. The adhesive was very 'sticky', ie it was in a **liquid-rubbery phase** and, as the flooring material was lifted, strands of the adhesive elongated and adhered to adjacent newspaper.

The two items of interest here are the brittleness of the material which had changed from being a flexible sheets and also the unexpected almost liquid state of the adhesive after such a long period (at least five years).

21

With many materials there is a tendency for 'like to dissolve like' and it appears that the plasticiser had migrated from the body of the tile into the adhesive and was helping to keep it liquid.

ADHESIVE TAPE STUDY

A small portable steel cupboard which had contained bottles of methylated spirits and white spirit for many months also contained some of the original packing material for shelving which was cardboard, wrapped with brown adhesive tape. In unwrapping the packing it was obvious that the tape now had very uneven patches of adhesive, with some areas that had become almost transparent. Where the brown adhesive coating had completely disappeared, any remaining was almost in a liquified state. The smell from the liquids contained in the cupboard was quite powerful. (In the section on adhesion, some mention has already been made of the different phases of a material.) The high concentrations of chemicals even in the gaseous phase was sufficiently strong in their concentration to change the surface wetting characteristics of the adhesive. It affected the ability of the adhesive film to such an extent that liquification had taken place from absorption of vapour which condensed on the adhesive tape. In solution the surface tension characteristics would have changed and the tape would lose its adhesive proper-ties. Some evaporation of plasticiser might also have occurred.

Reactions between materials are not often so dramatic or happen so quickly, but there are changes of materials by gaseous phases present that can affect the stability of flooring and roofing materials, particularly those that require intermediate bonding that is totally reliant on adhesion.

Chief points to remember are:

Compatibility between adhesive and the two substrates to be joined.

Isolation in situations where the constituents of background components are unknown, ie on previously carried out work. Refurbished materials should not be indiscriminately bonded on top of each other but separating layers or primers used to isolate the surface of any substrate of unknown origin.

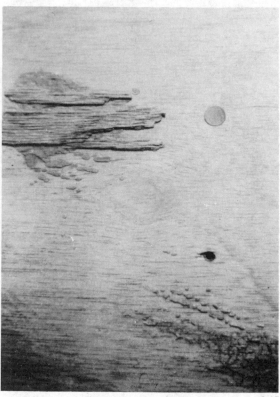

2.15

◄ **2.14** *Adhesive tape. The brown adhesive layer has destabilised and changed into a liquid phase, revealing the clear tape below after reacting with vapours from white spirit and methylated spirit*

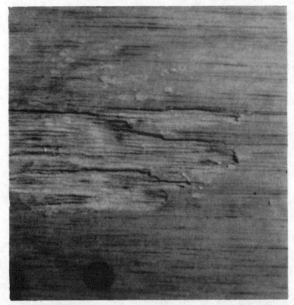 

2.15, 2.16 and 2.17 *Adhesion between two pieces of block-board. 2.15 and 2.16 show the one area where there had been true adhesion between the two faces (approximately 65 mm × 40 mm) on an area 1200 mm × 1200 mm. Adhesive had been applied to one surface and then the two surfaces had been scewed together. The two panels were separated four years* *later, and when the material was parted it was accompanied by a loud crack. Strong bonds were broken in the cellulose tubes as they split, and energy was released in the form of sound. Figure 2.15 shows the transfer of adhesive from one side to another, showing minimal surface wetting. The moral of applying adhesive to both faces is clear*

2.04 DEGRADATION OF POLYMERIC FILMS AS THIN SURFACE COATINGS

As paint films are the first layer of exposure in the building fabric, whether external or internal, they are subject to wildly fluctuating temperatures and conditions. The following categories of material performance should be used as a checklist for the expectation of film quality and its durability.

Mechanical wear and abrasion
The film should be hard but not to a state of being in danger of **embrittlement**. It should be **tough**; it may be necessary to evaluate its hardness by indentation testing.

Fracture development by expansion
Some substrates (especially timber) may have expansion cycles that must be tolerated by the film. Look for 'flexible films', and if critical find out their maximum extensibility.

Water absorption
Most polymers do absorb water but the degree to which they do this varies enormously, and nylon can show significant swelling. When polymers absorb water they can expand unevenly making them less resistant to bending and this in turn can promote the generation of hairline cracking under stress. Water absorption can also affect the glass transition temperature of a polymer by lowering this critical temperature. This can cause the polymer to move further into a liquid phase and show permanent deformation under stress in warm conditions. Look for 'microporous' paints which can assist the movement of water vapour across films without absorption.

Degradation under ultra-violet light
Polymers in paint films can be embrittled after stress cracking if they undergo excessive crosslinking due to the effects of energy bombardment from ultra-violet light. Look for *ultra-violet light stabilisers* which are

compounds that can absorb harmful energy at these wavelengths, change their molecular configuration, and then revert back to their original structure once the source of ultra-violet light (normally strong sunlight) is removed. This also explains why it is advisable **not** to paint in strong sunlight where variation in paint films can occur through the depth of the applied coating, as uneven reactions take place.

Ultra-violet light and heat can also accelerate the oxidation of polymers, which degrades the main polymer chains and is a prime cause of their ageing.

DEFECTS IN PAINT FILMS

Blistering
Blistering can occur for a number of reasons. One is the presence of moisture in the substrate which cannot migrate successfully through the finished film. Solvents can also be trapped by rapid surface hardening and reduce 'wet edge' time, preventing overpainting.

See figure 2.18.

Chalking
As defined in ASTMS D659 (1986) chalking is 'the formation on a pigmented coating of a friable powder evolved from the film itself or just below the surface'. It is common on exterior paints as a form of degradation. Paint itself has constituents which act as fillers, if the holding vehicle breaks down particles of this material as well as pigmentation particles can be released.

Checking
As defined in ASTM D669 (1981) checking is the 'phenomena manifested in paint films that do not penetrate to the underlying surface. The break should be called a crack if the underlying surface is visible.'

See figure 2.19.

Below
2.18 *Blistering. In this example, paint failure is occurring along the lines of map cracking in a plaster substrate. Moisture in the structure behind migrates through these cracks, and expands in the warmer internal environment. It cannot escape below a relatively impermeable film, causes blistering, which increases in size until the maximum extensibility of the film is realised, which then fails*

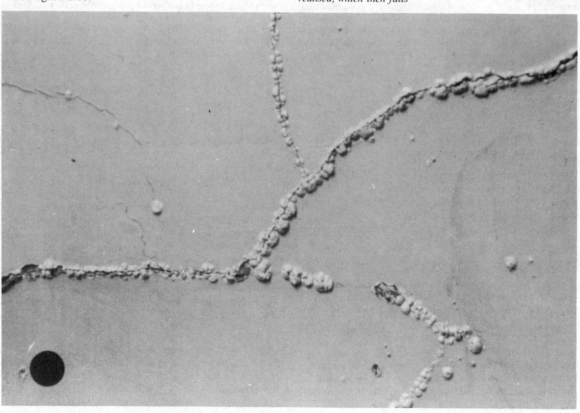

2.19 *Checking and cracking. On this wooden garage door there is checking and then cracking parallel to the grain showing lack of adhesion in line with grain detail. This could indicate an aged timber surface that should have been abraded/planed to remove surface defects, or filled and sanded to give a smooth/ homogeneous background, or replaced*

25

2.20 *Cracking. Paint on a wooden door, Smithfield Market, London. The paint coating was sufficiently thick to develop major cracking in line with the grain, after ageing of the film and subsequent embrittlement*

Cracking

As defined in ASTM D661 (1986) cracking is 'that phenomena manifested in paint films by a break extending through to the surface painted'.

2.21 *Paint as a sheet material. Paint had been applied to a rubber dustbin lid. Due to poor adhesion with the substrate the film had hardened, lifted, and in spanning then fractured in a brittle manner. The angular cracking patterns are similar to those in ceramics, the plastic has hardened to a 'glassy state'*

Erosion

As defined in ASTM D669 (1981) erosion is 'that phenomena manifested in paint films by the wearing away of the finish to expose the substrate or undercoat. The degree of failure is dependent on the amount of substrate or undercoat visible'.

Efflorescence

As defined in ASTM D1736 (1984) efflorescence is 'a condition that occurs when soluble salts in the dried paint film migrate to the film surface during exposure. Efflorescence is seen as either a light, medium or heavy deposits of crystals'. It often occurs in cyclical situations of low temperature and high humidity with condensation forming on the coating surface as an important factor. Testing for whether a particular paint film is susceptible and contains trace salts, imitates this process. Efflorescence can be a result of salts being present in the substrate.

Flaking

In ASTM D772 (1986) flaking is 'that phenomena manifested in paint films by the actual detachment of pieces of film itself, either from its substrate, or from paint previously applied'. Flaking (scaling) is generally preceded by cracking or checking or blistering, and is the result of loss of adhesion usually due to stress–strain factors coming into play. Loss of adhesion can be due to moisture being present, poor preparation of surfaces which contain contaminants such as dirt or grease. Poor preparation is usually the prime cause, or an incompatible coating and substrate.

See figures 2.18 and 2.19.

Defect	Typical causes	Remedial treatment
1 Adhesion failure	(a) Application to damp or dirty substrates; or subsequent entry of moisture, eg through open joints in woodwork	Flaking, peeling or poorly-adhering material should be removed. Where moisture is the cause, it should be ensured that the substrate is dry before repainting
	(b) Failure to prepare or pre-treat non-ferrous metals correctly	Defective material should be removed as above
	(c) Omission of primer or use of unsuitable primer	Defective material should be removed as above. Refer to appropriate substrate clause in section four for information on priming
	(d) Application to powdery or friable substrates	Defective material should be removed as above. Application of a penetrating primer or sealer may be necessary
	(e) Application to hard, dense substrates, eg glass or glazed surfaces	Defective material should be removed as above
	(f) Apparent loss of adhesion on iron and steel, may be due to detachment of mill-scale	See item 8 of this table
2 Blistering	Blistering is usually indicative of liquid or vapour beneath the coating. The presence of water is a frequent cause. On woodwork, resinous material may be responsible	Depending upon the extent and severity of blistering, preparation may be confined to removal of isolated blisters or complete stripping may be necessary Where moisture is the cause, time should be allowed for drying out Blistering on resinous external woodwork may be influenced by choice of finishing colour
3 Chalking, powdering	Slow erosion and chalking on lengthy exposure, especially externally, is a characteristic of many paints and wood finishes. It is not usually regarded as a defect unless it occurs prematurely and profusely, when the causes may be as follows: (a) conditions of exposure exceptionally severe; (b) earlier coats in system have failed to satisfy porosity of substrate; (c) incorrect or unsuitable formulation	In absence of other defects, lightly chalking surfaces may require only washing and light abrasion to provide a satisfactory base for further coats Heavily chalked or powdery surfaces will require more vigorous cleaning or abrasion combined if necessary with application of a penetrating primer
4 Colour defects, eg fading, staining, 'bleeding', or other forms of discoloration	(a) Some loss of colour of paint may occur on lengthy exposure to bright sunlight but is not usually significant. Early loss of colour may be due to use in unsuitable conditions, eg external use of a colour intended only for interior use Chemical attack may cause change or loss of colour	If necessary, consult manufacturers regarding selection of colours or types of finish for repainting

Table 2.1 *Defects in paintwork and remedial treatment*

Defect	Typical causes	Remedial treatment
4 Colour defects *continued*	(b) Oil-based finishes tend to yellow in situations where direct daylight is excluded. This is more obvious with white and light-coloured finishes	Yellowing is not usually sufficiently marked to be significant. If freedom from yellowing is important, consult manufacturers for guidance on selection of oil-free coatings
	(c) Apparent colour change may be due to masking of colour by surface chalking (item 3 of this table) to efflorescence especially on external rendering or, on external plywood treated with wood stain, to diffusion of water-soluble salts contained in adhesives	Normal cleaning usually removes surface deposits. Efflorescence and diffusion of salts on plywood may recur until source is exhausted
	(d) Failure of clear finishes on external woodwork may result in discoloration of exposed wood	Clear finish should be removed completely. Sanding or scraping may remove discoloration, but application of coloured wood stain may be necessary to achieve uniform appearance
	(e) Constituents of the substrate or previous coatings can cause discoloration	Wash with detergent, use alkali resisting primer, re-paint
5 Cracking, other than that due to structural movement	Cracking is usually indicative of stresses within the coating film, caused, for example, by applying hard-drying coatings over soft coatings. It may also be the initial stage in adhesion failure (item 1 of this table). Cracks may be confined to the finishing coat or extend through the thickness of the film	If cracking is slight and confined to the finishing coat, rubbing down may provide a satisfactory base for recoating. If cracking is severe or extends through the thickness of the film, complete removal may be necessary
6 Damage to coating	(a) Mechanical damage, eg by abrasion, impact or vigorous cleaning (b) Graffiti	Where surfaces are subject to hard wear, specialist coatings may be required. Consideration should also be given to the use of wear-resistant materials, eg ceramic tiles or plastics, where practicable
7 Gloss, loss of	Some loss of gloss after lengthy exposure, especially externally, is to be expected and may be the first stage in chalking (item 3 of this table). Where it occurs prematurely, possible causes are as described for premature chalking	Loss of gloss in the absence of other defects is not usually significant in relation to maintenance treatment
8 Millscale, detachment from painted iron and steel	Poor initial preparation leading to formation of oxide film below	Removal of millscale, eg by blast-cleaning or flame cleaning, may be impracticable as a maintenance operation and is costly, hence the desirability of effective initial preparation. There may be no alternative to manual cleaning to remove millscale as it loosens, but this may extend over several repaints

continued . . .

continued . . .

Defect	Typical causes	Remedial treatment
9 Organic growths, ie moulds, algae, lichen, moss	Micro-climate, poor maintenance	Consider modifications to design or environment which may eliminate or reduce causes of failure
10 Rust-spotting or rust-staining on painted iron and steel	This usually indicates that the thickness of the paint system is insufficient to provide protection on peaks and edges. It may result from application of an inadequate system initially or at the last repaint or from erosion of the film during exposure. A further possible cause is failure to use a rust-inhibitive primer	Depending upon the severity and extent of the defect, treatment may range from manual cleaning and priming of localised areas to overall removal of the coating and treatment as for new iron and steel Consideration should be given to increasing the film thickness of the system or to reducing the intervals between repaints until an adequate thickness has been built up

*'Paintwork' refers generally to paints, clear finishes and wood stains

Table 2.1 *Defects in paintwork and remedial treatment.* Based on Table 17 of BS 6150:1982

APPLICATIONS

2.1 SURFACE COATINGS TECHNOLOGY

INTRODUCTION

Finishing coatings are generally thought to combine protective and decorative functions to materials. However, their importance in terms of performing a vital protective function is often underestimated and they must have the ability to resist a great range of external stresses, whether physical, chemical or biological and must stay stable in a wide range of temperature conditions. This demands a high level of engineering on the part of the paint technologist. Also it is important that the coatings used are specified for the particular condition and that a specification will cover adequately the correct preparation of the substrate. To ignore the condition of the material to be coated is effectively to build in certain failure of the film and consequently an unexpectedly short life. As coatings are now so specialised it is important not to accept substitutions that do not meet the original specification on site and not allow the mixing of paint systems. Where transfer of moisture must be maintained across the structure, the coating system must be chosen to avoid the build up of moisture.

In conclusion, the technology of paint systems is complex and the full understanding of coatings and their application relies on a knowledge of their composition and their mechanics of adhesion. In return this requires some general knowledge of polymer chemistry, the understanding of the transition of the transformation of polymers from liquid to solid and an appreciation of some of the mechanisms of failure.

As a strategy for specification a major source of reference is the Code of Practice for *Painting of Buildings* BS 6150: 1982. This document covers the design and specification of coatings, the materials used, coating systems, application, maintenance and, lastly, health and safety. Although inspection sampling and testing is included as a section, for detailed descriptions of tests that are possible it is worth making reference to BS 3900 and to the ASTMS series of standards. One of the most important parts of the inspection is in establishing the moisture content of the substrate. This is a source of many coatings failures. A great deal of time and effort is spent in establishing the cause of failures in films with attempts at the apportionment of responsibility which could have been pre-empted by careful inspection prior to and during coating application. (See table 2.1 pages 28–30 which summarises the main defects and possible remedial action.)

TEXTURE AND COLOUR
Coatings and surface texture and resultant colour

The overall colour and opacity of a surface coating is dependent on the properties of pigments, and not just their body colour (ie the selective wavelengths of light they do not absorb) but the actual particle size of the pigment and how it physically distributes light. Textures of surfaces can be divided into rough and smooth.

Rough

These textures give a greater vibrancy to colour through giving uneven surface reflectances and hence a wide range of tones, eg as in hand-made bricks.

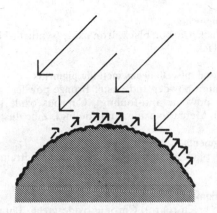

2.22 *Rough surfaces showing scattering of light*

Smooth (two categories)

1 Hard Hard surfaces have greater surface reflectance values and light is bounced back with a limited amount of absorbency by the substrate, eg as in marble and glass which exhibit a mirror-like quality.

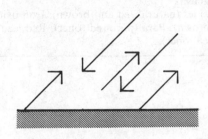

2.23 *Smooth but hard surface showing complete reflectance of light with no absorbency*

2 Soft Soft surfaces have small-scale surface irregularities which allow for a high degree of absorbency, and great intensity of colour is given to the material with very little reflection. The best examples of this surface texture behaviour is in soft fruits or flowers.

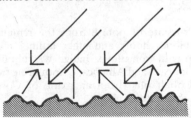

2.24 *Smooth but soft surface showing part absorption and a diminished reflectance of light*

This classification of colour as a major repercussion of surface texture is best understood by a comparison of artists' paints. Giant paintboxes with many colours (usually fairly cheap) yield a watery solution with disappointing covering power and have a noticeably 'gritty' appearance. More expensive paints are completely smooth in appearance and have a great covering power. The particle size of their pigments is far smaller and the greater expense is due to the refinement of ingredients and extraction of impurities.

Paints can be engineered in the control of pigment sizing to give a greater density of colour and hence covering power, by having the ability to scatter light internally with a minimum of reflection. This obviates the need for paint films to be 'thick' in terms of their effectiveness. The science of determining the hiding power of a paint by the physical qualities of the pigmentation is known as *reflectometry* and ASTMS standard D2805 (1985) estimates efficiency.

The colours of paints have been determined historically by pigments available. Some colours, such as red or purple, were extremely rare due to their limited source of supply, and today still have connotations or associations with the heads of social hierarchies. This explains the abundance of colours in the green, dark blue or brown ranges which were readily available from a great variety of natural pigments for ordinary usage before the First World War.

TRADITIONAL PIGMENT SOURCES

From Rivington 1901, *Paints and Varnishes*

Blacks Soot from oil, coal, resinous woods. Also bone black.

Blues Prussiate of potash from the remains of old leather, blood, hoofs and other animal matter was boiled up with iron filings. Indigo was obtained from plants from Asia and America, Ultramarine from Lapis Lazuli, Cobalt blue from an oxide of Cobalt, Blue ochre from a natural clay.

Browns Oxides of iron. Umber is a naturally occurring clay stained with oxides of iron, and was burnt to produce darker oxides. The same can be said for Sienna, hence Burnt sienna. Also Brown ochre.

Yellows Chromates of lead-dilute solutions of acetate, nitrates of lead, bichromate of potash. Yellow ochre natural clay stained by oxide of iron. Yellow Lake, made from tumeric, alum, etc.

Red From red lead and also from vermilion (naturally occurring sulphide of mercury known as Cinnabar—China). Also made artificially. Indian red—naturally occurring iron ore from Bengal. Venetian red obtained by heating sulphate of iron (waste product from tin and copper works).

Greens From copper compounds, arsenic, etc.

Limited colour sources from vegetables

Red	Madder root
Orange	Onion bulb
Yellow	Saffron
Dark brown	Walnut fruit

Rare colour sources

Red	Cochineal insect (Carmine)
Blue	Azurite (mineral)
Green	Malachite (mineral)
Purple	Murex (mollusc)

MODERN PIGMENT SOURCES

ASTM checklist page 1209 volume 06.01

Inert or low hiding pigments (fillers, extenders)
Aluminium silicate (anhydrous), Aluminium silicate (hydrous), Barium sulphate, Calcium carbonate, Diatomaceous silica. Magnesium silicate (talc), Pumice, Wet ground mica.

White pigments
Calcium borosilicate, Titanium dioxide, Tribasic Lead phosphosilicate (intent to withdraw). White base lead carbonate, Zinc hydroxy phosphate, Zinc oxide, Zinc sulphide.

Black pigments
Bone black, Carbon black, Iron oxide (synthetic black), Lampblack.

Bronze and miscellaneous metallic pigments
Aluminium powder and paste, Bronze powder (gold), Copper powder (anti-fouling), Cuprous oxide (anti–fouling), Mercuric oxide (anti-fouling), Zinc dust.

Blue pigments
Copper phtalocyanine blue, Iron blue, Ultramarine blue.

Green pigments
Chrome green (pure), Chrome oxide green, Phtalcyanine green.

Yellow orange brown pigments
Chromate (strontium), Chromate (Zinc yellow), Chrome yellow and Chrome orange, Iron oxide (hydrated yellow), Iron oxide (natural red and brown), Iron oxide (synthetic brown), Molybdate orange, Ochre, Sienna (raw and burnt), Silichromate (basic lead), Umber (raw and burnt).

Red pigments
Iron oxides (natural red and brown), Iron oxide (synthetic brown), Para (pure red toner), Red lead, Toluidine (red toner).

Colour today is defined chiefly by using the **Munsell system** which evaluates colour in terms of:

Hue   The actual colour ie name 'green' or 'red'.

Value   which measures brightness in terms of the degree of reflectance.

Chroma   Intensity of hue related to greyness.

It is worth mentioning that the BS 4800: 1981 range of colours is extremely limited and that major paint manufactures produce a far wider range of colours. The Royal Horticultural Society have just re-published their own colour referencing system which was originally designed to assist in the accurate recording of flowers and their colours for the duration of their lifespan. It was used widely by printers and traditional decorators for colour matching. As the colour of the samples is matched to the 'Smooth/soft' textures found in nature the quality (intensity) of colour is very high.

Colour can also be achieved by the physical splitting of white daylight through a diffraction grating, and further cancellation of colours can be achieved by the interference of different wavelengths of light. There are many examples in nature, ie the scales on a butterfly wing have fine grilles, and so do the wing cases on beetles, the resultant colour seen is nothing to do with pigmentation. Even bright surface colours on insects and birds may be from the holding of layers of moisture between laminations or feather hairs. These layers can act prismatically. If a bird dies, and the moisture evaporates, the feathers lose their colour and the body becomes dull. These physical mechanisms to achieve colour can be copied in architectural coatings. Some oxide films on metals are controlled so the depth of the oxidised layer can give the effect of colour by the physical phenomenon of interference. These colours are more permanent as they do not have to be engineered for chemical stability in the environment.

HISTORICAL BACKGROUND

Traditional paints were described in building textbooks in terms of their ingredients with advice and recipes for their making. Until the First World War it was quite common for contractors to have their own workshops which made up the paint. The mechanics of hardening and adhesion were not properly understood so the emphasis was on making up recipies that were based on tried and tested coatings. The early terminology used is still understandable today although the individual ingredients we use may have changed in complexity.

Rivington's *Notes on Building Construction* (1901) read:

'The paints used by the engineer and builder as a rule consist of a **base** (generally a metallic oxide) mixed with some liquid substance known as the **vehicle**; upon this, permanency of the paint depends.
'In most cases a **drier** is added to cause the **vehicle** to dry more quickly, and a solvent is sometimes required to make it work more freely. When the final colour required differs from that of the base used, the desired tint is obtained by adding a stainer or colouring pigment.
'**Bases**   white lead, red lead, zinc white, oxide of iron
Vehicles   water, oils, spirits of turpentine
Solvents   spirits of turpentine . . .'

The book then described how to make all of these ingredients, recognising to some extent their toxicity, ie on white lead paint:

'Where it is exposed, however, to the fumes of sulphur acids, such as are evolved from decaying animal matter in laboratories, and in some manufacturing towns, it soon becomes darkened by the formation of black sulphide of lead. It has also the disadvantage of producing numbness and painters' colic in those who use it.'

Sometimes it may be necessary to match traditional paints and, even though the information may be out of print, it is still accessible due to the meticulous recording of recipes at the time. However, the heavy emphasis on lead ingredients, and some of the acids needed to modify them, indicates the handling of materials which is either now minimised or barred altogether. It is worth stating that in conversion work the stripping of paint back to the original layers will reveal heavy lead-based coatings that are still a health risk owing to the accumulation build up of lead possible in the body. Safety measures for undertaking this kind of work cannot be overstated.

COATING SYSTEMS

Coatings to materials normally have specific functions depending on their position with regard to the substrate. Initial coatings or primers should have good **adhesion** and immediately be able to protect the material against natural decay. Metal primers carry pigments that help achieve this, for example red lead or zinc powder. The primer should also cover imperfections and bridge minute cavities that could engender corrosion fatigue. Top coats are not just chosen for their brilliance of finish but for their hardness against erosion, ie resistance to scratching and stability against aggressive environmental conditions.

Coating thickness
Initial protection is given by the thickness of coatings and this is dependent on the severity of conditions in the atmosphere.

Minimum layer thickness
Clean country air	125 microns
Polluted city air	180 microns
Corrosive sea air	250 microns
Industrial air	300 microns

As film thicknesses individually are so thin this means that layers of coats must be built up for adequate protection.

Thicknesses of some typical coatings
Acrylic resin	25–30 microns
Alkyd resin	25–30 microns
Chlorinated rubber	150 microns
Polycyclic latex	15–25 microns
Traditional oils	35–40 microns

Primers have the function of adhering well to a substrate and in turn providing an efficient base for adhesion by undercoats. Their importance cannot be overstressed, and failure of the primer will immediately mean failure of the whole coating system. Unfortunately primers are varied in their performance and must be specified adequately. They also have to resist substantial strains, especially in timber where seasonal movement can give a strain figure of up to 5.3% for the coating performance.

NB The extent of movement will vary according to the timber species and its method of sawing. See *MBS: Materials*, Timber section.

Permanence can vary in different primers and failures have been recorded by BRE that vary from one week to six months. General points to note are that slow drying primers give good results, primers even without lead content can still be perfectly adequate and any timber should be treated with preservative prior to priming by immersion or vacuum methods. Permanence can be a particular problem with factory primed joinery and care should be taken to ensure that nominated suppliers are adhering to standards specified.

2.2   ORGANIC COATINGS
This category refers to the group of compounds in surface coatings that are carbon based. Many of the applied finishes today in this category are in the realm of the polymer science.

ORGANIC COATS AND THEIR CLASSIFICATIONS
Paints are generally classified according to how they harden, transforming from liquid (vehicle and pigment) to solid (binder or matrix composite).

A   EVAPORATIVE DRYING (non-convertible)
In this category the film hardens with no chemical reaction taking place. The paint constituents are suspended in a **medium** commonly referred to as the **vehicle** and evaporation occurs of a particular solvent with no chemical reaction.

Polymer constituents commonly found in solution in organic solvents
Cellulose group	Cellulose nitrate
	Cellulose acetate
	Ethyl cellulose

PVC   Polyvinyl (chloride co-vinyl acetate)
These are commonly embraced in the term *vinyl resins*. PVC is insoluble in ordinary solvents and highly resistant to alkalis and acids as well as oxidising agents. PVC can be degraded by energy inputs from heat and light. It is a linear thermoplastic and commonly used as a copolymer with vinyl acetate. It has a tendency to crystallinity.

Acrylic   Poly(methyl methacrylate)
Acrylic resins have a high softening point (T_m) and can be easily converted to thermosetting resins by the addition of other monomers, eg styrene. It is soluble in a variety of solvents and is a common binder in paints.

Polyvinyl butyral
Polyvinyl butyral is common in metal pre-treatment primers (etch primers) and helps give good adhesion for successive undercoats.

Rubber   Chlorinated rubber is dissolved in a medium of hydrocarbon solvents and will give some of the thickest coatings available, providing substantial protection to metals.

NB   The loss of solvents in evaporative mixtures can be a health hazard. Instructions should be followed and work carried out in factory controlled conditions or well ventilated spaces. Toxicity can lead to permanent damage to living tissue.

Polymer constituents dispersed in water

These are all *emulsion* types with one solution suspended in another, or latex types with fine particles dispersed in water. As the water evaporates particles come closer together and coalesce to form a continuous film. Plasticisers are often present in these films and work by depressing the T_g (glass transition temperature) of the main polymeric compounds so the film stays in a rubbery state (ie non-brittle) at ambient temperatures. Paint films lose their plasticisers over time as they migrate into the atmosphere. This causes the film to become hard and ultimately brittle. The setting of these films can be critical with regard to temperature. Hardening in low temperatures ranges (ie close to the glass transition temperature) could cause hardening of dispersed particles before they coalesce and form a film. This would give a 'powdery' finish instead of a continuous hardened film from the solidification of an even liquid coating. The most commonly used are:

Poly(styrene-co-butadiene)
Poly(vinyl acetate) and co-polymers
Poly(methylmethacrylate) and co-polymers
PVC organsols

B CONVERTIBLE COATINGS

All of these coatings undergo a chemical reaction when they are applied and as they change their state from liquid to solid.

Oxidative polymerisation

These films actively combine with oxygen molecules in the atmosphere to make their transformation from monomers to polymers. They include most of our traditional **oil paints**, and give chiefly crosslinked polymers. Examples are:

Fatty drying oils
Oleoresinous coatings
Air drying alkyds

Oleoresinous binders are vegetable in origin (ie linseed oil from the flax plant) also from the olive, soya castor, coconut and cotton seed plants. These films, by the addition of natural/synthetic resins and the omission of pigmentation, will give oleoresinous varnishes. To speed up the hardening process, mixtures include salts of lead, cobalt and manganese but any of these accelerators should be avoided as they cause overhardening and give a more brittle film.

The alkyds (polyesters) contain between 35 and 80% oleoresinous components. They can be degraded by alkalis. Different categories of alkyd resins vary according to the ratio of oleoresinous components used. Short oil ratio alkys are used in specific solvent which can be cured at high temperatures ie suitable for baking or stoving processes. Those oils with medium and long oil ratios can be cured in the atmosphere. Categories known as *modified alkyd resins* can incorporate chlorinated rubber to improve corrosion and fire resistance, and to accelarate hardening; cellulose nitrate to increase hardness; amino resins to increase hardness and improve resistance to alkalis; and lastly silicone resins to improve water and heat resistance.

Coatings can harden by a chemical reaction within the film used in '2 pack' systems. Conversion (or curing) is often assisted by the input of external energy, ie ultra-violet light. Examples are:

Epoxy EP
Unsaturated polyester
Polyurethane
Urea and Melamine formaldehyde

CLEAR FINISHES: natural finishes or varnishes

These often consist of the same ingredients as a paint film but lack any pigmentation or fillers. Although they provide a high gloss finish to a material and some protection against solvents, especially water, they often cannot filter out the ultra-violet radiation components in daylight that a pigment would normally absorb. This leads to a degradation of the film by excessive crosslinking, making the film more rigid and brittle. The film ceases to be able to move at the same rate as the substrate, and once crazing begins, light waves are scattered along the edges of cracks causing opacity.

Examples of typical clear finishes in the non-convertible category of films are shellac, bitumen and cellulose nitrate (commonly known as *cellulose lacquers*). They are non-convertible as they can be re-dissolved in their original solvents. This is an advantage in the repair of french polish which is simply shellac dissolved in methylated spirits. The polymeric coatings that are convertible are then more stable but once damaged have to be replaced in their entirety.

STAINS

These can be a one or two coat application and, if made up of two coats, it is likely the first coat will have a lower solid content for greater penetration.

Low solids < 30%
High solids > 40–50%

Stains are traditionally thought of as being more economical than paint films as the labour content in number of coats applied becomes less. The higher the solids content, the greater the ability of the film to resist degradation through ultra-violet light as there is greater opportunity for absorption of light.

The main resin vehicle usually just has pigmentation and a fungicide. Very dark colours, ie black, brown, dark blue, can act as a heat sink and cause excessive shrinkage in the timber below. The mid range of colours, ie blues or greens can be most effective for protection without causing complications from heat gain.

The penetration of stains is often high relative to paints which allows for the passage of water vapour but can increase the movement of jointed components from the additional water penetration. Preservatives incorporated into stains are not effective as long-term protection to timber (eg pentachlorphenol, tributyl tin oxide) as they only prevent mould growth on the finished film and should really be regarded as anti-fungicidal. Separate impregnation of timber prior to staining with a specification to approved British Standards should always be carried out.

Good maintenance is still required to stained treatments and is carried out usually at the first signs of any noticeable loss of gloss or sheen and before any noticeable deterioration. Once colour deterioration is seen damage will already have occurred to the timber substrate and there will be loss of adhesion of subsequent coatings of stain. This can only be rectified by substantial preparation of the timber.

The aim in staining is for a minimum life of five years and some stains give a performance (often with two coats) that can be twice as long. Deep penetration of the substrate can be disappointing from current stains and the penetration power no deeper than regular paint systems.

Note In external joinery windows when glazed with putty rely on paint for protection. When staining timber joinery the glazing compound used must change to a butyl, polyisobutylene, polysulphide or similar, adhesive. These compounds can react unfavourably with compatible paint films used internally and in some situations neoprene gaskets may have to be specified. (This is common practice for proprietary window products in Scandinavia.)

2.3 INORGANIC COATINGS

This category covers the coatings which are not carbon based and whose basic constituents are inorganic, metallic, or a combination of both. Because of their chemistry they are often found as the basic coatings used to protect metals.

Conversion coatings
These coatings undergo a reaction when applied which can chemically combine with a metal substrate. This makes them ideal as primers. They often form oxide coatings which can also be regarded as engineering a form of controlled corrosion. They usually have the ability to react with the metal, allowing positive metallic ions to be available for combination with other ions in the coating, and so forming a new metallic compound. The pH usually rises as the new metallic compound is formed, so changing the immediate environment around the metal from an acidic one (which encourages corrosion) to a more passive alkaline one. The coatings formed are very thin, perhaps some 2 microns thick. It is important that the full coating system is applied soon afterwards.

Metal   Coating   Atmosphere

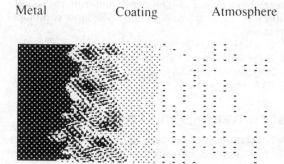

2.25 *Inorganic coatings. An ideal situation, a coating that is already oxidised and has some compatibility with the atmosphere, and provides an intermediate compound which exhibits chemical bonding back to a metal substrate*

Integrated controlled corrosion
Some metals (especially steel) have additional alloying elements which ensure that surface corrosion is limited and a corrosive layer builds up which protects the metal from further corrosion. All stainless steels use this technique by varying the percentage content of chromium, which oxidises rapidly in the atmosphere to form a strong coating that can be polished. *Cor-ten* contains approximately 0.2–0.5% copper and will form a weathering steel. Care should be taken in its use, as rainwater run off can stain adjacent materials. *Phosphorous* is also commonly used as a controlled corrosion element.

All coatings which depend on controlled corrosion engineering must be comparable in terms of their molecular sizing and atomic spacing with the parent metal, ensuring a good degree of inter-metallic bonding. Incompatibility in sizing will cause stress cracking, and the new exposed surface will cause further corrosive deposits to grow. This can give a patchy and unsightly layering to material. It is thought that the success of some of these finishes may be due to the phenomenon of the additional alloys causing 'growth poisoning' and inhibiting the normal crystalline formation of the oxide layer of the parent metal.

The oxidation of iron is unacceptable because the corrosive deposits formed are large in scale with the parent metal and have voids, further exposing the metal and leading to continuing and progressive corrosion through the whole body of a section.

Enamels
Vitreous enamel coatings normally applied to steel are extremely thick, up to 0.8 mm. They are applied as a powder which is fired and then fuses to the metal. Although they are resistant to most chemicals, especially acids, they are susceptible to alkali attack. (Note the effect in hardwater areas on bath enamel.)

Cement based paints
These contain white Portland cement with or without pigments, water repellants, fillers and plasticisers. They are water based and can only be used on brickwork, concrete and renders. They are being replaced now by proprietary masonry paints which are acrylic emulsions with alkali resistant large scale pigments and fungicides.

2.4 SPECIAL COATINGS

This is a new category of coatings to consider and can encompass some of the traditional ceramic coatings used, as well as suggesting strategies for the future that will take into account new developments in ceramics. Historically the discussion of thin surface finishes deals chiefly with organic coatings and this emphasis has been unchanged for about 25 years.

Research and development
There is also a great deal of money invested in research and development in polymers in an attempt to perfect the technology of engineering organic coating systems. This means a huge investment on the part of manufacturers in maintaining an interest in the use of organic coatings in the building industry. Also those films may be getting better, but the industry is built around a policy of renewal and expectation of a large and constant supply of these surface coatings. To some extent the specification of these finishes is self perpetuating unless attention is drawn to other options.

Vulnerability
As paint coatings are only microns thick they present a finish that is vulnerable unless the film is well engineered for its stability under stress, whether through dimensional movement or a range of temperatures from -10 to $+40$. It must also resist direct abrasion and ingress from water molecules.

Adhesion
The film should also not depart from its background and to avoid this it must have properties of adhesion to the substrate. This leads into an examination of adhesion and to reconsider the following subject areas:

Surface wetting
Thermodynamics
Surface chemistry and possible bonding.

If this is done successfully it can be established why different films are engineered in the way they are and the precise function of primers. The mechanical notion of bonding can almost be completely disregarded, especially if the topography of metal surfaces is looked at in detail.

Degradation
There are also problems with organic coatings. Most research and development is devoted to the stabilisation of primarily unstable materials. Ultra-violet light as a source of radiation can cause further reactions in polymers and extensive crosslinking that can cause embrittlement.

These are problems of chain scission of polymers under ultra-violet light and ultra-violet stabilisers are introduced to combat this by changing their structure under the energy of light, and changing back when the source of ultra-violet is removed, emitting heat at the same time. There is also the notion of water absorption in plastics, the resultant swelling in plastics and films as the possible cause of hairline cracking through embrittlement by stiffness.

These points appear obvious but it seems to be going to a great deal of trouble to make a usable product from a material that is inherently unstable in the atmosphere. In a particularly aggressive environment, or one that demands a very high expectation of a surface coating finish, a specification should be considered:

(a) Not advocating the use of finishes which are fraught with problems and lead to failure of the building fabric if they are not well maintained (timber, etc).

(b) The use of finishes that were already environmentally stable, ie they were relatively inert and would decay or deteriorate no further.

37

(c) The specification of a finish that was able to form a chemical bond with a substrate.

Priorities

The most urgent application for this line of thought is for metals. Their rate of decay is not only costly in terms of renewal but also dangerous. The failure of films will lead to the initial corrosion of steel through intergranular corrosion, possibly leading to more severe failure of the material, certainly significant in highly engineered structures.

The best candidates for stable coatings are ceramics. They are inert and will not change in the atmosphere as they are already in an oxidised state. There is also a proven compatibility between metals and ceramics; most ceramics have metallic elements as part of their bonding. The following categories show some variety in the possible use and application of ceramics, some of which are still developmental:

(a) Glass type coatings

Good surface 'wetting' of the metal to be coated is important as well as cleanliness of the metal surface. Although the metal may be cleaned to a state of brightness with the complete removal of oxidised material, the metal may then be left for a short while for controlled depth of oxidation to take place. This does assist adhesion. Sometimes intermediate oxide coatings are applied to bright surfaces and may require an intermediate firing. After surface preparation, powdered glass is applied to the surface and then heated. It is important that the glass types used can liquify at temperatures that do not cause phase transformations in the metal substrate. It is important that the glass and metal do have similar co-efficients of thermal expansion. These types of coatings require control and a manufacturing process that relates to particular components which can be fairly large, eg cladding panels. Common known applications are in signage and also in the manufacture of steel and cast iron baths. The technology of these coatings is improving as the controlled oxidation of the parent metal is optimised, and the depth of the coating lessens. Old porcelain ceramics were very vulnerable to chipping because of the depth of the coating.

There are some problems of deterioration with these kinds of coatings which can lead to loss of gloss, and the resulting surface imperfections can give rise to a significant loss of strength. There are common environmental conditions that can degrade materials. Water is not a problem with most of these coatings but solutions which are alkaline can permanently alter the structure of Si-O configurations and dissolve the material, the severity of which increases with the concentration of OH$^-$ ions. Although more resistant to acid solutions, glasses can suffer severe degradation from hydrofluoric acid. As detergents also give an alkaline reaction they should be avoided, particularly as they may precipitate silica deposits.

(b) Composition coatings inhibiting iron migration

These compositions were originally developed and patented for the food industry after complaints by customers who could detect a change in taste of the liquid if there was a concentration as low as 60 ppm of iron in beer. The sealant around the ends of the cans was the basic problem. As many foods are acidic, if they came into contact with material that had some defect, as in the second ends of the pack, iron migration was a possibility and this was modified. The material used was an organic enamel based on polyvinyl chloride, with a plasticiser. A metal oxide (aluminium, zinc, magnesium, or calcium) is now added to this enamel coating and it inhibits soluble iron migration by acting as an acid scavenger. (Patent protected invention. Billings *et al.*, USA 4, 278, 718, 14.7.81.)

(c) Weather resistant coatings

Look carefully at the components in paint coatings and consciously choose compounds that will make effective bonds with metals to provide an environmentally stable coating. Some reseach is concentrating on calcium and strontium oxalates and group 1B or IIB metal oxides or sulphates mixed with water soluble silicates. The greatest difficulty is in finding compounds that will bond effectively at ambient temperatures. Most work undertaken was concentrated on the fusion of ceramic/metal interfaces by heat, laser or an electric field. In effect, this is a similar process to the making of particle composites, and is an expensive procedure, not a site application.

The search for effective compounds in coatings is making an evaluation of some materials that were traditionally used and referred to as pigments. Pigments were often inorganic compounds suspended in organic matrices or solvents, but their properties were never properly evaluated except as colouring agents. The best known reactive compounds made very effective primers, as in the case of red lead.

Although red lead in epoxy binders today does not undergo a reaction with the substrate, it 'is encapsulated in a chemically resistant binder and is rendered to the level of an inert extender'.[1]

(d) Long life inorganic coatings

One major drawback to organic coatings is their

[1]'A Paint Manufacturer's Viewprint: Painting for Protection', R W Green, *Corrosion Prevention and Control* February 1986.

limited life. They have a limited 'pot life' and degrade over a long period of time. Development work is being carried out on inorganic coatings composites with a long pot life which contain, for example, condensed phosphates in an aqueous silicate solution.

(e) Sagging resistant coatings

Organic coatings need control to ensure they stay in a 'rubbery' phase and that their weight is low, so that in a normal application, sagging will not occur before proper hardening has taken place. When thick coats need to be built up for heavy duty protection, special coats using water soluble silicides, or silica solvents with a hardener solution containing phosphate and aluminium, are now seen as alternatives.

TEXTURED FINISHES

Hammer finishes

Hammer films are popular today because of their durability and physical appearance. They provide a 'beaten' dimpled surface. The whole effect relies on the method of evaporation of the solvents used in the paint. This happens at great speed causing a vortex effect and Bernard cell formation. Bernard cells are characterised by hexagonal geometries which take least amount of surface energy to form. These films contain metallic powders, usually aluminium, and the flake-like parti-

cles, when rotating in the vortex action align themselves with the sides of cell walls and intensify light reflection. These finishes can be sprayed and should not be applied thickly (approximately 25 microns) as this can inhibit good cell formation and leave the lower part of the film less rigid. Hardening time is fast, in the region of 15 minutes.

Binders include styrenated alkyds, vinyl toluene co-polymers, chlorinated rubber polyurethanes, epoxide esters and nitrocellulose.

Wrinkle finishes

These kinds of finishes were commonly used on metals post war and for small artifacts ie typewriters. They are very durable and should be applied by spraying. The mechanism for hardening now accepted is that a smooth crosslinked film forms on the surface after rapid oxidative polymerisation. The lower layers are starved of oxygen and individual monomers are absorbed by the surface skin, swelling it, but as the skin is floating on a liquid surface and still attached, the swelling deforms into wrinkle formation. This effect can be inadvertently achieved when using a paint that softens an underlying coat, the new top coat can then wrinkle from the same mechanism and is seen as a defect.

Binders include oleoresinous varnishes, phenolic resins (modified) and alkyds, and vinyl resins. An alkyd wrinkle is approximately 50 to 80 microns in thickness

2.26 *Hammer finish on surface of gas fire appliance*

which is significantly larger than individual coatings in paints (of the order of 25 microns) and so can be more effective protection.

Intumescent paints

On heating, components in the film react giving off gaseous phases which cannot escape due to the strength of the polymeric materials involved. The gases used are non-flammable and are usually carbon dioxide or ammonia. The coating then often expands by an order of 10^2 converting from a film into a thick rigid foam. This would give an expansion of 100, ie from 0.1 mm to 10 mm. Some surface thicknesses can be as much as 1.5 mm (1500 microns). The thickness will depend on the degree of fire protection required and the structural member type to which it will be applied. For example, columns are required to have a more substantial coating than tie struts.

NB These coatings are often water sensitive and may not be suitable for external use. Individual requirements should be checked with the manufacturers concerned.

Powder coatings

There are two main categories of powder coatings which can be divided conveniently into *thermosets* (epoxy resins) and *thermoplastics* (chiefly acrylics and polyesters).

These are often a mixture of polymeric materials, commonly referred to as co-polymers which form hard resins. They are ground into fine particles and applied to metals (often electrostatically for even coating) and then heated in ovens which cause the particles to coalesce. These polymers are commonly thermosets and show good powers of adhesion. Thicknesses between 80 to 90 microns can be achieved and they set quickly, (commonly between 6 and 30 minutes). Their original development shows a response to the elimination of toxic evaporants in cellulose paints which were in widespread use by the automobile industry. The development was probably encouraged by the high cost factors involved in installing air handling equipment to existing premises if fumes were to be properly controlled, as well as union pressure representing operatives in the USA. Organic solvents of this type are also derived from the distillation of crude oil, and as the costs of this raw material fluctuates, this encourages the development of alternative products.

The thermoplastics give a characteristic smooth and glossy film surface but it is not as durable and does not bond as well to metal substrates or show as great a resistance to organic solvents as the thermosetting powder coatings. The disadvantage of thermosets is in their surface finish which, due to a phenomenon of setting during heating before attaining complete fluidity, have slightly rougher surface and hence less gloss.

Both categories of powder coatings have a complex mixture of ingredients which would include the following:

Flow control agents
Anti-static agents
Pigments
Plasticisers

In fact the coatings have a sufficient mix of ingredients as to fall into a category of particle composite technology. (See section 4.0 of this volume.)

The engineering of these coatings can sometimes be similar to the development of conventional paint systems where within the coating are discrete layers. These are known as *multi-layer powder coatings* and can still be applied in a one spray operation which contains opposing electrically charged powdered components. These have clear separate functions. For example in pipe interiors zinc particles coat first to give a galvanising layer to the metal (steel). A surface layer of epoxy resin will then protect the zinc coating from abrasion and electrolytic corrosion. Sometimes components are sprayed in such a way that component particles become suspended in a matrix, commonly an epoxy resin.

There is an alternative to spraying powders cold onto substrates and then heating them. If the material, usually metal, is heated first then, as spraying occurs,

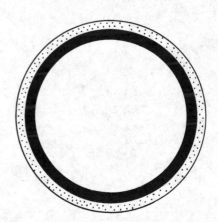

2.27 *Multi-layer coatings on pipes*
(a) *Pipe exterior*
The total powder mixture is blown onto a pre-heated pipe (above the T_m of the powder. There is instant fusion (70–120°C) and good resistance to future de-bonding. The epoxy here is polyglycidal ether with barium sulphate and calcium carbonate filler in epoxy resin matrix

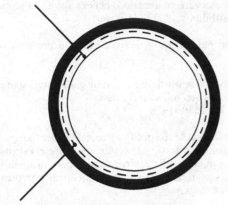

Epoxy layer protecting zinc from abrasion/electrolytic action

Zinc particles (galvanising layer)

(b) *Pipe interior*
This multi-layered coating is applied in one spray treatment. Electrically opposing properties of the different powders give a layering separation. This means the coating will have appropriate properties for the substrate as well as the exposed surface

fusion is instantaneous (70–120°C). This gives an overall long-term better resistance to de-bonding.

Anti-fouling paints

These paints are commonly used on marine structures. They contain toxic material which is part of the anti-fouling mechanism. Consequently these products should be handled with caution and not used in situations where maintenance of the ecological balance is a major consideration.

Fungicidal paints

The prevention of mould growth can be a parameter in the choice of paint films, not just in housing but in situations generally where the microclimate favours the growth of micro-organisms. These paints should not be used as a remedy for existing problem situations where checks on ventilation and the diagnosis of condensation, if present, should still be carried out. The Building Research Establishment have published lists of coatings that have proved effective on the basis that if they remain mould free for three months it is unlikely that mould growth will begin. There are also anti-condensation paints that prevent mould growth. (These probably work on the principle of manipulating the surface tension of water droplets making it impossible for spheroids to form and so keeping the water in a vapour state.) See BRE *News of Construction research*, October 1986.

2.5 PREPARATION OF SURFACE BACKGROUNDS

Prior to painting all surface backgrounds should undergo preparatory treatment to eliminate grease, or old defective paint. Backgrounds should be thoroughly cleaned, not simply brushed down, as the paint will only be adhering to loose particles and not a solid substrate. Preparation is the most important part of the coating process. Often the substrate, (especially in the case of plasters and renders) has not fully hydrated and there may still be some additional moisture loss. Checks should be made on the moisture content of the surface to be coated:

1 by hand-held instrumentation

2 in sealing off an area of approximately 300 mm square (recommended in BS 6150: 1982) and taking measurements in the centre with moisture sensitive papers

3 by using a hygrometer (as described in BRE Digest 55). This method can be applied to all large-scale surface finishes that involve wet trades. See ASTM D4263 for the equivalent moisture test which uses 450 mm square sampling surfaces.

Removal of old material

Burning off

Existing paint films can be removed by heat treatment. Blowlamps can produce burn marks if used carelessly but hot air paint film softeners are less likely to mark timber.

Solvent and chemical removers

These solutions are very aggressive chemically and should not be used in confined spaces. Instructions should always be carefully followed. If these solutions are used the surfaces should always be washed clean. See BS 3761: 1970.

Physical removal of paint films

Methods of sanding timber, working from coarse to fine grades, produce good results as loose fibres and debris are removed from the timber substrate. Sand-blasting methods are also effective, although samples should be tried first, as the coarser the particles used, the higher the rise of grain as softer pulp is removed.

Removal of fungal and algae growth on paintwork and related coatings

Exact guidance for this can be taken from ASTM D4610 (1986) from which the following is taken as a guide or BS 6150: 1982 (53.8). This is a problem especially in micro-environments which foster biological growth. Sodium hypochlorite (NaOCl) solution can be used as 5% aqueous solution in conjunction with trisodium phosphate, also as a 5% aqueous solution (non ammonia-containing laundry detergent).

The surface can be tested first with a drop of the sodium hypochlorite solution; if it bleaches, micro organisms are present. The surface should first be washed with the trisodium phosphate solution, thoroughly washed with clean water and then one part sodium hypochlorite solution for 10–15 minutes before thoroughly rinsing the surface again with clean water. After the surface is completely dry it can be painted.

TIMBER

Most timber used in building has to undergo some form of surface protection.

One of the chief problems with timber is that it absorbs moisture from its surroundings and this creates an environment conducive to the support of life forms. If the timber is dead, and there is no growth then these life forms whether insect or fungal will start to break down the structure of the timber and return it to the natural food cycle. This is an inevitable process and our use of timber simply delays the cycle for a time, which will vary according to how impenetrable our coating systems are, or how lethal the constituents are that they carry.

The second major problem with timber is that all untreated timber will bleach and eventually turn grey under the effects of ultra-violet light. Very few timber species stay stable in these conditions as the ultra-violet radiation destroys the lignin content in the timber. When this binding material (also a polymer) degrades only loose cellulose fibres are left and the surface delaminates.

Preservation

Before any surface coatings are applied it is fundamental that the timber has already been treated against decay and there should be evidence of certification of the timber supplier, contractor or joinery subcontractor. The most effective treatments contain salts that are toxic to the living organisms of fungi and pests. Double vacuum methods of absorption of the liquid are the most effective. See BS 4072: 1987 for treatments for external woodwork in buildings (excepting ground contact) which use copper chrome arsenate (CCA) water-bourne preservatives, applied using the vacuum method; and BS 5056 for copper napthenate and BS 5707: 1986 for pentachlorophenol organic solvents.

Timber with ground contact details should use creosote preparations as detailed in BS 5589.

If preservatives are used, checks should also be for compatibility and should cover:

1 The paint/coating system and the preservative in use.

2 Any effect on fixings, ie thin gauge steel gang nail plates, ferrous nails, and screws.
See BS 5589: 1978

It is advisable to specify all metal timber fixings to be corrosion resistant, as systems of preservation can create a milky acidic environment. This will act as weak electrolyte, risking the electro-chemical corrosion of ferrous fixings.[1]

Moisture content

The moisture content should be checked prior to coating which is relatively easy for a contractor to carry out using hand-held instrumentation. It should not exceed approximately 18% for general woodwork but in constantly centrally heated environments the moisture content may have to go down to as low as 10% depending on the continual temperature to be achieved in a building all the year round. (See *MBC: Materials* chapter 2 *Timber*). Generally the procedure for painting timber should follow section 25.4 in BS 6150: 1982. The following checklist outlines the work.

General repair

The wood should be checked for soundness with a knife or hat pin. A strip of Sellotape can be applied and pulled away to establish if there are any loose fibres. If this is the case the wood must be sanded or planed to achieve a smooth sound surface. If the wood has been repaired and pierced in, check that no surfaces are proud or need further sanding. Sandblasting is also an optional preparation treatment but will sometimes remove the weaker and pulpy cellulose tubes leaving a ridge-like character to the wood.[2]

Sanding

All surfaces should be sanded with fine glass paper in the direction of the grain, coarse grades will only detach sound fibres and damage the surface. Surfaces

[1] 'The corrosion behaviour of certain metals in CCA treated timber,' D W Simm and H E Button, *Corrosion Prevention and Control*, April 1985
[2] Kaare Kleive of Jotun Paints.

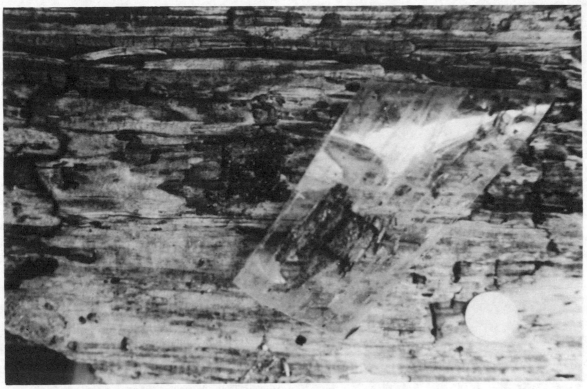

2.28 *Using Sellotape to detect loose and fibrous material. Although this is an extreme example, it is a very useful site test for the surface preparation of timber. Any loose fibres picked up indicate a surface too poor to accept coatings without further preparation*

are normally dusted off but today hoovering is more convenient and would remove dust from the painting area. At this stage some oily hardwoods (teak, aformosia, gurjun and makore) can be washed with white spirit, which helps to prevent loss of adhesion on these particular timbers.

Knot treatment
Knotting, the stabilisation of knots, must be carried out to seal the consistent seeping of natural resinous matter from the end grain features of branches/twigs, etc. Preservative will also seep from these end grain features and knots have to be sealed to prevent any damage to new coatings. See BS 1336: 1971 for the specification of 'knotting' (shellac in methylated spirits). Aluminium primers may be adequate indoors to seal knots but not externally, where under conditions of intense sunshine resinous knots may de-stabilise.

Priming
It is essential that primers are applied soon after the timber has been dried to its correct moisture content. End grain must also be fully primed as the ingression of moisture along open cellulose tubes can be as much as 100 × the moisture gained from the side of material. Most paint failures are due to the quality of the substrate of the timber surface. There is no point in painting over rotten and decayed wood, it should be systematically prepared and if necessary stripped out and replaced.

BS 6150 outlines three primer types for use in wood work, see table 2.3. Ref 1/1 is for a low-lead (less than 1%) oil-based primer to BS 5358: 1986 and for general use. Ref 1/2 is for an aluminium wood primer to BS 4756/1983 and suitable for resinous woods. Ref 1/3 is for a water-thinned primer to BS 5082: 1986 and has rapid drying qualities. All primers must be compatible with the system of finishing coats to be used, and a check should be made on the primer manufacturers' compliance on a relevant British Standard. Finishing coats should be applied as soon as possible after priming and after checking the moisture content of the substrate.

43

Description	General composition	Characteristics and usage
Low-lead, oil-based primer to BS 5358	Drying-oil/resin type binder with 'low lead' pigmentation	Primers of this type have a lead content of less that 1% (as determined by the method described in BS 4310) but are equivalent in performance to the traditional 'pink' (white lead/red lead) wood primers. They are suitable for general use on wood not highly resinous and not treated with metallic naphthenate preservatives; also for fibre boards and wood chipboards not fire-retardant treated. *Colour*: Typically white or pink
Aluminium wood primer to BS 4756	Drying-oil/resin type binder with aluminium pigment	Alternative to 1/1, and more suitable for woods which are resinous or have been treated with metallic naphthenate wood preservatives or creosote. May also be used as primers for fibre boards and wood chipboards (not fire-retardant treated) and as 'sealers' for surfaces that have been coated with bituminous materials. *Colour*: Aluminium
Water-thinned primer to BS 5082	Eulsion-type binder (typically based on acrylic polymer) with lead-free pigmentation	These primers dry more rapidly than 1/1 and 1/2 types, usually allowing same-day recoating if required. They do not contain flammable solvents and permit tools and equipment to be cleaned with water. Their durability without top coats on exterior exposure is equivalent to that of 1/1 and 1/2 types but, as they are more permeable, they may be less effective in excluding moisture from primed joinery stacked in the open. They are more prone to raise grain than oil-based primers. They may also be used as primers for fibre building boards and woodchip boards not fire-retardant treated. *Colour*: Typically white, light grey or pink

Table 2.2 *Primers for wood.*
Based on Table 1 of BS 6150:1982

Stopping and filling
Cracks and holes should be filled after priming with oil-based compounds which are more compatible with finishing coats. Putty is a traditional filler and should conform to BS 544: 1969. If applied prior to priming its binder can be absorbed into the timber leaving a friable surface to paint over. Water based fillers will need re-priming prior to painting. It may also be necessary to 'flat down' with fine glass paper prior to painting.

Undercoats
Two coats should be applied for external work, but this is optional internally and depends on the final quality of the work. Undercoats should be flatted down if a high gloss is required on the top coat.

Top coats
Externally, two coats are ideal, and if two are applied, one undercoat may be omitted. Internally, one gloss coat is usually sufficient unless very high quality work is required. Gloss finishes are more suitable for use externally as they are more effective in allowing the run-off of moisture.

Maintenance and cleaning
It used to be common practice that two years after coatings were applied, they were completely washed down with soapy water and 'leathered off', in a similar way to cleaning windows. This work used to be undertaken by the decorator and increased the service life of the paint films, especially externally. The deposition of sooty dust in rainwater creates aggressive solutions which degrade paint.

Natural finishes for wood
For timber the main finishes of varnishes, stains and french polish have been mentioned in 2.12 to achieve a natural finish but there are other methods.

Application	Requirement for preservative treatment (note 1)	Primers and references in table 2.2	Finish systems and product	Typical life to first maintenance (note 2)
Window joinery, softwood, internal and external	Essential	Low-lead, oil-based (1/1). Aluminium (1/2) (preferred for resinous woods, eg Douglas fir, and possibly for timber treated with metallic naphthenate preservatives). Water-thinned (1/3) (compatibility with water-repellent organic solvent preservatives should be checked)	*External gloss* 1 coat undercoat 2 coats alkyd gloss finish (Or 2 undercoats and 1 coat finish)	3 years to five years
			Internal gloss 1 coat undercoat 1 coat alkyd gloss finish	5 years or more
			Internal mid-sheen 2 coats alkyd mid-sheen finish	Up to 5 years
			Internal matt 2 coats alkyd matt finish	As mid-sheen finish
External sills, hardwood	Optional but necessary if excessive sapwood present	Low-lead, oil-based (1/1). Aluminium (1/2). Filling necessary with open-grain timber	As for *external gloss* above	Generally as for window joinery but depending on species and nature of timber
Doors and frames internal	Optional	As for window joinery		
softwood			As for window joinery	As for window joinery
plywood	None	As for window joinery. Filling recommended on open-grain veneers		
Doors and frames, external softwood	Desirable	As for window joinery	As for window joinery	As for window joinery
plywood	Optional; required if it contains non-durable species	Low-lead, oil-based (1/1). Aluminium (1/2). Filling recommended on open-grained veneers or if checking has occurred		
Skirtings, softwood	Desirable	As for window joinery	As for window joinery	As for window joinery

Table 2.3 *Paint systems for wood, internal and external (excluding hardwood surfaces not usually painted)*

continued . . .

45

Application continued . . .	Requirement for preservative treatment (note 1)	Primers and references in table 2.2	Finish systems and product	Typical life to first maintenance (note 2)
Cladding barge-boards, fascias and soffits	Required by Building Regulations for some species (not Western red cedar)	As for window joinery. Back-priming desirable	*Gloss finish* As for window joinery	As for window joinery
softwood			*Textured coatings* Finish types may be suitable for use on timber cladding; consult manufacturers	Op to 10 years
plywood	Optional; required if it contains non-durable species	Low-lead, oil-based (1/1). Aluminium (1/2). Paper overlay desirable and may allow primer to be omitted		
Gates and fences softwood	Essential	Low-lead, oil-based (1/1) Aluminium (1/2)	*Gloss finish* As for window joinery	Up to 5 years, depending on design and degree of exposure
hardwood	Desirable and may be essential in some circumstances; see BS 5589	*Note.* Unless painting is necessary for appearance, consideration should be given to preservative treatment of gates and fences initially and for subsequent maintenance		

Note 1 Reference should also be made to BS 5589:1978.
Note 2 Life expectancies shown assume application to dry, sound woodwork which, if necessary, has received appropriate preservative treatment and are based on performance in 'moderate' environments as defined in Table 9, of this standard.

Table 2.3 *Paint systems for wood, internal and external (excluding hardwood surfaces not usually painted).* From Table 10 of BS 6150:1982

Oils
These treatments help in water resistance but a good number of coats have to be rubbed in with time allowed for hardening in between.

Wax polishes

Rubbed finishes of undercoat

French polish

Acrylic emulsions

All comments given so far are also relevant to plywood, but if used externally the correct grade should be used with weatherproof adhesive and durable grades of timber veneer, ie Gaboon or African mahogany and generally hardwoods and not softwoods.

Application	Product type and reference in table 2.5	System	Typical life to first maintenance (note 1)
EXTERNAL WINDOW JOINERY, DOORS AND FRAMES			
	Varnish Not recommended	—	—
	Exterior wood stain Low solids High solids Opaque	2 to 3 coats	Variable according to product type but unlikely to exceed 3 years on full exposure
Hardwood	Varnish Exterior grade, full gloss	4 coats	Unlikely to exceed 3 years
	Exterior wood stain As for softwood	2 to 3 coats	As for softwood
Plywood, eg door panels	Varnish Not recommended	—	—
	Exterior wood stain Low solids	2 to 3 coats	As for softwood. Salt-staining possible
EXTERNAL BOARDING, CLADDING, BARGEBOARDS, SOFFITS, FASCIAS			
Softwood	Varnish Not recommended	—	—
	Exterior wood stain As for window joinery Also 'Madison formula'	2 to 3 coats	As for window joinery
Hardwood	Varnish Exterior grade, full gloss	4 coats	As for window joinery
	Exterior wood stain As for window joinery Also 'Madison formula'	2 to 3 coats	As for window joinery
Plywood	Varnish Not recommended	—	—
	Exterior wood stain As for window joinery Also 'Madison formula'	2 to 3 coats	As for window joinery. Salt-staining possible
GATES, FENCES, HANDRAILS See also note on these items in table 2.3			
Softwood	Varnish Not recommended	—	—
	Exterior wood stain Low solids	2 to 3 coats	As for window joinery

continued . . .

Table 2.4 *Natural finish systems for wood, external and internal*

Application continued . . .	Product type and reference in table 2.5	System	Typical life to first maintenance (note 1)
Hardwood	Varnish Exterior grade, full gloss	4 coats	As for window joinery
	Exterior wood stain Low solids	2 to 3 coats	As for window joinery
INTERNAL GENERAL JOINERY SURFACES, LININGS AND FITMENTS			
Softwood, hardwood, plywood (note 2)	Varnish* Interior grade, full gloss or mid-sheen. Polyurethane, two-pack or moisture-curing for exceptional abrasion resistance.	2 to 3 coats	Variable according to type and service condition but typically up to 5 years in 'average wear' environments
	Wood stain Some exterior wood stains may be suitable for interior use but refer to manufacturer's recommendations	1 to 2 coats	Variable according to type and service condition. May give lifetime service in some situations

Note 1 Life expectancies shown assume application to dry, sound timber which, if necessary, has received preservative treatment and are based on performance in 'moderate' environments as defined in table 9 of BS 6150:1982
Note 2 When a high standard of finish is required on internal hardwood surfaces, special-purpose wood finishes, eg french polish or lacquer, are generally used.

Table 2.4 *Natural finish systems for wood, external and internal.*
From Table 11 BS 6150:1982

Description	General composition	Characteristics and usage
Varnish, exterior grade, full gloss	Typically, drying-oil/phenolic or alkyd resin	This provides a tough, flexible, water-resistant coating, used principally as a clear protective finish for exterior hardwood
Varnish, interior grade, full gloss	Typically, drying-oil/alkyd, urethane or urethane/alkyd resin	Harder than exterior grade type and is more suitable for use on interior hardwood joinery. Some types may be sufficiently abrasion-resistant to be suitable for use on hardwood floors, counter tops and similar 'hard wear' locations
Varnish, eggshell, satin or matt finish	Composition generally as for 6/2 but adjusted to provide a lower level of gloss	Generally as for interior grade varnish but is likely to be less suitable for use in 'hard wear' locations

Table 2.5 *Natural finishes for wood*

continued . . .

continued . . .

Description	General composition	Characteristics and usage
Varnish, polyurethane, two-pack or moisture-curing one-pack	Two-pack types are supplied as separate base and 'activator' which are mixed before use to initiate chemical curing. With one-pack moisture-curing types, the reaction is initiated by absorption of moisture from the atmosphere or from the surface to which the material is applied	These coatings provide extremely hard, strong films with exceptional resistance to abrasion. The stresses set up within the film may lead to peeling and flaking especially on exterior woodwork whose surface, through long exposure without protection, has become degraded. In general, the use of this type of coating is best confined to interior woodwork where exceptional resistance to abrasion and possible chemical attack is required
Decorative wood stain	Drying-oil, spirit or water media with coloured pigments or dyes	Used essentially to modify or enhance the appearance of wood without obscuring its grain and is usually overcoated with clear finishes
Exterior wood stain, semi-transparent, Madison formula	Drying-oil binder (boiled linseed oil), paraffin wax, fungicide and pigment	Water-repellent penetrating stain that imparts an 'oiled' appearance to the wood. Suitable for brush application. Film remains soft and slightly tacky so will retain dirt and is not suitable for situations where it is likely to be abraded or come in contact with clothing. Wax component may cause difficulty if over-painting is subsequently required
Exterior wood stain, semi-transparent, low solids	Resin solution of low viscosity with fungicide and pigment	Water-repellent penetrating stain suitable for brush application. Imparts little or no sheen to surface of wood. Because of very low film thickness, offers little resistance to passage of water vapour and, in consequence, moisture content of wood may fluctuate considerably. Stains of this type can be used on interior woodwork but before doing so, it should be ascertained from the manufacturer that the fungicide contained does not constitute a health hazard
Exterior wood stain, semi-transparent, high solids	Generally as for low solids but higher resin content	Because of its higher resin content, this type of stain will normally impart a noticeable sheen to the surface. It is less penetrative than low solid stain and offers greater resistance to water vapour movement, so fluctuations in the moisture content of the wood are less pronounced
Exterior wood stain, opaque	May be a solvent-thinned resin solution or an emulsion-type, with pigment and fungicide	This type may be regarded as intermediate between a stain and a paint. It has low gloss, but the texture of the wood remains evident because of the differences in penetration within the growth rings. Some opaque stains may be used over weathered but sound paintwork

Table 2.5 *Natural finishes for wood.*
From Table 6 of BS 6150:1982

2.29

2.31

◀ **2.30**

2.29 *Pope House now relocated at Woodlawn Plantation Virginia by Frank Lloyd Wright 1940. One of the Usonian Houses, showing careful choice of materials so that applied finishes are minimised or avoided altogether. The timber is cyprus wood from Florida*

2.30 *Fishermen's drying sheds at Hastings, Kent. Maintenance of these structures is by a mixture of creosoting and straightforward patching with new timber when needed*

2.31 *Timber fence post detail. As timber ages softer material is eroded creating greater surface areas for exposure to ultraviolet light and cavities for water penetration. Consequently deterioration becomes faster as crevices provide opportunities for infestation. Painting on this surface would be unthinkable but this degree of surface irregularity does exist on badly or unprepared timber visible under a microscope and affects the adhesion of paint which is only microns thick (10^{-6} mm)*

50

METALS

Most problems relating to the successful coating of metals and protection of them can only be appreciated by an understanding of the mechanisms of corrosion. These mechanisms are outlined in *MBS: Materials* chapter 9 but it is worth stating that every metal in use in building is a highly processed material which is in an artificially alloyed state. The natural state of all metals is in their original found forms in the earth's crust. They may be oxides or sulphides but in this natural state they are stable compounds. After refinement metals are unstable materials and actively seek to recombine with oxygen or other elements. We call this process *corrosion*.

The most stable coatings are those that can form an oxidised layer on the surface and that layer should be thick and even to prevent further corrosion. Paint coatings only work because they have a thickness which prevents oxygen from reaching the metal layer within an acceptable period or they combine with the metal in such a way as to form a new chemically inert coating. Whatever mechanism is used to protect metal from decay it must be applied quickly before extensive corrosion products form on the parent metal (otherwise coatings are adhering to these weaker deposits and not the substrate). Consequently the cleaning metallic of surfaces is not to do with removing foreign debris but primarily to remove initial corrosion and to inhibit temporarily the formation of any new deposition. Cleaning can be done mechanically (blast cleaning) or chemically (pickling and etching).

Inspection

In the application of coatings to metals care should be taken that the work is checked by an inspector who is independent of the contractor carrying out the work. This is standard practice in America and is also recommended in BS 5493 Section Four: 1977. ASTM standard D3276 gives a checklist of applications with a very detailed account of methods of cleaning metals. This is paralleled by CP 3012: 1972 which gives very detailed methods for cleaning all types of metals. There are guidelines for making observations at particular stages of the coating process with reference to tests that can be undertaken on site to check quality, at every one of these stages. This is to ensure longevity of the film with particular regard to the repercussions of failure. Corrosion fatigue will often have its origins in the failure of coatings.

Testing

For example in ASTM D3359 failure of adhesion in coatings is measured in a tape test, method A, where a cross cut is made, a figure **X**. The tape is placed carefully over the **X** and then pulled away. The degree of film material that comes with the tape and its position relative to cut indicates a grade of adhesion. British equivalent tests use a grid system. There are also non-destructive tests which can measure thickness of paint films using electromagnetic pulses. In standard D3363 film hardness can be checked on site by using pencil tests with known grades of lead (from 6H–6B). Tests are carried out until a grade is found that will not mark the paint. This determines the relative softness of the film and hence the degree of hardness. These standards must be read carefully as the instructions for making the tests are very precise. The principles outlined above are only valid if testing is carried out in the exact manner described in the standard, otherwise comparative values are invalid.

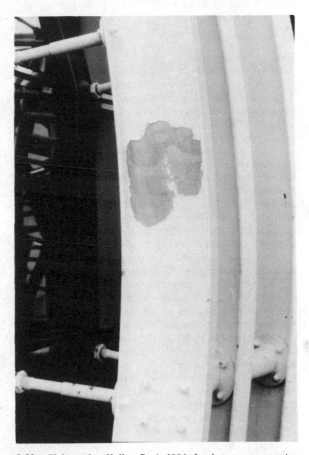

2.32 *Flaking, Les Halles, Paris 1986. Inadequate preparation to the galvanised substrate has resulted in loss of adhesion and embrittlement of the coating*

Iron and steel (ferrous metals)

BS 5493 (Amd 1984) is a comprehensive code of practice for the *Protective coating of iron and steel structures against corrosion*. It is a complete guide for the design, specification, inspection and maintenance of coatings systems and is a fundamental reference book.

The preparation of steel surfaces is critical and however good the surface cleaning from impurities, initial corrosion, etc, initial protection must be carried out as soon as possible as preparation and certainly not later than four hours after cleaning, otherwise surface coatings will be adhering to an increasing and thickening oxide layer, and not the substrate at all. All steel is best treated in controlled conditions before delivery to site. For the surface preparation of steel see section three of BS 5493: 1977 and CP 3012: 1972 which gives specific cleaning methods for all metals. See also Swedish Standards SFS 055900 (1967), *Rust grades for steel surfaces and preparation grades prior to protective coating*.

General preparation

Solvents are used to dissolve oil and grease, and surfaces should always be well rinsed after application. Aggressive *alkali cleaning* will take off old paint and if used, surfaces should also be washed after application. *Wire brushing* and scraping with metal tools is a fairly crude and unsatisfactory method for preparing metal surfaces. *Blast cleaning* is more effective in removing dirt and corrosion and can use metal shot or varying particle sizes of sand or grit in a stream of air or water. It will also give a surface topography that improves adhesion. (See BS 4332 and BS 5493: 1977 for further advice and specification on blast cleaning.) *Pickling* and *acid etching* will remove scale. *Flame cleaning* is used to evaporate moisture from the face of metals and can help to detach light corrosive deposits but it should be used with caution. It could affect the strength of metals locally by raising metals to their T_m (melting temperature) and possibly initiating re-crystallisation and probable loss of strength especially on metals below 5 mm in thickness. Priming can be carried out on metal that is still warm to the touch, but not hot.

Atmospheric parameters

In the surface coating of metals it is fundamental that the surface is dry. Any moisture on the face of the metal, if trapped, can initiate corrosion below the paint film and cause intergranular corrosion, this can cause flaking-off paint and spalling of finishes generally, leading to pitting in the surface of the material. To avoid condensation on the face of the metal, the temperature of the metal must be above the air dewpoint. It is advisable only to carry out surface coating if the air temperature is above 5°C and the relative humidity is below 80%.

Priming

Priming should follow quickly after surface preparation of the metal. There is general agreement in Britain and the USA that this should happen within four hours of preparation. It is recomended that priming should be carried out within one hour of surface preparation on metal that has been blast cleaned, because the nature of the surface has then a fine micro topography with a greater surface area available for corrosion.

The priming coat must be good enough to resist normal weather conditions for some time, especially as steel in a primed condition may stay exposed because frame structures are often erected before finishing coats are applied. See tables 2.6 and 2.7.

COATINGS ON WET TRADE FINISHES

There are some general points to be made with regard to plaster, cements, concrete and brickwork mortar. All these materials set by the mechanism of hydration, ie the chemical reaction with water which provides new compounds. Rates of hydration are slow and cannot be hurried. There is no point applying heat in new buildings to 'dry out' the fabric. This will take away moisture that is needed to assist the process of hydration and will leave the surfaces of materials more friable and more likely to give poor results. An approximate time for proper hydration is about five weeks for 25 mm of wet construction. Full set plasterwork will take about three weeks before decoration is programmed and screeds will take ten weeks if 50 mm in thickness. See BRE Digest 163 for advice about 'drying out' buildings. Moisture meters or hygrometers should be used to check the moisture content and humidity of the construction before finishing coats are contemplated.

The materials used in wet construction often have salt impurities which after wetting with water re-crystallise and are seen as efflorescence. Depending on the salts present, either hard glassy skins will form (potassium sulphate), or the more recognisable white fluffy compounds (sodium sulphate, magnesium sulphate). Any efflorescence that has occurred is also likely to damage new coatings and should be removed, and the surface brushed down every few days until the reaction ceases.

Any form of construction using Portland cement or lime will be alkaline in nature and care should be taken that finishing materials are compatible. A 'saponification' reaction can occur with oil compounds in coatings, where paint films effectively turn into soap. The

Continued on page 55

Description	General composition	Characteristics and usage
Pretreatment, wash or etching primer, two-pack As above, one-pack	Typically, polyvinyl butyral resin solution with phosphoric acid (as separate component) and zinc tetroxychromate pigment Typically, polyvinyl butyral/ phenolic resin solution with tinting pigment	The main function of these primers is to improve adhesion of paint systems to non-ferrous metals. They may also be used to provide temporary protection to blast-cleaned steel and sprayed-metal coatings. The two-pack types generally give superior performance but may be less convenient to use. Application of primers of this type does not usually obviate the need for the application of a normal type of primer subsequently. Most pretreatment primers may be used in conjunction with conventional and specialist coating systems. *Colour*: Typically low-opacity yellow (two-pack types) or blue (one-pack types)
Red lead primer to BS 2523: type A Red lead primer to BS 2523: type B Red lead primer to BS 2523: type C	Linseed drying-oil type binder with red lead (types A and B) or red lead/white lead (type C) as the sole pigments	These are primers of traditional type for iron and steel especially in new construction when there is likely to be a lengthy delay between erection of the steel and completion of painting. More tolerant of indifferent surface preparation than most other metal primers, they are slow in hardening which is disadvantageous when early handing or recoating is necessary. *Colour*: Orange red
Red lead/red oxide primer	Typically, drying-oil/resin type binder with red lead/red oxide pigmentation	These primers for iron and steel are quicker in drying and hardening than 2/2 primers and are therefore more suitable for use in maintenance work or when early handling or recoating is necessary, although they are of lower durability on exposure without top coats. *Colour*: Red-brown
Zinc phosphate primer	Typically, drying-oil/resin type binder with zinc phosphate as the main inhibitive pigment. Other tinting pigments may be incorporated	Zinc phosphate offers advantages over other inhibitive pigments in being non-toxic and neutral in colour. Zinc phosphate primers are fairly quick-drying and can afford protection without finishing coats for reasonable periods. Established usage is for priming steelwork, but some types may be suitable for non-ferrous metals; refer to manufacturers' recommendations. *Colour*: Typically light grey
Chromate primer	Typically, drying-oil/resin type binder with zinc chromate as the main inhibitive pigment. Red oxide or other pigments may be incorporated	Characteristics and usage vary according to formulation, but chromate primers are usually fairly quick-drying and suitable for use on ferrous and non-ferrous metals. *Colour*: Typically yellow, red-brown or grey-green
Calcium plumbate primers to BS 3698: types A and B Calcium plumbate primer, alternative to above	*BS 3698 types.* These have a linseed drying-oil binder. Type A contains 48% calcium plumbate; type B, 33% *Alternative types.* Typically, binder is of the drying-oil/resin type with calcium plumbate content similar to that of BS 3698 types	The main use of calcium plumbate primer is on galvanised steel; for this purpose, primers having the lower proportion of calcium plumbate are satisfactory. They may also be used on composite wood/metal components, eg galvanised steel window frames in wood sub-frames. BS 3698 types are fairly slow-drying, and the alternative quicker-drying types are frequently used. Not all

Table 2.6 *Primers for metal*

continued . . .

Description	General composition	Characteristics and usage
Calcium plumbate primers continued . . .		paints adhere well to calcium plumbate primers, and compatible undercoats and/or finishes should be specified. *Colour*: Typically cream or light grey
Metallic lead primer	Typically, drying-oil/resin type binder with at least 25% metallic lead pigment	Metallic lead primers are relatively tolerant of indifferent surface preparation and can protect iron and steel for reasonable periods before application of finish coats. They may show advantages over red lead primers in chemically-charged atmospheres and are quicker-drying than the 2/2 types. *Colour*: Merallic grey
Zinc-rich primer to BS 4652: type 1 Zinc-rich primer to BS 4652: type 2 Zinc-rich primer to BS 4652: type 3	Types 1 and 2 are based on a non-saponifiable medium, eg chlorinated rubber. Type 1 is supplied in two-pack form (zinc paste and thinner), type 2 in one-pack form. Type 3 is based on epoxy resin and is supplied in two-pack form (zinc paste and curing agent)	These are quick-drying primers for iron and steel with excellent rust-inhibiting properties. They should be applied only to well-prepared (eg blast-cleaned) steel. They may also be used for touching up damaged zinc coatings, eg zinc-sprayed or galvanised surfaces. Type 3 is frequently used as a prefabrication primer. Spray application is recommended, except on small areas. *Colour*: Metallic grey

Table 2.6 *Primers for metal.* Based on Table 2 of BS 6150:1982

Surface condition, primer	Finishing system	Total film thickness *(μm)*	Typical life to first maintenance in environments indicated
Blast-cleaned 1 coat zinc-rich primer and 1 coat oil-primer	(a) 1 coat oil-based undercoat and 2 coats alkyd gloss finish or 2 undercoats and 1 coat of gloss finish	170 to 205	*Exterior 'moderate'.* Up to 10 years
	(b) 2 coats micaceous iron oxide paint		*Interior 'moderate'.* Over 10 years
	(c) 2 coats aluminium paint (d) 1 coat oil-based undercoat and 1 coat alkyd gloss finish or 2 coats of gloss finish (e) 2 coats micaceous iron oxide paint	115 to 145	*Exterior 'moderate'.* Up to 5 years for film thicknesses exceeding 125 μm *Interior 'moderate'.* Up to 10 years
Manually-cleaned 2 coats Red lead primers to BS 2523 Zinc phosphate	As (c), (d) or (e) above	125 to 150	*Exterior 'moderate'.* Up to 5 years *Interior 'moderate'.* Up to 10 years
1 coat Chromate metallic acid	As (c), (d) or (e)	85 to 115	*Exterior.* Not recommended *Interior 'moderate'.* Up to 5 years

Table 2.7 *Paint systems for iron and steel.* From Table 12 BS 6150:1982

54

effect is not quite so literal, but oil films will soften as a result. Alkali resistant primers should be specified if oil-based coatings are to be used. To avoid this situation entirely, use only finishing coatings that are designed for these kinds of backgrounds and are classed clearly as masonry paints.

Substrate condition	Finish type	Primer	Finish system	Typical life to first maintenance (note 2)
DRY R.H. below 75% (note 1)	Alkyd gloss, mid sheen or matt	Alkali-resisting primer or, plaster only, water-thinned primer	(a) *Gloss finish* 1 coat oil-based or emulsion undercoat 1 coat alkyd gloss finish	5 years or more
			(b) *Mid-sheen finish* 2 coats alkyd mid-sheen finish	5 years or more
			(c) *Matt-finish* 2 coats alkyd matt finish	Up to 5 years
	Emulsion paint	Primer not usually required A well-thinned first coat of emulsion paint may be required on surfaces of high or variable porosity	(d) *Matt or mid-sheen finish* 2 or 5 coats general purpose emulsion paint, matt or mid-sheen	5 years or more
			(e) *Matt, high-opacity finish* 2 coats 'contract' emulsion paint 1 coat, spray-applied, may suffice in some situations	Up to 5 years
	Multi-colour	Primer or basecoat as recommended by manufacturer	(f) Usually 1 coat *multi-colour finish* spray-applied but refer to manufacturer's instructions	10 years or more
	Textured	Primer not usually required but refer to manufacturer's instruction	(g) *'Plastic' texture paint* Normally 1 coat but may require over-painting (h) *Emulsion-based masonry paint, heavy-texture* Normally 1 coat but refer to manufactuer's instructions	Indefinite in environments in which normally used but likely to require periodic over-painting to maintain appearance
	Cement paint (not on gypsum plaster)	Primer not required	(i) 1 or 2 coats *cement paint*	5 years or more in situations for which cement paint is generally used
DRYING Some damp patches may be evident R.H. 75% to 90%	Emulsion paint	As for 'DRY' substrates	As (d) and (e) above	Generally as for
	Multi-colour finishes possible but consult manufacturer	As for 'DRY' substrates	As (f) above	similar systems on 'DRY' substrates but some risk of failure at higher moisture levels

continued . . .

Table 2.8 *Paint systems for plaster, concrete, brick, block and stone, internal*

Substrate condition	Finish type	Primer	Finish system	Typical life to first maintenance (note 2)
DRYING continued . . .	Textured paints possible but consult manufacturer	As for 'DRY' substrates	As (g) and (h) above. If over-coating is necessary, emulsion paint should be used	
	Cement paint (not on gypsum plaster)	Primer not required	As (i) above	As for 'DRY' substrates
DAMP Obvious damp patches R.H. 90% to 100%	Emulsion paint possible	Primer not recommended	As (d) and (e) above. 'Contract' types are usually more permeable than general purpose types and less prone to failure on damp substrates	High risk of early failure
	Cement paint (not on gypsum plaster)	Primer not required	As (i) above	As for 'DRY' substrates
WET Moisture visible on surface R.H. 100%	Cement paint (not on gypsum plaster)	Primer not required	As (i) above	Generally as for 'DRY' substrates but some risk of failure

Note 1 'R.H.' refers to the relative humidity in equilibrium with the surface. Moisture content measured as in BS 6150:1982
Note 2 Life expectancies shown assume application to dry, sound substrates, qualified as indicated for other substrate conditions, and are based on performance in 'moderate' internal environments as defined in Table 9, of BS 6150:1982.

Table 2.8 *Paint systems for plaster, concrete, brick, block and stone, internal.* From Table 14 BS 6150:1982

Substrate condition	Finish type	Primer	Finish system	Typical life to first maintenance
DRY R.H. below 75% (note 1)	Alkyd gloss	Alkali-resisting primer	(a) 1 coat oil-based undercoat 1 or 2 coats alkyd gloss finish	3 years to 5 years or more
	Emulsion paint, general purpose if suitable for external use	Primer not usually required	(b) 2 coats general purpose emulsion paint	Up to 5 years
	Masonry paints, solvent-thinned	Alkali-resisting primer or as recommended by manufacturer	(c) *Smooth or fine-textured types, solvent-thinned.* 2 coats	5 years or more
			(d) *Thick, textured types, solvent-thinned.* Usually 1 or 2 coats applied by spray, often by specialist applicators	10 years or more

Table 2.9 *Paint systems for renderings, concrete, brick, block and stone, external* continued . . .

Substrate condition	Finish type	Primer	Finish system	Typical life to first maintenance
DRY continued . . .	Masonry paints, emulsion-based	Primer not usually required	(e) *Smooth or fine-textured types, emulsion-based.* 2 coats	5 years or more
		Primer not usually required but refer to manufactuer's instructions	(f) *Heavy-textured types, emulsion-based.* Usually 1 coat applied by roller	10 years or more
	Cement paint	Primer not required	(g) 2 coats cement paint	Up to 5 years
DRYING Some damp patches may be visible R.H. 75% to 90%	Emulsion paint, general purpose	As for 'DRY' substrates	As (b) above	
	Masonry paints, emulsion-based	As for 'DRY' substrates	As (e) or (f) above	Potentially as for 'DRY' substrates but high risk of earlier failure
WET Moisture visible on surface R.H. 100%	Cement paint	Primer not required	2 coats cement paint	As for 'DRY' substrates but some risk of earlier failure

Note 1   'R.H.' refers to the relative humidity in equilibrium with the surface. See BS 6150:1982 for methods of measuring moisture content.

Table 2.9   *Paint systems for renderings, concrete, brick, block and stone, external.*
From Table 15 BS 6150:1982

PLASTER

Ideally all plasterwork should be fully dry before applying any paint coatings. Most paint films are compatible with plaster and there is an increase in using paint finishes as a specification.

There are significant differences between types of plaster used that may affect the performance of coatings. Using BS 1191: 1973 as a classification for plasters, gypsum plasters are in their four categories of A B C and D. *Grade A* is pure plaster of Paris and can be treated as *Grade B* which are both 'soft' plasters with good but variable absorption. Over wetting is not recommended. *Grade C* plasters are harder but if they have been artificially dried before hardening, there will be particles of plaster open to chemical reaction once water is applied, causing expansion and blistering.

They are also very slightly alkaline which should not prove a problem unless lime has also been added, increasing workability. *Grade D* (Keene's Cement is the hardest plaster available and the surface can be so dense that adhesion for paints can prove difficult when used on squash courts, etc). It has been the practice to prime this particular plaster 'following the trowel' ie immediately after the initial set, usually within three hours. The primer used is well thinned with only a small amount of oil and is traditional and not a modern remedy. (It must be recognised that not all classes of plaster specified in the British Standards are now readily available. See section 3.13 in this volume.)

External renders (Portland cement)
Repairs to old renders should be carried out in accordance with BS 5262: 1976.

2.33 *Flaking, finish on external render. There are a number of separate checking patterns that mirror directions of induced stress (top left). As the paint films ages and hardens adhesion is lost and the film cracks in characteristic hexagonal patterns typical of fracture in sheet-like materials. Note how the generation of the large fractures in the surface coating follows cracking in the render below*

Most external renders are alkaline due to their portland cement base and sometimes integral lime constituents. If these renders are new, and not fully hydrated a saponification reaction can occur.

Prime with alkali resisting primer or use a base coat recommended by the paint manufacturer. Finish with alkyds, emulsions, masonry paints, cement paints.

Concrete

The painting of concrete should be avoided. Concrete presents a durable exterior if properly specified and painting can sometimes lead to the harmful entrapment of moisture. There is some movement of free water in and out of the gel pores, and if this is inhibited by using paint films that are permeable, blisters can occur. However, in order to give protection to re-inforcement in the body of the concrete that may be only lightly embedded (especially on existing old concrete) films have to be impermeable and it is recommended to use chlorinated rubber and bituminous coatings. Here is a dilemma, and one that highlights the problems in coatings in general.

Concrete first has to be properly surface cleaned before coating. Brush cleaning will remove dust and debris initially but air blast cleaning operating between 80–100 psi should be used 600 mm from the surface to remove all surface dusting. It should then be cleaned with water and then if necessary with detergents or steam cleaning (often thought more effective) to remove any oil or grease.

If all that is wanted is to improve an existing concrete surface, it is worth investigating two other methods first before resorting to paint. The first one is to abrade the surface mechanically or to acid etch the material to gain a different surface roughness/texture. Acid should only be used after the surface has been cleaned to a certain standard (ASTM D4258). Acid etching uses different concentrations of hydrochloric, sulphuric or phosphoric acids. Acid concentration varies according to the depth of etching required, and after application can be brushed down to give surface textures that will vary from fine to coarse grades of sandpaper. It is worth mentioning that the less smooth the surface topography the greater the likelihood of entrapment of dust and grime, which can deteriorate the surface further in the future.

BRICKWORK AND STONEWORK

It is not advisable to paint either brickwork or stonework. They are usually durable enough materials and any coatings will often create new problems. There should be a free movement of moisture through a masonry building structure and paint can do a great deal to inhibit the passage of water vapour which can become entrapped. Because of the degree of porosity, especially in brickwork, frost action can be more noticeable on externally painted walls, and free moisture can also encourage latent efflorescence. In the case of sedimentary stone this can be evident as subfluorescence.

Before painting concrete, cements, brickwork, or stonework, a full investigation should be made as to whether the surface can be cleaned, whether mechanically or chemically. Often paint is used as the first 'cost effective' solution to impoving the look of an external surface. The problems caused by applying paints indiscriminately can cost far more in terms of new defects and repeated maintenance than careful and effective cleaning. For specialist advice in restoration contact the Society for the Protection of Ancient Buildings. (SPAB is at 37 Spital Square London EC1 and publish a range of material helpful in understanding the detailing and restoration of ancient buildings.)

Architectural wall coatings (similar to industrial floor finishes)
These are hard finishes and use two-pack resin systems such as epoxy polymides, or polyester epoxy coatings are now in wider usage. These particular finishes are seen as a viable alternative to tiling in some public areas, as they have a lower initial cost and require little maintenance. They show good adhesion, are chemically resistant, and can be made on these particular coatings with regard to flame spread.

Type of board sheet	Primers	
	With alkyd and oil-based finishes	With water-thinned finishes*
Fibre hardboard, medium board and insulating board	Primer-sealer/stabiliser Water-thinned primer Aluminium wood primer	Not usually required, but, for absorbent board, first coats may need additional thinning
As above, flame retardant treated	Alkali-resisting primer	Alkali-resisting primer
Insulating board, bitumen-impregnated	Aluminium wood primer	Not usually required
Wood chipboard	Oil-based wood primer Primer-sealer Water-thinned primer Aluminium wood primer	Not usually required except possibly that oil-based primer is recommended for single layer boards to prevent swelling of chips
Plasterboard	Primer-sealer/stabiliser Water-thinned primer	Not usually required

Table 2.10 *Site priming of fibre building board, wood chipboard, and plasterboard*

Other backgrounds

The backgrounds dealt with so far cope with the basic range of materials used in building. There are a number of other materials, such as composite boards, hardboards, paper, fabrics and plastics which will need a particular specification. It is best to take manufacturers' advice after choosing a paint system. There are well known problems in applying new paint systems to backgrounds which have been coated with bituminous coatings, especially old timbers. Aluminium primers are advisable in this instance. For other general advice BS 6150: 1982 should be the first source of reference. With any unusual material, particularly composites materials, the most important decision is in the priming system, which has to relate to the degree of absorption of the material as well as chemical compatibility. This is why advice is given more specifically on priming in table 2.10.

3 CERAMIC MATERIALS

3.01 INTRODUCTION

Ceramics cover a range of materials that all have a similar range of properties and behaviour. This widens the traditional classification of ceramics to cover materials that vary in their origin and appearance. Ceramics can cover natural resources such as rocks and their minerals, or man-made materials which can include cement gels, glassware, as well as sintered clays giving the range of materials now called 'traditional' ceramics. These traditional ceramics are derived from the mining of clays which are fired to give pottery, bricks and tiles and are a combination of flint, feldspar and clay. It is important that ceramics are properly understood as covering a wide ranging group of materials. They are all:

Inorganic (One exception is diamond-carbon which is sometimes classified as a ceramic) and have

Nonmetallic properties (but metallic elements may be present) are **Ionically or Covalently bonded** with often a combination of **Metallic/Oxygen atoms** (More generally gaseous and metallic elements can be in combination, for example nitrogen can be substituted for oxygen in many alumino silicates which are then called *sialons*.)

Ceramics share a range of properties which include being:

Hard

Thermal insulators (good fire resistance)

Electrical insulators (density is important here for effective insulation and temperature is now relevant with regard to the development of super cooled semi-conductors)

Chemically stable (sometimes described as inert within the range of weak compounds which they may come into contact)

Brittle but with **high compressive strengths** (fracturing without plastic deformation)

Multiphase materials (a phase will be a different mineral/micro-structure)

The ceramic materials used in building exhibit all these properties. The advantages of using many ceramic materials is that they are already environmentally stable and will not oxidise further in the atmosphere. Unlike metals, which generally exist in an instable state and must be protected, ceramics are unlikely to react with elements in the atmosphere and are normally used in their natural state, ie their body composition can be their finished skin. This makes them economic in terms of maintenance. Problems are more likely to occur when they are combined with other materials to give different properties. For example when concrete is in combination with steel, initially to improve tensile strength by making a composite, carbonation and the subsequent corrosion of re-inforcement will make the whole material unstable. Mechanical fixing details generally are also a source of failure. The basic ceramic material usually degrades slowly, and is a long life component, whereas the fixing mechanisms are often highly stressed and if corrosion occurs, failure is more dramatic.

As the strength of ceramics improves, their performance starts to be comparable to metals. The difference in the materials is then limited to their mode of failure, or how they fail. Metals are capable of some degree of ductility or plastic deformation before failure occurs, whereas ceramics will fracture directly after reaching the end of their elastic limit, and so their failure is immediate and brittle.

Traditional ceramics

This category applies when considering fired clay products. A combination of materials are used with three main components, ordinary clays, calcined flint and feldspar minerals. Depending on the clay bodies used, the proportion of the two other components, and the degree of firing and type of cooling, the phase micro-structure of ceramics can be manipulated to give a range of materials with quite different properties and eventual usage. Most of our bulk building materials such as brickwork, tiles or pipes, use proven sources of clay without any further additions, and the place of manufacture is usually situated within the boundaries of the clay mining area. It is the increasing proportion of the other components, the feldspar and flint that give the finer tiles, pottery ware and electrical goods, taking ceramics into the harder porcelains and vitrified ware.

Earthenware clays will produce a soft porous material after firing at low temperatures. On fracture the material will show cleavage around individual particles. Glazed material shows a noticeable boundary between glazed and unglazed sections. It will have a Mohs hardness of about 4 or 5.

Stoneware clays are fired at higher temperatures with a hardness of 7 or 8. If fractured, the material will break as a glassy body with a continuous fracture plane. A stoneware glaze has the appearance of fusing with the clay body, which is extremely dense and non-porous. The silica in the stoneware forms the glassy matrix in which other particles are suspended.

Porcelain is the most glass-like body, with a glaze appearing completely integral with the body. Although a fine-grained material, it is extremely tough and durable as the microstructure of porcelain reveals needle-like crystals of mullite in a glassy phase matrix which prevent crack propagation.

Increases in the strength of ceramic materials can be achieved by minimising glassy regions, through which crack propagation is dramatic, and also by manipulating the size and structure of crystals. Fractures require more energy to propagate through crystalline rather than glassy regions and if the crystals are small the work of fracture is higher. Even if there is only a partly crystalline region as in porcelain, there is a toughening capability. The heat resistant ceramic hobs appear to be glassy but are a carefully controlled crystalline material. The material is seeded with nuclei for crystal growth and exact temperature control produces a completely crystalline material with strengths far exceeding that of porcelain. These materials are known as *glass ceramics* and their main feature is high temperature strength and resistance to thermal shock, due chiefly to the inclusion of high quartz phases. Even stronger glass ceramics can be made from the introduction of keatite crystals and other ranges are even machinable, their fracture toughness is so high.

New ceramics
The new ceramics, also sometimes referred to as technical ceramics, or engineering ceramics, are polycrystalline micro structures and so have several components. Their purity is far higher than traditional ceramics, and instead of using raw clay mined directly from the ground, the components used are pure compounds with no unwanted elements or impurities. Powders are

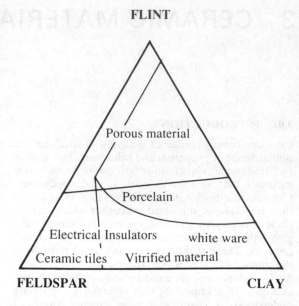

3.01 *Traditional ceramics. Relation of materials used to products obtained.* Redrawn from: *Ceramic Science for Materials Technologists* by I J Mcholm 1983, Leonard Hill, Blackie & Son Ltd

formed from these ingredients and are then cast, pressed, extruded or moulded into shape. These powders may also be set with organic binders. At this stage they may undergo machining before final sintering, sometimes in combination with additional applied pressure. It is the combination of pure materials, and exacting production techniques that ensures the very high strength of these materials. 'Ceramics in a Metals World', James A Spirakis in *Advanced Materials and Processes* 3/87).

Because of their very high strength chemical bonding at an atomic level, pure ceramics can be used as fibres, whiskers, or as toughening particles in composite materials. To optimise these materials very specific elements are used which show this type of strong convalent bonding and also have very low atomic weights. Elements that fit this criterion are beryllium, boron, carbon and silicon and when combined, as in boron carbide or silicon carbide, give an extremely strong group of materials.

3.02 GLOSSARY

Bonding
See 3.03

Calcination
Materials that have been calcinated have been heated to sufficiently high temperatures to give off water, organic contaminants and in some cases (especially in metallic ore extraction), carbon dioxide.

Cermets
This is a general term that relates to ceramic/metallic particle composites, but initially and more specifically to tungsten (W-Co) 'cemented' materials. In this instance the metallic phase forms the matrix, and is sintered from a powdered form of the metal.

Clastic material
This refers to the construction of new stones from older material by natural earth processes.

Faience
These are glazed terra-cotta (earthenware) tiles used on buildings. The word, although from popular French usage, originates from 'Faenze' in Italy, historically a centre for the production of fired ceramics which were chiefly tin glazed. The proportion of iron oxide present determines the degree of pink or red colouration.

Composition outlined from *Advanced Building Construction* George A Mitchell and A M Mitchell, Batsford 1947, as follows:
Silica 75.2%
Alumina 10.0%
Ferric oxide 3.4%
Calcium oxide 1.2%
Magnesium oxide (traces)
Alkalies and alkaline chlorides 0.5
Water 5.9%
Organic matter 7.7%
(**Note** these original figures do not total 100% but have been kept as originally printed as they reflect broadly the nature of the material.)

Glass
Glass refers generally to non-crystalline solids, sometimes called *amorphous solids* as they have no regular structure. They have the random order of molecules normally associated with liquids, which is why ordinary glazing glass is sometimes referred to as a *supercooled* liquid.

Mohs' scale of hardness
This is a scale of hardness that relates to the ability of a material to resist a scratch defect from a mineral. The tests should be made by hand and the examination for scratch deformation is by eye. To test a material, minerals that have been recently fractured with a sharp edge of increasing hardness are drawn over the test surface. This method of testing is described in BS 6431 Part 13: 1986 relating to ceramic floor and wall tiles.

1	Talc	Can be scratched by fingernail
2	Gypsum	Can be scratched by fingernail
3	Calcite	Can be scratched by a copper coin
4	Fluorite	Can be scratched by steel
5	Apatite	Can be scratched by steel
6	Feldspar	Scratches steel with difficulty
7	Quartz	Scratches steel with ease
8	Topaz	Scratches steel with ease
9	Corundum	Scratches steel with ease
10	Diamond	Scratches steel with ease

The above list shows a rough and ready equivalent with common objects if the correct minerals for testing are not to hand.

Multiphase materials
In solid materials there may be different regions of molecular structure. In many rocks these would be seen clearly as different mineral forms with individual, identifiable characteristics. Most ceramic materials could be called multiphase solids, as they usually are composed of particles, with their own individual structures, set within a matrix which may be glassy but also have its own identifiable structure.

Salts
These are compounds resulting from the replacement of one or more hydrogen atoms in an acid by metal atoms, or electropositive radicals. They can be crystalline at ordinary temperatures and include carbonates, chlorides, nitrates, phosphates, silicates and sulphates.

Sintering
Sintering is the fusing of particles together, they may be metallic, ceramic or a mixture of both. The mixtures, usually in particulate form are heated to a point where they can fuse and coalesce with adjacent particles. Materials in a powdered form have a far greater surface area. This is important in fusion processes where the greater surface area gives a more efficient transfer of heat and faster and more controllable material change. There are characteristic gaps in sintered bodies giving a degree of porosity. If these are filled after firing then it

is indicative that another component must have been present in the manufacturing process which liquified and filled pore vacuoles.

Suction

Suction is often referred to as a 'property' of cementitious materials in their take up of water and material. It is not a mechanism in itself and should be regarded as the rated ability with which a material can absorb liquids, usually due to the actual mechanics of capillary action.

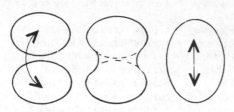

3.02 *The sintering of two particles*

Terra-cotta

The term is from the Latin meaning 'baked earth' but is used loosely and now relates to the use of hollow ceramic fittings imitative of stone introduced towards the end of the nineteenth century on a large scale. These fittings were made from graded clays often incorporating some reground material from earlier fired but substandard products.

Vitrification

Materials that are fired at very high temperatures and fuse to give a glassy state are said to be vitrified. They are in effect, supercooled liquids with very little porosity and particles coalesce to the extent of losing their individual microstructure.

3.03 BONDING, PHYSICAL AND CHEMICAL

Physical

Bonding is a term that has several different definitions according to which discipline is using the term. In building it relates to 'the securing of a bond between plaster and backing by physical means as opposed to mechanical keys'.[1] Mechanical keys or mechanical bondings refers to a physical locking of parts by their profiling. The physical means refer to a good take up of the backing material wth the substance and good adhesion. Adhesion varies in its definition according to the scientific discipline concerned, but in physics is generally defined as:

'Intermolecular forces which hold matter together, particularly closely contiguous surfaces of surrounding media, eg liquid in contact with a solid.'[1]

Adhesion in bonding of cementitious type materials is often achieved by a physical attraction through van der Waals' forces between pore walls (usually displaying electronegativity from compounds containing oxygen) and the initial attraction with water molecules in solution (which are dipoles with positively charged hydrogen ions).

Chemical

In ceramics there are two systems of bonding, covalent and ionic. Covalent bonding is by far the strongest of all chemical bonds, involving the pairing of electrons shared between two atoms. The pairing structures try and attain the most stable of all configurations, ie that of the noble gases, which are the most stable elements. Consequently it requires great energy to split these bonds, which in normal materials processing is usually carried out by heat.

Ionic bonding is the second strongest configuration and describes the transfer of electrons from a metal to a non-metal. The loss of electrons (negative particles) will make an element strongly positive, whereas the gain of electrons will make an element strongly electronegative. Consequently the ionic bond relies on strong electrostatic attraction between oppositely charged bodies. The final distribution of electrons also seeks to attain that of a noble gas.

A great deal of the bonding occurring in compounds is intermediate in nature between the two pure bonding types. The only other type of bonding, not found in ceramics is metallic bonding where although metallic atoms occupy regular positions in the formal geometry of the atomic lattice, the electrons act like a cloud and move freely through the lattice. This cloud interferes with wavelengths of light absorbing energy from light photons, but reflecting some, hence their opaque quality with some degree of lustre.

[1]*Dictionary of Science and Technology*, Chambers, 1981 edition.

3.04 FRACTURE MECHANICS AND CERAMICS ENGINEERING

There is a commonality about the methods of fracture in ceramic materials. Most traditional building materials fall into the category of being brittle. This tendency towards a brittle state determines the method of fracture. Most traditional ceramics can display particular flaws which can be crack imitations. Even if these flaws are extremely small they can be effective as crack initiators by acting as stress concentrators. Accordingly those ceramics which have small pores in the body of the material, have in effect, built in stress concentrators, which will make the material predictably brittle. A A Griffith developed his famous theorem relative to crack propagation in the 1920s and his formulae (modified) are still used as a powerful model or the prediction of crack behaviour.

Fracture toughness is a property now commonly measured in conjunction with compressive strength, where notched specimens are used for testing to initiate crack propagation. Materials are then modified or reinforced to minimise crack propagation and so increase toughness. When ceramics are reinforced, which can be on a large scale as in reinforced concrete, or on a small scale by using ceramic fibres in high quality engineering ceramic, they also become composites.

STONE

There is a great variety in the structure of rocks and strength is also dependent on orientation, not just the orientation of particular crystals, but also the orientation of bedding planes. For example, in shales, strength may increase by a factor of ten if stress is applied perpendicular to the grain rather than parallel to the grain. Surprisingly, perhaps, rocks do behave elastically, and there is always some extension prior to fracture. There is no plastic behaviour however and so no yield point, fracture occurs directly after a rock has reached its elastic limit. In compressive testing, branch cracks are produced which gradually become orientated in the direction of the applied stress, then they terminate. If the stress is increased more branching of cracks starts until there is such a great network of cracks that large-scale failure takes place between lightly cracked and heavier cracked regions. Stress is progressively increased until there is a total failure of the specimen being tested. This final stress value becomes the compressive strength of the material although obviously there has been substantial deterioration of the material before that final point is reached. ('Brittle fracture of Rock' by Leonard Obert, chapter 3 of *Fracture* Volume 7 by Llebowitz 1972, Academic Press Ltd).

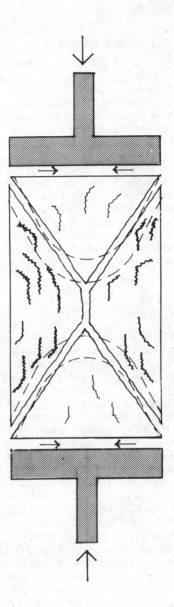

3.03 *Fracture in Compression specimens. After Paul and Gangal 1966. Complete failure stems from regions of macro cracks growing adjacent to areas which are lightly micro cracked. Note how the cracks will orientate themselves in the direction of the applied stress*

65

POLYCRYSTALLINE CERAMICS

These ceramics have a great range of micro-structures, of different grain sizes, sometimes include a glassy matrix and generally relate to porcelains as well as the wider range of alumina ceramics. There are so many components in these materials that fracture mechanisms are often hard to predict but it is generally known that materials in this category will fail at a strength far lower than their predicted theoretical strengths. There is general agreement that flaws dictate the strength of the whole material. Flaws relate to voids as well as surface defects. In fracture mechanics a high degree of porosity means a far greater number of flaws and hence a considerable reduction in possible strength. If materials have porosity values of less than 10%, values for elastic moduli and strength can decrease exponentially giving a more dramatic relationship with regard to failure.

FINE CERAMICS

Fine ceramics are materials with the highest purity, often single or dense polycrystals, with a high degree of control with respect to density, usually with only a few minor pores. Their application is in the field of electronics or high quality engineering. In these fields the control of flaws is fundamental and the concern with flaws relates not to structures that can be seen with the naked eye but to microcracks and other defects that could propagate further cracking.

Beta-Sialon ceramics showed an unexpected low fracture toughness that was investigated by Kishi (*et al* 1986 of the National Industrial Research Institute of Kyushu, GIRI Kyushu) who found internal defects between 50 and 100 microns in size below the surface where particles had not fully sintered due to non-homogenous mixing of particles. By making materials in this group with solution additives rather than sintered additives, the scale of defect was eliminated. The strength of the material was increased by 70% and after annealing improved by a further 53%. This example and work in this new field of fine ceramics is recorded in 'A perspective on new ceramics and ceramic composites' by H Suzuki (Philosophical Transactions, Royal Society London A322. 465–478 (1987.)

With these fine ceramics performance can be improved by producing an immaculate surface. Special coatings are being designed as protectors to this kind of finish. This development parallels the success found in treating roofing tiles to improve frost resistance. (See Section 3.05 *Frost and freezing mechanisms.*)

Stress concentration factors will alter a predicted strength and these relate to the geometrical shape of the flaw modelled as being either spheres, (most stable) cylinders or elliptical slots (edges can act as stress concentrators). Typical flaw sizes for these types of voids vary from 1 to ten microns, and as actual particle sizes of powder used might well be below 53 microns, this gives an idea of the scale of engineering involved.

CONCLUSIONS

Due to the brittle nature of our ceramic materials, if they are needed to take high loads, care must be taken in the design and placing of the ceramic material, so that there is no undue stress. If the material is to take loads in tension then, those materials must be reinforced in the same way as steel is used in concrete. Cracks cannot propagate in these reinforced materials, energy is needed to divert the crack around the reinforcement and this has the effect of crack stopping. Aggregates also act as crack stoppers by diverting cracks around the aggregate, again taking a greater amount of energy to do so. The number of voids in a material must be minimised, and the size of those voids controlled. In the placing of materials such as concrete, the action of placing must be as carefully specified as the materials themselves.

In polycrystalline and fine ceramics performance can be improved by fibre reinforcing. This brings these particular ceramics into the categories of being composite materials. Developments in fibres which include silicon carbide yarn and alumina and aluminium borosilicate fibres provide a better chance of increasing the toughnes of ceramic materials. Formerly carbon fibres were used, but unsuccessfully. They have a tendency to oxidise with resultant loss in strength. Fibre reinforcement can improve figures for the work in fracture relating to unreinforced glass and ceramics (measured in energy units of Joules per sq m) from 10^1 or 10^2 to 10^4. (See 'Fibre Reinforced Ceramics' by D C Phillips, chapter 7 volume 4 *Fabrication of Composites* edited by A Kelly and S T Mileko 1983, Elsevier Science Publishers.)

A broad understanding of fracture mechanics helps in determining their proper usage. Loads should be evenly distributed, point loads should be avoided or at least spread by an intermediate and dense material. Designers do not often think of fixing positions as point loads, which they certainly are, and act as stress concentrators often by causing further internal defects. Using fixings that are too strong are to no advantage as they will put additional stress on a material and be a cause of fine cracking that can lead to premature failure.

One fundamental point about using ceramic materials is ensuring that they have high degree of purity. This is why on a large scale the ingredients for making concrete must be strictly specified, large-scale failure can often be traced back to small-scale defects.

As the need for finer engineering increases in ceramics, this raises expectations in that raw materials from the earth's crust have to undergo greater refinement. It becomes rarer to find natural deposits with the right degree of purity or particle size and further processing will raise costs. Often, materials of known compositions are actually waste products from other industries. Investigations are currently being undertaken to establish the possibility of using bauxite waste from the making of aluminium to make high quality ceramics. The 'red mud' waste from the alumina industry in Jamaica has a high haematite content, low silica content but has three major oxides that can form glassy matrices after firing (SiO_2, P_2O_5, CaO). The waste also has most of the particle sizes (70%) at 5 microns, ideal for sintering. High firing produces material of a high enough quality for engineering ceramics. ('The Mechanical Properties of Ceramics from Bauxite Waste' by J C Knight, Arun S Waugh, W A Reid. *Journal of Materials Science* 21 1986 2179–2184 Chapman and Hall Ltd). If waste products can be used in this way it will make high quality ceramic components more accessible for the building industry.

3.05   FROST AND FREEZING MECHANISMS

It is well known that water will expand on freezing by approximately 9%, and this has been given as probably the major cause for the mechanical spalling of material in ceramic bodies. It was assumed that certain traditional ceramics could absorb an amount of water and become saturated on the surface. If this saturated water then froze, the change of the state from liquid to solid with the accompanying increase in volume, would be sufficient to force materials apart. This broad explanation for 'frost damage' is now under question. It is also unlikely that a material could be so fully saturated and freeze totally, as the freezing of water is pressure dependent. It is more likely that there will be some ice formation on the external face of the material, but chilled water will still be present in the body of the material.

3.04   *Brick arch St Pancras Station, London. Extensive erosion of soft red bricks and stone is accelerated by continual frost action causing spalling of both materials, although more extensively, of the brickwork. Note the dark encrustations of sooty material, forming a hard skin in sheltered regions through the combination of salts, pollutants and water vapour held in this more sheltered area*

Attention has now focused on the *pore system* of a material and the pressures that can be exerted within those pores, not just by crystal growth of ice but by the pressurisation of trapped chilled water. This can be hydraulically rammed by adjacent crystal growth, and be the real cause of mechanically applied pressure. Also, as ice crystals form, they continue to grow and be fed by adjacent chilled water. In this instance the mechanics of fracture may be due to prolonged crystal growth and not volumetric expansion of an original source of chilled water. There is also a capillary theory for frost action which is explained by the thermo-dynamics of a liquid/solid interface. The characteristic feature of this situation is that a curvature is developed at the interface and this can exert pressure on the side walls of a pore system.

Capillary suction depends on water being attracted to the walls of pore structures. Most ceramic walls whether silicates, carbonates or aluminium oxides have either a slightly negative charge from oxygen atoms or a positive charge from hydroxyl groups. As water molecules are polar (meaning they have negative and positive parts in the molecule) they can be attracted to pore side walls and this is the basic mechanism of hydrogen bonding. It means that many materials (notably concrete) always hold an amount of moisture in the pore walls which is weakly bonded and so not removed by the simple mechanism of evaporation.

However, it is unlikely that one factor alone will cause frost damage and there is likely to be a combination of mechanisms. For a discussion on this topic see 'Frost Action as a Capillary Effect' by J M Haynes, *British Ceramic Society Journal*, volume 63 *Transactions* 1964. For a more general overview see 'Frost Resistance: A Discussion' by Baldwin, West and Clews *British Ceramic Society Journal* volume 2–3 1956–66, volume 3 (i) pp 145–6.

The kind of pressures that can be exerted relate to pore size and also pore size distribution. In turn these also determine other properties, which include strength, water absorption, saturation coefficients, rate of absorption and capillary effects.

Test procedures to predict frost failure through pore size and distribution have not been over successful, and do not seem to be able to imitate the failure of the material in practice. The only way of establishing quality is still by use of freeze-thaw test cycles. The British Standards (BS 6431: 1968 Part 22 *Method for determination of frost resistance*) talk about satisfactory frost resistance being expected of tiles which survive 15 freeze-thaw cycles.

Destruction of ceramic materials by cyclical freezing usually starts from the glazed surface with fine crazing, rounded cracks then lead to a tear out of material, the rounded micro cracks transform into shallow tips and the degradation is progressive, ie there is an increase in the surface porosity, a greater ability to take up water and the damage continues. The early development of these cracks cannot be seen with the naked eye and the number of cycles of freezing is minimal in comparison with cycles of testing that are in the order of 10^2. Egerev's paper[1] concludes that the integrity of the glaze coating is all important and the most critical aspect to consider with regard to frost protection. In a paper published in 1986 Nakamara and Okuda[2] experimented with boiling clay roofing tiles in n-butanol for at least 24 hours to form a Butoxy group within the outermost skin of the tiles, giving less water absorption and enhanced durability. A later paper by Romanova[3] confirms the value of improving the formation of a strong intermediate layer between tile and glaze to improve frost resistance. Another paper by Nakamura[4] confirms several indirect evaluation factors which can influence frost susceptibility in clay roofing tiles. These

3.05 *Brickwork, St Pancras Station, London. Frost action has damaged the surface of this brick, and the spalling patterns echo the irregularity of the inner pore structure of the material*

are stated as being due to water absorption, bending strength, capillary water saturation and pore size distribution.

Prediction of possible behaviour is difficult but there is growing proof that denser tiles, ie fully vitrified with a minimum pore diameter, may theoretically be at greater risk from frost damage. By capillary action, penetration is more likely if the pore is completely full. A pore with a greater size in diameter has room for expansion when water changes its state from liquid to solid, and is also able to cater for evaporation of excess moisture.

Another variation of the hydraulic pressure theory describes how, in a highly porous material, the growth of ice crystals puts pressure on adjacent unfrozen water which may be unable to flow.

Instead of understanding frost action as the expansion on freezing of ice, if ice crystals grow with a source of unfrozen water still available then new crystal growth will put additional pressure on capillary side walls (similar to frost heave in soils). This requires regions of coarse pores adjacent to microporous regions for this particular phenomenon to happen. Proof that this combination is critical to initiate frost damage can be seen in stone with this kind of pore distribution. Portland stone is prone to frost damage whereas sandstone with an overall coarse size of pore diameter is more resistant to frost damage.

A related observation with regard to frost resistance, but this time in relation to concrete, is discussed in a Finnish paper on Arctic concrete technology. Tests were carried out in extreme conditions using freeze-thaw tests within a range of $+20°C$ to $-60°C$. Concrete types tested include mixtures with and without air entrainment and also those with hollow plastic microspheres. The concrete mixes that had been air entrained showed a better frost resistance. Concrete without air entrainment and with the microspheres showed an appreciable decrease in strength.[5]

Most work on frost resistance has centred on tiling because of the degree of exposure, and also their saturation, giving ideal conditions for studying freeze thaw conditions.

References
[1] *Effect of the quality of glaze coating on the frost resistance of façade tiles.* Egerev V M, (Scientific Research Institute of Building Ceramics USSR) Zotov, S N, Romanova, G P, Lykhina N S, *Glass Ceramics* volume 42 numbers 7–8 Jul Aug 1985 pp 351–372.
[2] *Enhancement of frost durability by modifications of internal surface of clay roofing tiles.* Nakamura (Masahiko), Okuda (Susuima) in *Yogyo Kyokai Shi* v 94 n12 1986 pp 1239–1242.
[3] *Increasing frost resistance of façade glazed tiles.* Egerev V M, Zotov S N, Romanova, G P, *Glass Ceramics* v 43 n1–2 Jan Feb 1986 pp 66–68.
[4] *Indirect evaluation on frost susceptibility of clay roofing tiles.* Nakamura (Masahiko), Mama (Akinoi) Matsumoto (Shin-ichi) Okuda (Susuima) in Yogyo Kyokai Shi v 94 n12 1986 pp 1239–1242.
[5] *Arctic Concrete Technology.* Kivekas, Lauri, Huovinen, Seppo, Hakkarainen, Tapani, Leivo, Markku. n305 1984 p 149. *Valt Tek Tutkimuskesku Tutkimuksia.*

APPLICATIONS

3.1 INTERNAL AND EXTERNAL TILING

There is an historical usage of tiling which is worth considering. The application of a new solid skin allowed for a richness of decoration and an opportunity for an applied finish that had a developed craftsmanship, whether by painting or the choice of inlaid marbles, or selected mosaics.

Although the history and usage of roof tiling is well documented with details for fixing that have not changed a great deal, there have been changes in the way people have used tiles as walling materials.

Early uses of vertical wall tiling, including mathematical tiles, is related to a localised vernacular that might use timber frame construction. The tiles were fastened with pegs onto battens, fixed to the main frame. The joints were pointed up afterwards to give the appearance of brickwork. There was a popular misconception perpetrated for many years that their use was deliberately to avoid a brick tax, introduced by Pitt the younger in 1784 (estimated at 3 shillings a thousand). In *Mathematical Tiles* by Maurice Exwood (*Vernacular Architecture* volume 12 1984) the author proves that mathematical tiles were more expensive than most plain tiles and bricks at that time. He quotes London area prices in 1862 as follows:

Plain tiles per 1000	£2 4 0d
Malm stocks (bricks)	£2 7 0d
Common stocks	£2 2 0d
Mathematical tiles (red)	£3 0 0d
Mathematical tiles (white)	£3 10 0d

The data shows how that mathematical tiles cost approximately 28% more. They were often used to modernise and improve the property. Any savings made in construction would be by the use of a timber frame. The quality of the tiles was such that they were often regarded as lasting longer than normal brickwork. Mathematical wall tiling is basically imitative of roofing technology, with the same principle of lapping one tile over another on battens. The only major difference is that the tiles are rebated and so in lapping over each other give the appearance of brickwork. Framing methods used should be stiffer to allow for the use of pointing which needs a more inflexible structure. The mortar mixes should also be on the weak side for flexibility and should also include lime. Any movement that may occur might then be rectified by the slight dissolution of lime in rainwater to heal hairline cracking.

The only other major use of tiles that are dry fixed and not bedded, is in the pegging or nailing of flat tiles to a wall surface. The most successful seem to be fixed on the diagonal, leaving a narrow gap between the tiles, which is then mortared over in a half round section, resembling rounded bars. This type of detail appears in Japan and also in Northern Europe, eg Belgium.

The Victorian use of terra-cotta owed more to the successful imitation of stone components, as a 'kit' alternative. The price was approximately half that of using stone (Rivington 1901). At the turn of the century this use of fired clay products became more developed as an expression of decoration related to the period.

Terra-cotta refers to fired but unglazed ware which will have a proportion of iron oxides present. The clays are generally earthenware with a significant addition of ground glass, sand and recycled substandard pottery (ground) which help to minimise distortion in firing. The body colour of the clay will vary according to how much iron oxide is present. There are also colour changes depending on the degree of firing.

The best terra-cotta clay products have an even body composition from carefully selected and well graded material. Some terra-cotta clays have a body of coarse clay and a face of finer clay. The whole tile is backed with another layer of finer clay to act as a compensating layer and to prevent warping. Sometimes the layers of finer clay were too thin and could spall away from the main body of the tile from differential movement. This method of making tiles is similar to 'encaustic tiles' where the fine baking and facing layers were pigmented and then pressed, the pressed part then filled with coloured slip for contrasting colour. Burnt tiles were then glazed by dipping into a mixture of powdered glass and water and reheated. (It was noticed that the more successful and durable coatings were formed from tiles glazed whilst still hot from the first biscuit-fired process.) Some terra-cotta is often referred to as having a vitrified skin, possibly because of smaller particles on the outermost layer having a greater ability to sinter successfully apart from the choice of materials used for the facing.

3.06 *Terra-cotta cladding, office building Surbiton. Aggressive cleaning has removed the vitrified skin from these pilaster details. Water is now more easily absorbed through the face, taking salts and impurities from adjacent mortar and fixings, encouraging severe discoloration*

The use of terra-cotta and the techniques of being able to make highly individual components was used to great effect in not only large buildings such as the Natural History Museum, Kensington, but also later on small scale but special constructions like the Michelin Building, Chelsea. Built in 1910 and restored 1987 it is an outstanding example of Art Deco building. The architect M. François Epinasse of Clermont Ferrand used a Hennebique ferro-concrete system but the tiles, made by Gilardoni Fils et Cie of Paris, are unique from the individually depicted racing scenes, to the tile details based on automotive parts. The fixing of these tiles is worthy of comment. The complex shapes, are three-dimensional and were expected to be filled with mortar and weighty pieces restrained by additional metal cramps. These can corrode if exposed to water and air, and any refurbishment should allow for their replacement.

3.08

3.07 *Natural History Museum, South Kensington, London. Cleaning has made these cill details less resilient to water penetration, and subsequent efflorescence and some discoloration is now apparent (1984)*

3.08, 3.09 and 3.10 *Michelin Building, Chelsea, London 1984 (prior to restoration by Conran Roche and YRM) L G Mouchel 1911. Built using the Hennebique ferro concrete system the terra-cotta tiles still retained when these photographs were taken (1984) and were in good condition figure 3.07, although where the vitrified skin had been eroded (by whatever means) there was significant discoloration*

◄ 3.09   3.10

The next major use of tiles in wall claddings occurred in the 1920s and '30s. They were known as *faience* (a fresh word for earthenware) although they consisted chiefly of flat earthenware tiles as used for the Odeon cinemas. The term became synonomous with tiles which held a more highly coloured and more obvious glaze.

Our twentieth century aesthetic (which currently dominates with plain colour applications as a skin to building) probably owes much more to the rigours of the early modern movement, obsessed with the sterile façade of medical technology and science than the continuation of a decorative tradition. Our inheritance of that aesthetic is the concept of 'grid' which is limiting. For a grid to be successful on a building façade it means that the dimensional co-ordination of the building should, ideally, be designed from the outside in and the internal finishes set out accordingly.

'Smooth and sensible functioning of daily life is not an end in itself, it merely constitutes the condition for achieving a maximum of personal freedom and independence. Hence, the standardisation of the practical processes of life does not mean new enslavement and mechanisation of the individual, but rather frees life from unnecessary ballast in order to let it develop all the more richly and unencumbered.'[1]

[1] Walter Gropius from v. 12 of the Bauhaus books. The quotation is shown adjacent to a house (1926) with a completely tiled kitchen.

3.11 *External tiling detail. History Faculty Cambridge (James Stirling 1964–7). Water penetration through a horizontally tiled surface and a critical edge junction encourages the leaching out of calcium hydroxide from concrete/cementitious material. In combination with carbon dioxide in the atmosphere this will form insoluble calcium carbonate. The projecting window detail acts as an inevitable splash zone for this sequence of events and cannot be cleaned*

3.12 *Vulnerable edge detailing in tiles, Cité de Refuge 1933 (Le Corbusier). The junction of several different materials, shapes and services is a potential site for failure*

3.13 *External tiling detail. Failure of these tiles has revealed only a small area that gave proper bonding and adhesion*

BS 6431: 1982 is a comprehensive set of standards dealing with all aspects of external and internal tiling. There are great problems in tiling which relate not so much to the tiled component as to the supporting building fabric. In effect, the tile is the final component of a composite system of construction and is usually an integral part of the fabric. The specification for tiling cannot be thought of in isolation, and although the tile is fixed last specifications must be developed at an early stage so that repercussions of shrinkage of backing materials, ie cements and concrete frames, are fully understood and catered for. Another factor to influence early decision making is the long delivery period that some tiles might need. Often the best tile to specify is unavailable due to delay in supply and a compromise decision is reached which is entirely unsatisfactory.

3.14 and 3.15 *St Thomas's Hospital, London, (YRM)* (photograph taken 1984.) *Careful detailing showing how tiling is thought of as a composite with the structural fabric. Tiles are clad over individual structural elements with clear separation inbetween. There are no horizontal exposed surfaces and cills weatherproof the tops of infill panels*

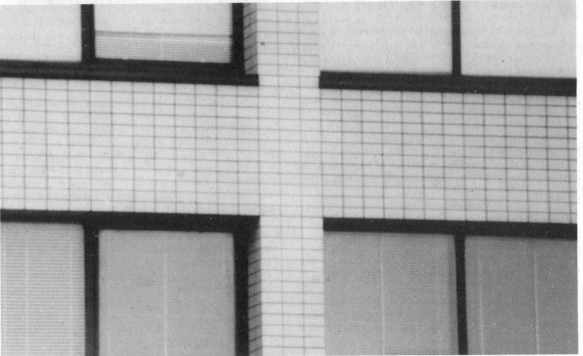

Categorisation

The European Committee for Standardisation (CEN) have agreed a classification for tiles, is based on water absorption which is related to porosity and method of manufacture.

Shaping	Water absorption	Group I $E \leqslant 3\%$	Group IIa $3\% < E \leqslant 6\%$	Group IIb $6\% < E \leqslant 10\%$	Group III $E > 10\%$
A		Group A1 EN 121	Group AIIa EN 186	Group AIIb EN 187	Group AIII EN 188
B		Group BI EN 176	Group BIIa EN 177	Group BIIb EN 178	Group BIII EN 159
C		Group CI ...	Group CIIa ...	Group CIIb ...	Group CIII ...

Table 3.1 *Classification of ceramic tiles according to their groups and their specific product standard.* From BS 6431 Part 1: 1983, EN 87 Table 2

All tiles submitted for inclusion under this standard have to satisfy dimension and surface qualities which include the actual dimensions of length, breadth and width, rectangularity, surface flatness and quality as defined by the test methods in EN 98. In every case thicknesses of tiles are specified by the manufacturer, but in order to conform to the tests undertaken for degree of warp or physical strength, it should always be possible to produce a tile of adequate thickness. As a result, there is no clear guidance as to likely thickness from a particular tile size given in the British Standards. The thickness can only be determined after a manufacturer is chosen.

Every category of tile will have a recognisable grouping of types which also relate to their quality and ultimate performance. Every group will also have its own modular and non-modular preferred sizes for that grouping.

Group AI: extruded ceramic tiles with low water absorption of E < 3%

The extruded tiles may be single and subsequently pressed into shape or double (and subsequently spilt in two after firing) and as the highest category is suitable for all uses, internal or external, 'in all climatic conditions'. They also have the highest resistance to chemical attack, Certain quarry tiles can also come into this category if their composition and manufacture is of a high enough standard.

See tables 3.3(a), (b), (c) and (d).

Group IIIa: extruded ceramic tiles with water absorption of 3% < E < 10%

The extruded tiles relate only to split tiles or quarry tiles which may be subsequently pressed. They are suitable for internal and external use but specifiers should satisfy themselves as to the degree of exposure they can sustain.

Group AIIb: extruded ceramic tiles with a water absorption of 6% < E < 6%

The extruded tiles relate only to split tiles and quarry tiles. The quarry tiles may initially be formed by extrusion but can be die-pressed into their final shape at a later stage. They are suitable for internal and external situations but used mainly for flooring. This Standard is in two parts with Part 2 relating to *terra cuite* produced in France and Belgium, *cotto* in Italy and *baldosin catalan* in Spain. These are slightly softer and less resistant to constant wear.

Group AIII: extruded ceramic tiles with a water absorption of E > 10%

The extruded tiles refer to split tiles and quarry tiles. Quarry tiles in this category may also have a later shaping by die-pressing after extrusion. They should not be used where there is a risk of frost.

All **A** category tiles will satisfy standards whether they are glazed, fully or partly, with glossy or matt finishes, or *unglazed*.

Group BI: dust pressed ceramic tiles with a water absorption of E < 3%
These are pressed tiles of high quality and can be classed as fully vitrified if their water absorption is less than 0.5%. They can also include mosaic tiles and tiles fitted with spacer lugs. They are suitable for interior or exterior use on walls and floors.

Group BIIa: dust pressed ceramic tiles with a water absorption of 3% < E < 6%
These tiles are suitable for interior and exterior use on walls and floors.

Group BIIb: dust pressed ceramic tiles with a water absorption of 6% < E < 10%
These tiles are suitable for interior and exterior use on walls and floors.

Group BIII: dust pressed ceramic tiles with a water absorption of E > 10%
Although used for walls and floors, they are not advised for use where there could be considerable floor loading or in areas where frost is likely.

The standards all relate to tiles that may be glazed, glossy matt or semi matt, or unglazed except in the group BIII which do not have an approved unglazed category.

Accessories
There are a number of fittings that can be obtained for tiles involving coves, round edges, angle junctions (internal and external), beads channels, water outlets, etc. Some of the most complex accessories are to be found in specialist usage for laboratory fittings or swimming pools, but could also be used for domestic fittings to comply with austere functionalism. Other domestic fittings include soap dishes (integral to a tiled wall), dado features, rails, toothbrushes and toilet roll holders, etc.

Physical properties
Physical properties have to satisfy standards related to water absorption, modulus of rupture, scratch hardness, linear thermal shock or crazing, frost resistance, and moisture expansion characteristics on unglazed tiles with a water absorption equal to 6% or more. In addition flooring tiles have to satisfy set standards with regard to surface and deep abrasion.

Chemical properties
Chemical properties are evaluated on resistance to staining, use of household chemicals and swimming pool water cleanser, as well as the usual resistance to alkalis and acids.

Although this seems a formidable range of criteria, it is in fact a fairly basic list. Any tiles which come from outside the European Community should be checked as to whether they can conform to these criteria as a precaution against failure. Designers should also familiarise themselves with the ASTMs set of standards for these materials if importing from the USA.

Tile dimensioning
Tiles today are manufactured in a wide range of sizes. 'Modular' tiles are manufactured in obvious metric dimensions, and with face sizes in increments of 100 mm or multiples or subdivisions of those increments, ie measuring $100 \times 100 \times 5$ mm or $200 \times 100 \times 6.5–8$ mm. 'Non-modular' dimensions relate to tiles which have metric equivalent dimensions to imperial sizes in England, ie 152×152 mm (6 in. $\times$ 6 in.), or are sizes historically produced in other countries but do not fit 'modular' dimensioning. In working out tolerances and joint widths it is more critical to understand how the tile was made than its overall sizing. Pressed tiles, made from ground particles of clay compressed into a mould are dimensionally more stable than extruded tiles, where green clay is drawn through a mould giving characteristic directional dovetailed ribbing on the rear of the tile. The action of drawing the clay through the mould with consequent directionality of deformation will give pronounced shrinkage and movement in that direction. Hardline functionalists could reflect this as the differentiation of mortar joint width. Joint width has also been

Dimensions	Symbol	Modular	Non-modular
Coordinating dimension	C	$W + J$	$N_2 + J$ or $W + J$
Nominal dimension	N_1	$W + J$	—
	N_2	—	$N_2 \simeq W$
Work dimension	W	W	W
Joint width	J	J	J

Table 3.2 *General definition of dimensions.* Table 1 EN 87 *In all cases the thickness of the tile is to be specified by the manufacturer and this is dependent on the tile size, and the most economic section that complies with all the physical properties required by BS 6431:1983*

| Co-ordinating size (C) cm | Work size (W) mm | | Thickness mm (d) |
	Length (a)	Width (b)	
M10 × 10			
M15 × 15			
M20 × 5			
M20 × 10			
M20 × 20	According to manufacturer.		The thickness shall be specified
M25 × 6,25	The manufacturer shall choose the work size in		by the manufacturer
M25 × 12,5	order to allow a nominal joint width of		
M25 × 25	between 5 mm and 10 mm		
M30 × 7.5			
M30 × 10			
M30 × 15			
M30 × 30			
M40 × 20			

Table 3.3(a) *Modular preferred sizes for split tiles*

| Nominal size (N) cm | Work size (W) mm | | Thickness mm (d) |
	Length (a)	Width (b)	
20 × 20			
21,7 × 10,5			
21,9 × 6,6	The manufacturer shall choose the work size		The thickness shall be specified by the
22 × 11	in such a way that the difference between		manufacturer
24 × 7,3	the work size and the nominal size is not		
24 × 11,5	more than ± 3 mm		
30 × 30			
40 × 20			

Table 3.3(b) *Non-modular sizes for split tiles*

| Co-ordinating size (C) cm | Work size (W) mm | | Thickness mm (d) |
	Length (a)	Width (b)	
M10 × 10			
M15 × 15			
M20 × 5	According to manufacturer.		The thickness shall be specified
M20 × 10	The manufacturer shall choose the work size in		by the manufacturer
M20 × 20	order to allow a nominal joint width of		
M25 × 12,5	between 3 mm and 11 mm		
M25 × 25			
M30 × 15			

Table 3.3(c) *Modular preferred sizes for quarry tiles*

| Nominal size (N) cm | Work size (W) mm | | Thickness mm (d) |
	Length (a)	Width (b)	
10 × 10			
13 × 13			
14 × 14			
15 × 15			
15,2 × 7,6	The manufacturer shall choose		The thickness shall be specified
15,2 × 15,2	the work size in such a way that the		by the manufacturer
18 × 18	difference between the work size and the		
20 × 10	nominal size is not more than ± 3 mm		
20 × 20			
20,3 × 20,3			
22,9 × 22,9			
26 × 13			
28 × 14			
30 × 30			

Table 3.3(d) *Non-modular sizes for quarry tiles*

Table 3.3 *Sizes for split tiles.* From EN 187-2 BS 6431:1983

calculated as a function of water vapour loss from the fabric, often negated by mortar specifications made more impermeable by proprietary additives. Also see page 88.

Movement and substrates
To minimise any movement in tiling, backgrounds should be completely stable. This is the most difficult criterion to achieve. Backgrounds should be structurally as well as chemically stable and not subject to deflection in use. The whole building fabric should be fully hardened, not just the immediate backing material, ie renders, and this implies allowing for the hardening of all concrete structural components in the building. Consideration should be given to the natural shrinkage of all cemetitious materials, including block-work and, where possible walling components should be chosen to minimise future material change and movement. Framed construction systems are usually unsuitable unless proper precautions are taken. Even on a domestic scale it is preferable to tile on renders which are reinforced with a metal mesh which is made from wires welded together, and are either stainless steel (austenitic) or galvanised to BS 729: 1986.

Expanded metal is not as suitable due to the possibility of deformation in the direction that the metal was originally expanded. There should be a distinction between using metal mesh as a key or as a stabilising frame to prevent further movement. As this is the type of reinforcement commonly fixed on stud partitions (whether metal or timber) it can significantly affect the degree of movement. Tiles fixed on frames should have expansion joints where framing systems make connections to other frames or adjacent solid elemental components.

As the use of polymeric adhesives becomes more common, they can generate different considerations in application. Some resins can expand (possibly through moisture absorption) and this can generate stress on tiling, eventually causing cracking. It is difficult to detail against this type of failure and any adhesive materials specified should have proven usage.

Class or type	Details	Drying shrinkage movement	Surface characteristics	Preparation for rendering
Dense, strong and smooth	(a) High density clay brickwork and clay blocks	Negligible	Low suction and generally poor key	May require more than raking back of joints, eg hacking, spatterdash, bonding agent, lathing or netting. Walls constructed of keyed bricks need no raking back
	(b) Dense concrete either precast or in situ	May vary from low to medium but usually moderate*	Low suction and poor key	Remove any ridges and fins from in-situ concrete before cleaning down. Remove grease and mould oil. May require hacking, spatterdash, bonding agent, lathing or netting
	(c) Hard natural stone	Negligible	Low suction and poor key	May require more than raking back of joints, eg hacking, spatterdash, bonding agent, lathing or netting
	(d) Glazed brick and tiles	Negligible	Very low suction and poor key	None
Moderately strong and porous	(a) Clay bricks and blocks	Negligible	Moderate or high suction and reasonable key	Rake back joints
	(b) Concrete (natural aggregate)	May vary from low to high*	Moderate suction and reasonable key	May require hacking, spatterdash, bonding agent, lathing or netting
	(c) Soft natural stone	Usually negligible	Moderate or high suction and reasonable key	May require hacking, spatterdash, bonding agent, lathing or netting
	(d) Concrete bricks and blocks (natural aggregate)	May vary from low to high*	Moderate suction and reasonable key	Rake back joints

Table 3.4 *Backgrounds: summary of data and various materials for tile fixing*

Rendering: mix proportions	Additional comments	Materials for fixing tiles		
		Cement-based adhesives	Organic-based adhesives	Cement and sand mortar
Portland cement and sand 1:3 to 4 by volume. Alternatively masonry cement and sand or plasticised† cement and sand mixes of equivalent strength may be used	Direct fixing may sometimes be adopted for (a), (b) and (c), provided the surface is suitable. In cases where adhesive is used, drying out may be delayed and grouting should be deferred for as long as practicable	S	S	S
	New concrete should be left for at least 4 weeks before rendering or direct fixing is commenced. Cement/sand mortar rendering should be left for 1 to 2 weeks before tiling is applied	S	S	S
		S	S	S
None	Clean down existing surface to remove grease, grime, condensation, etc. Check that old tiles/bricks are firmly bedded, remedy isolated loose areas. Drying time of adhesive may be extended. Delay grouting as long as practicable	NS	S	NS
Portland cement and sand 1:3 to 4 by volume. Alternatively masonry cement and sand or plasticised cement and sand mixes† of equivalent strength may be used	Direct fixing with a thick-bed adhesive may sometimes be adopted provided the surface is suitable	S	S	S
	New concrete, concrete blocks and bricks and calcium silicate bricks should be left for at least 4 weeks and any cement/sand mortar rendering for a further 1 to 2 weeks before fixing is commenced	S	S	S
		S	S	S
		S	S	NS

continued . . .

Class or type	Details	Drying shrinkage movement	Surface characteristics	Preparation for rendering
continued . . .	(e) Calcium silicate bricks (hard)	May vary from low to high*	Moderate suction and reasonable key	Rake back joints. With some types of extremely smooth and dense bricks, hacking, spatterdash, bonding agent, lathing or netting may be used to obtain a good key
Moderately weak and porous	(a) Blocks and concrete containing lightweight aggregate with open surfaces*	May vary from moderate to high†	Moderate to high suction and good key	None, except for some unusually smooth blocks which may require special treatment, eg spatterdash, bonding agent, lathing or netting
	(b) Blocks and concrete containing lightweight aggregate with closed surfaces*	May vary from moderate to high†	Moderate suction and poor key	May require hacking, spatterdash, bonding agent, lathing or netting
	(c) Autoclaved aerated concrete	Moderate to high†	Moderate suction and reasonable key	None
	(d) Calcium silicate bricks (soft)	May vary from low to high†	Moderate suction and reasonable key	Rake back joints. With some types of extremely smooth bricks, hacking, spatterdash, bonding agent, lathing or netting may be used to obtain a good key
No-fines concrete	(a) Dense	Varies from low to moderate according to aggregate used*	Suction varies from low to moderate, and usually good key	Should not require further keying

Table 3.4 *Backgrounds: summary of data and various materials for tile fixing*

Rendering: mix proportions	Additional comments	Materials for fixing tiles		
		Cement-based adhesives	Organic-based adhesives	Cement and sand mortar
		S	S	NS
Portland cement and sand 1:4 to 5 by volume. Alternatively masonry cement and sand mixes of equivalent strength may be used	Walls should be kept dry and should be left at least 4 weeks before any rendering is applied	S	S	NS
		S	S	NS
Portland cement and sand 1:4 by volume for concrete having a density above 625 kg/m³. A 1:5 masonry cement and sand mix, by volume, for concrete having a density below 625 kg/m³		S	S	NS
Portland cement and sand 1:4 to 5 by volume. Alternatively masonry cement and sand or plasticised cement and sand mixes‡ of equivalent strength may be used		S	S	NS
Portland cement and sand 1:3 to 4 by volume. Alternatively masonry cement and sand or plasticised cement and sand mixes† of equivalent strength may be used		S	S	S

continued . . .

83

Class or type	Details	Drying shrinkage movement	Surface characteristics	Preparation for rendering
continued . . .	(b) Lightweight aggregate	Varies from moderate to high*	Suction varies from moderate to high, and usually good key	Should not require further keying
Sheets and boards	Plasterboard	Negligible	True and smooth	Direct fixing to the decorative side of plasterboard can be carried out. Alternatively joints scrimmed and skim coat of finish plaster applied. Skimmed board should receive binding coat of suitable primer before tiling
	Asbestos board Asbestos-cement sheets Plywood Chipboard Fibreboard Blockboard	May have large moisture movement	True and smooth	Seal exposed edges and back against water absorption. Asbestos board and asbestos-cement sheets should be brushed and primed or prior to tiling
Other backgrounds	(a) Plasterwork	Negligible	Dependent upon age and condition but usually smooth with good suction	Clean or strip if painted, distempered or otherwise decrated Binding coat of suitable primer prior to tiling
	(b) Paintwork	According to background	Dependent upon age and condition. Low suction. Suitable for direct fixing	Clean and degrease
	(c) Metal surfaces (iron/steel)	Nil	Low suction and poor key	Clean to remove rust, grease, etc.

Table 3.4 *Backgrounds: summary of data and various materials for tile fixing.*
Based on Table 2 BS 5385 Part 1:1976

Rendering: mix proportions	Additional comments	Materials for fixing tiles		
		Cement-based adhesives	Organic-based adhesives	Cement and sand mortar
Portland cement and sand 1:4 to 5 by volume. Alternatively masonry cement and sand or plasticised cement and sand mixes† of equivalent strength may be used		S	S	NS
None	All boards should be rigidly braced	NS	S	NS
None		NS	S	NS
None	New plasterwork should have been completed at least 4 weeks and should be dry throughout. Tiles should only be fixed to the finish coat, never direct to the backing coat. Plasterwork is unsuitable as a base for tiling in wet areas	NS	S	NS
None	If paint is flaking it should be stripped off mechanically. Emulsion paint, limewash, distemper and similar finishes are best removed since they may possess poor adhesion to backing. Solvent-based adhesives should not be used	NS	S	NS
None	For metals other than iron/steel or in any case when abnormal conditions apply, obtain additional advice from adhesive manufacturer	NS	S	NS

Note 1 In describing the properties of backgrounds the terms used are intended to indicate only relative characteristics of the various materials.

Note 2 S denotes 'suitable' and is used to indicate the most commonly used groups of adhesives. All adhesives within a particular group may not be suitable and selection of the appropriate adhesive is necessary (see table 3.6). NS denotes 'not suitable'.

Class or types of background	Details		Drying shrinkage movement	Surface characteristics	Materials for fixing tiles and mosaics		
					Cement and sand mortar	Cement-based adhesives	Organic-based adhesives
Dense, strong and smooth	(a)	High-density clay brickwork	Negligible	Low suction and generally poor key	S	S	S
	(b)	Dense concrete either precast or in situ	May vary from low to high but usually moderate*	Low suction and poor key	S	S	S
Moderately strong and porous	(a)	Clay bricks and blocks	Negligible	Moderate or high suction and reasonable key	S	S	S
	(b)	Concrete (natural aggregate)	May vary from low to high*	Moderate suction and reasonable key	S	S	S
	(c)	Concrete bricks and blocks (natural aggregate) (BS 2028 type A)	May vary from low to high*	Moderate suction and reasonable key	S	S	S
	(d)	Calcium silicate bricks (hard)	May vary from low to high*	Moderate suction and reasonable key	NS	S	S
Moderately weak and porous†	(a)	Blocks and concrete containing lightweight aggregate with open surfaces (BS 2028 type B)	May vary from moderate to high*	Moderate to high suction and good key	S‡	‡	‡
	(b)	Blocks and concrete containing lightweight aggregate with closed surfaces (BS 2028 type B)	May vary from moderate to high*	Moderate suction and poor key	‡	‡	‡
	(c)	Autoclaved aerated concrete (BS 2028 type B)	Moderate to high*	Moderate suction and reasonable key	‡	‡	‡
	(d)	Calcium silicate bricks (soft)	May vary from low to high*	Moderate suction and reasonable key	‡	‡	‡
No-fines concrete	(a)	Dense natural aggregate	Varies from low to moderate according to aggregate used*	Suction varies from low to moderate; usually good key	S	S	S
	(b)	Lightweight aggregate	Varies from moderate to high*	Suction varies from moderate to high; usually good key	S	S	S

Table 3.5 *Backgrounds: summary of data and relevant clause numbers*

continued . . .

Class or types of background *continued . . .*	Details	Drying shrinkage movement	Surface characteristics	Materials for fixing tiles and mosaics		
				Cement and sand mortar	Cement-based adhesives	Organic-based adhesives
Sheets and boards	Asbestos-cement sheets. Marine plywood	May have large moisture movement*	True and smooth	NS	NS	S
Other backgrounds (a)	Metal surfaces (iron/steel)	Nil	Low suction and poor key	NS	NS	S
(b)	Glazed and unglazed tiles and glazed bricks	Negligible	Very low suction and poor key	NS	NS	S

In this summary S denotes 'suitable' and is used to indicate the most commonly used groups of bedding materials. All adhesives within a particular group may not be suitable and selection of the appropriate adhesive is necessary (see table 3.6). NS denotes 'not suitable'.

*The amount of drying shrinkage movement to be expected may vary according to the particular grade and/or degree of saturation.

Table 3.5 *Backgrounds: summary of data and relevant clause numbers. From Table 2 of BS 5385 Part 2:1978.*
Detailed advice should be sought from this standard where this table gives specific clause references

Type	Chemical nature of adhesive	Dry backgrounds and service conditions of varying dampness	*Damp backgrounds and service conditions of varying dampness	Dry backgrounds and warm service conditions (up to 60°C)† of varying dampness	Permanently wet conditions (after fixing on dry background)	Where flexibility is required (backgrounds where appreciable vibration or large size changes are expected)
		Appropriate backgrounds All those listed in table 3.5 except that lightweight concrete, calcium silicate bricks, sheets and boards are of limited suitability	*Appropriate backgrounds* All those listed in table 3.5 except rendered or unrendered lightweight concrete. Sheets and boards. Rendered or unrendered calcium silicate bricks	*Appropriate backgrounds* All those listed in table 3.5 except sheets, boards and metal surfaces. Lightweight concrete and calcium silicate bricks are of limited suitability	*Appropriate backgrounds* All those listed in table 3.5 except rendered or unrendered lightweight concrete. Sheets and boards. Rendered or unrendered calcium silicate bricks	
Thin-bed Capable of application in a maximum thickness of 3 mm	Natural rubber latex cement	S	R	S	S	S
	Synthetic rubber latex	R	R	S	R	S
	Elastomer (solvent based)	S	NS	S	S	S
	Epoxy resin (epoxide)	S	R	S	S	R
Cement-based adhesives	Cement	S	S	S	S	NS

Table 3.6 *Adhesives classification*   *continued . . .*

Type	Chemical nature of adhesive	Dry backgrounds and service conditions of varying dampness	*Damp backgrounds and service conditions of varying dampness	Dry backgrounds and warm service conditions (up to 60°C)† of varying dampness	Permanently wet conditions (after fixing on dry background)	Where flexibility is required (backgrounds where appreciable vibration or large size changes are expected)
continued . . .		Appropriate backgrounds All those listed in table 3.5 except that lightweight concrete, calcium silicate bricks, sheets and boards are of limited suitability	Appropriate backgrounds All those listed in table 3.5 except rendered or unrendered lightweight concrete. Sheets and boards. Rendered or unrendered calcium silicate bricks	Appropriate backgrounds All those listed in table 3.5 except sheets, boards and metal surfaces. Lightweight concrete and calcium silicate bricks are of limited suitability	Appropriate backgrounds All those listed in table 3.5 except rendered or unrendered lightweight concrete. Sheets and boards. Rendered or unrendered calcium silicate bricks	
Thick-bed Capable of application of 3 mm thick. The upper limit given by the manufacturer must not be exceeded. All thick-bed adhesives are usually used over uneven surfaces	Natural rubber latex cement	S	R	S	S	S
	Epoxy resin (epoxide)	S	R	R	S	NS
Cement-based adhesives	Cement	S	S	S	S	NS

S denotes 'suitable', NS 'not suitable'; R signifies that reference to the manufacturer's instructions is required to determine suitability. Some of the type are suitable, some are not.

Table 3.6 *Adhesives classification.* From BS 5385 Part 2:1978

Joints

Guidance on joints for tiling is often vague and sometimes contradictory. There is an attempt to specify a weather-tight construction to protect the building fabric, as well as consideration for the passage of water vapour from internal walls to the exterior. However, diffusion of gaseous material is a two-way process and dependent on many factors, including differential pressure between either side of a material. A general rule is given in BS 5385 Part 2: 1978 to allow for a jointing area equivalent to at least 10% of the tile area. This is based on the unlikely passage of water vapour through a fully glazed/vitrified tile. In reality, the joints specified for extruded tiles if at 10 mm will easily exceed this minimum area. A joint of 10 mm is often specified as it does allow for good quality pointing although they may be unnecessarily thick.

In BS 5385 Part 2: 1978 Section 16.2.3 the advice given is:

'Glazed tiles are impermeable at their surface and vitrified tiles, even when not glazed, have a negligible rate of transfer of water and water vapour. Consequently the size and nature of the joints has to allow for variation in tile size, protection from outside water penetration, and passage of any water vapour from the wall to the outer atmosphere.'

3.16 *Clay ridge tile. These cavities are caused by erosion but show clearly the finer vitrified skin on the surface and the coarser backing material in the body of the tile*

Unfortunately these functions are not at present given numeric terms and mathematical relationships which would allow the optimum joint width to be calculated. Likely performance depends on experience through usage and, unless a specifier has proven information, manufacturers' recommendations should be followed.

Tile composition

All ceramic tiles are made from clay and other minerals usually in proximity to the source of particular clays. Hence kilns and the clay manufacturing industries have historical locations, and so economise on the transport of raw materials. From their basic raw materials clays vary in their texture and mineral composition and their colour, depending on their geological location. There are characteristic clays falling into earthenware or stoneware groupings. The earthenware range of clays is recognisable by varying from reds through to browns. There is a classification of white earthenware which is creamy in colour. Stoneware is normally fired at higher

temperatures and becomes vitrified to some extent, producing a stronger more durable and less porous material. Stoneware is recognisable by the body clay varying from light greys to light browns or 'taupe'.

Grading and forming

The raw clay material is usually sieved, sorted and ground to get a known range of particle sizes that will produce a homogenous mixture with a measured water content. In any one quarry where the raw clay is mined there will be considerable variation from top to bottom of the clay layers, in terms of particle sizing and general consistency. Clay is usually scraped vertically from top to bottom of the open mine to achieve as good a mix as possible before grading. The material is then formed into regular shapes by being pressed or cast into moulds, or extruded through controlled section profiles and cut to the required length. The products formed are then left to become leather hard following natural water loss through evaporation with subsequent shrinkage. After this the tiles are then fired and the clay particles will sinter until they partly fuse or completely coalesce to give the hard and rigid final product. There is a category called *split tiles* from extruded forms, where double tiles are split after firing.

Firing

The first firing can produce a coloured tile if slip colours are used. It is possible to use 'slip', (a fine slurry of clay) to give an integral colour to tiles if applied at the leather-hard stage. Glazing is usually applied on the first fired 'biscuit ware' and then a subsequent firing at a higher temperature will take place to fuse the glazed coating on to the body of the biscuit ware. The glaze applied is a solution with a combination of silica (silicon dioxide) and one or several basic oxides to alter the actual colour with alumina (aluminium oxide) to give some viscosity to the solution. Calcium, barium, lead, magnesium, potassium, sodium, zinc are the main oxides used.

Materials for fixing

Care should be taken in the specification of mortars and all their constituent ingredients. The performance of tiling relies on a very exacting specification. Care should be taken not just in the correct specification of tiles but also in the materials used for their fixing. Some of the main causes of failure are rooted in the impurity of materials used or an incompatible specification with tile and background material. All ingredients for mortar must be clearly referenced back to British Standards (eg cement to BS 12: 1978) for purity. Sand is the most likely source of contamination, whether of salts or other matter that can effect the final dimensional properties of the joint by unpredictable shrinkage.

Backing coats and pointing mortars as well as the aggregates for these mixes should be inert to minimise chemical degradation. Fine particles of opaline silica is a constituent found in chert, flint, shale sandstone or limestone, and lead to the formation of an impure gel with a greater volume in an alkali/aggregate reaction. In fixing their tiles, Langley recommended the use of a chromalith mortar which is highly refined and is imported from Luxembourg, containing quartz silver sand, limestone, pigment and a waterproofer.

The treatment of joints is critical to assist for a maximum of water run off. Recessed joints should be avoided and flush faced or bucket handled joints are preferable.

Refer to BS 5385 Part 2: 1978 (and June 1986) for advice on backgrounds, treatment, backing materials, bedding methods and adhesion. Refer to table 14 abstracted from BS 5385.

3.17 *Parc Guell (Gaudi). Extraordinary though technologically sound detailing. Exposed surfaces are curved so deposition and water are naturally flushed away. The ceramic pieces are small and already fractured into energy efficient shapes*

3.2 CONCRETE FINISHES

To obtain a good finish, whatever the texture, it is fundamental to specify quality ingredients and a sound specification for formwork and the placement of concrete. In using concrete there are often a whole range of blemishes that can be unsightly which can all be traced back to poor mix design or bad workmanship. Failure in terms of unacceptable appearance are usually from a combination of factors rather than one factor, involving mix design, curing, release agents, retarding agents, weathering in the course of setting, excessive vibration or striking formwork too early or too late. All of these factors can be controlled but need a good specification and supervision.

For a complete introduction to concrete see *MBS: Materials* chapter 8. Also refer to *Introduction to Concrete* and *Concrete Practice* (originally by the Cement and Concrete Association).

References
The following are relevant titles published by the British Cement Association. Reference numbers:

1 *Visual Concrete: design and production*, William Monks
3 *The Control of Blemishes in concrete*, William Monks
4 *Efflorescence on Concrete*, D D Higgins
7 *Textured and profiled concrete finishes*, William Monks
8 *Exposed aggregate finishes*, William Monks
9 *Tooled concrete finishes*, William Monks
Structural concrete finishes: a guide to selection and production, William Monks

The prevention of major blemishes can be summarised as follows:

FORMWORK

This should be stiff enough, ie inflexible with a uniform face and very little absorbency, (the water is needed in the chemical reaction for the mix). The joints should be tight and not able to leak, the formwork should be evenly coated with a release agent and free from any material that can stain the mix, eg fixings from the formwork. All formwork should be sealed, especially timber which should have lapped joints where possible to avoid excessive water absorption.

It is also surprising how many designers will specify the British Standards without realising that the materials for the formwork may be still be unspecified and left to a contractor unless defined precisely by the designer. If the formwork is struck and the finish found to be unsatisfactory, it is very difficult to make good, so care must be taken in the drawings and specification to ensure that the right finish will be achieved. It is worth including in a specification, that sample panels should be cast for fairfaced work for approval, before proceeding with the work.

A variety of materials can be used for formwork as long as they are constructed to be stiff enough to take the weight of wet concrete. Standards of formwork should be high, as the skills required are those of a joiner rather than a carpenter for the best finishes. Timber, metals, plastics, rubber, polystyrene and even hardboards can be used for formwork and very fine textures can be reproduced. Timber is often sandblasted so the grain can be emphasised. Finishes should also be designed to take account of weathering. Very smooth surfaces are unsatisfactory in this country. Textured surfaces with a vertical emphasis are better for deliberately channelling water flow. Horizontal features will cause streaking unless proper drips are introduced.

Retarders
Chemical retarders are applied on formwork to ensure that although the body of the concrete has set, there is a slurry on the surface of the concrete that can be removed easily to expose the underlying aggregate. Most of these retarders are sugar based and are difficult to use, results are not always predictable and retardation can inhibit in-depth setting of the mix.

Acid etching
Fine surface detail can be achieved by etching with a 5% solution of hydrochloric acid. The length of time left on the surface will determine the degree of etching. This type of finish is probably more useful for altering the texture of an existing building, as the same degree of control can be reproduced by careful choice of formwork. Surfaces treated in this way need through rinsing and protection of adjacent surfaces, especially glass.

CONCRETE MIX

It is important that the precise mix proportions are used, a low sand content will create voids and a cement rich mix will be more likely to craze. Dry or porous aggregates will take too much of the water content of the mix leading to a less dense mix with a friable and sometimes powdery surface. Too much water will also lower the strength and produce voids. The mix must be consistent and excessive vibration should be avoided.

See BS 8110 Part 1: 1985 *Code of Practice for design and construction*, BS 5328 1981 *Methods for specifying concrete including ready mixed concrete.*

CURING

Most problems in curing concrete stem from inadequate understanding about how concrete hardens. The action of mixing water and cement is to initiate a *chemical reaction* known as *hydration*. The water is an essential component which has to be mixed in the correct proportions specified, and never to achieve a degree of workability. As the water is needed for the reaction steps must be taken to ensure there is no appreciable water loss, so concrete is protected to prevent loss of water from evaporation.

Curing should be even as too rapid or inadequate drying will give differential moisture loss. Weather conditions should be carefully monitored otherwise uneven hardening will take place.

WHITE CONCRETE

For white concrete white cements should be specified but all the aggregates should also be specified as lighter colours, eg light limestones and granites, calcite spar or calcined flint with fine silica sand as the fine aggregate. This does lead to an expensive and possibly uneconomic mix and demands a greater degree of control to minimise rates of shrinkage that are prevalent with white cements.

SUMMARY OF BLEMISHES

Hydration discolouration
There are often variations in colour which can be detected at joints of formwork or sometimes as patchiness, echoing the grain in timber or plywood or as a shadow pattern of aggregates. All of these colour variations are due to *hydration discoloration*. If there is a differential moisture loss from the body of the concrete while it is in the process of setting there will be a high concentration of cement and a marginally lower water content in that specific region. This means a slight change in the type of compounds formed and a greater proportion of teracalcium aluminoferrite, which has a characteristic darker grey colour than normally set ordinary Portland cement with its correct water cement ratio. So areas where moisture is lost will always be a slighter darker colour. If different veneers or timber is used and not properly sealed there will be different rates of absorbency which will also give a different colour to the finally set cement. Aggregates close to the surface of the concrete that absorb moisture from the mix will give a colour difference and a shadow effect for the same reason. Sometimes this is called *segregation discoloration*.

Lime bloom
In the hydration of compounds tricalcium silicate and dicalcium silicate can liberate free lime (calcium hydroxide) which can be leached out of the concrete by rainwater or moisture and then harden by reacting with carbon dioxide in the atmosphere to form the more insoluble calcium carbonate. This deposit can be removed with a 5% solution of hydrochloric acid but if the concrete is continually saturated the fault may persist and may be reflecting a detailing problem.

Crazing
This is a pattern of fine shrinkage fractures on a cement rich skin to the concrete. It will probably be due to using too smooth a formwork finish. More absorbent formwork surfaces can raise fine aggregates to the surface but these have crack stopping capabilities, preventing large areas of cement rich skin from being under stress. It can also be due to an excess of water in the mix. Rather than repairing the surface, fine sandblasting or acid etching to form a slight texture may be more successful.

Blow holes
These defects can be caused by using surface formwork which has no absorbency. Inadequate vibration is also a cause and leaves air pockets trapped against the side of the formwork.

Scabbing
On striking the formwork a very rough face to the concrete showing a tearing of the material indicates a poor application or performance of release agents.

Pyrites
These are iron rich aggregates (iron sulphide crystalline mineral) that can be the cause of streaking stains down the face of the concrete and are rust brown in colour. They can also react expansively with free lime in the concrete forming iron hydroxide. The increased volume of material can cause cracking. It is difficult to detect these aggregates prior to staining or reaction and the only remedy is to pick them out. If the area locally is examined and the source of the staining seems to be a soft grey material then this is confirmation of the reacting aggregate. (Staining of this nature can be confused with the remains of small wires as re-inforcement ties.) Prevention should be by checking the purity of aggregates.

Dusting

If the concrete is not properly dampened down, excessive water loss can cause rapid hardening with a friable surface.

3.18 *Unite d'habitation Firminy Vert. Le Corbusier, built 1967. This concrete wall is on top of the building on the high roof terrace and shows a number of faults. Age enhances the definition of formwork joints (hydration discoloration). Mirror cracking repeats the structural form on the other side of the wall giving pathways for the external deposition of lime bloom (deposits of insoluble calcium carbonate)*

MAJOR DETERIORATION AND REPAIR

The first step in the remedy of reinforced concrete that has deteriorated, is in establishing a diagnosis. First indications of failure are usually cracking and/or spalling of the concrete. If cracking is parallel with the reinforcement it is indicative of expansive corrosion of reinforcing steel. The depth of cover can be established using a cover meter and the reinforcement plotted. If the cracking patterns do not follow the reinforcement then a separate structural investigation needs to be carried out. As a brittle ceramic, it is more likely that cracking will occur in directions that are perpendicular to the tensile stress causing cracking.

Concrete cover to the concrete should be carefully removed to look at the nature of corrosion. Corrosion of reinforcement that is even, ie of the same depth to the steel along its length, will suggest carbonation whereas corrosion showing severe pitting will indicate chloride attack.

Carbonation

Carbonation is used as a term to describe the progressive change of calcium oxide in the original concrete mix into calcium carbonate. This change affects the pH of the porewater from a value inbetween 12.5 to 13.6 (alkaline) down to a value of 3 (acid). This change affects reinforcing steel, which in a *passive* alkaline environment is not susceptible to corrosion. The relevant reactions are as follows:

$$CO_2 + H_2O \rightleftarrows 2H^+ + CO_3^{2-}$$

$$CaO + H_2O \rightleftarrows Ca^{2+} + 2OH^-$$

$$Ca^{2-} + CO_3^{2-} \rightleftarrows CaCO_3$$

$$H_2O \rightleftarrows H^+ + OH^-$$

As our supply of carbon dioxide is guaranteed and there is already a supply of calcium oxide which can supply calcium ions, then the reaction will proceed. The critical point to establish is the rate at which carbon dioxide will travel through the concrete. This will be the rate of diffusivity and it should define the depth of cover needed. The code of practice for the recommended depth of cover changed from 25 mm in 1948 to 50 mm in 1972.

To determine the extent of carbonation that has already taken place in a sample of concrete surrounding corroded reinforcement, the technique using a solution of phenolphtalein in diluted ethyl alcohol, is described in BRE Information paper IP 6/81. If sprayed on a freshly fractured surface, it should change to a healthy pink if the concrete is still alkaline. It will stay colourless if the concrete has a pH value of less than 9. If the test is alkaline then samples of concrete should be tested for chloride content. (BRE Information sheets IS 12/77 and 13/77 and BS 1881:1986.)

To illustrate the scale of the problem, Teesside Polytechnic underwent extensive repairs after deterioration of the concrete frame was confirmed as being due to carbonation. The building was 20 years old and carbonation was found to have occurred at least to a depth of 8 mm and in some cases up to a depth of 40 mm. Concrete cover varied from 10 to 40 mm for main steel, and nil to 12 mm for secondary steels. The general strategy for repair allowed for exposing all the reinforcement where corrosion was taking place, cleaning, which was undertaken by grit blasting and then making good. This was achieved by initially protecting the reinforcement with a cementitious grout with a corrosion inhibitor, giving a new alkaline environment to the steel, then applying a slurry with a bonding agent, before finishing with a repair mortar. The whole frame was finished in an impervious coating to inhibit the passage of carbon dioxide but which also allowed the diffusion of water vapour. The coating is anticipated to last for 10–15 years before reapplication (Source: 'A new lease of life for a reinforced concrete building' by Charles Morris, *Construction Repairs and Maintenance*, July 1986.)

Chloride attack

The concrete may be alkaline but corrosion can still occur if there are free chloride ions. Chloride ions can form stable compounds with calcium aluminate already in the mix, but there is a limit to the amount of chloride ions that can be accommodated in this way. Excess ions are free to travel and affect pore water by making it an effective electrolyte, dissolving metal ions. Chlorides may have been introduced into mixes as contaminants in aggregates (sea dredged) or as an accelerator in the form of calcium chloride, from proximity to marine environments or from the de-icing of roads in winter. Calcium chloride was banned as an accelerator in 1977 but remedial work has to tackle the repercussions of earlier usage. From BRE Digest 264 and in relation to the cement content for dense aggregate concretes to BS 12, the following categories of chloride content apply:

Low chloride ion content up to 0.4% by weight of cement

Medium chloride ion content from 0.4 to 1%

High chloride ion content over 1%

Corrosion of the reinforcement is likely if the ion content is over 1%.

Alkali aggregate reactions
These reactions show that concrete has the capacity for further change by the action of alkaline pore fluids in the concrete on siliceous aggregates. The end product is a calcium silicate gel which absorbs water and swells, causing cracking. This is not a common reaction and not many cases have been reported in the United Kingdom, they are also confined to the South-West and Midlands in England, and need several common factors including high alkalinity, high cement content and exposure to water.

Core samples from suspected cases may be coated with gel, and so be confirmed. Alternatively sections may be taken for microscopic examination and cracked aggregate particles with their cracks filled with gel can be clearly seen.

There is little experience in repair work to structures damaged by this reaction but if diagnosed, efforts should be made to improve the water resistance and water penetration to avoid absorption by the newly formed gels.

Prevention can be through aggregate selection as well as the use of low alkali cements and cement replacement materials. The most reactive aggregates are opaline silica which are not common in the UK. The most reactive aggregates are likely to be found in sand and gravel off the South Coast, the Bristol Channel and the Thames Estuary and in parts just inland from these areas. They include microcrystalline and cryptocrystalline silica, chalcedony and some quartz. (*Alkali aggregate reactions in concrete*, BRE Digest 330 March 1988.)

REPAIR AND GUIDANCE

BRE Digests 263, 264 and 265, *The durability of steel in concrete*, Parts 1, 2 and 3, outline the two major causes of corrosion to reinforcement (carbonation and chloride attack) and recommend strategies for repair. The Concrete Society Technical Report 26 (October 1984) elaborates on these strategies.

If carbonation has been diagnosed, then repairs are possible and increase the longevity of the building. The treatment follows the case study but the following points apply:

1 Cutting back all concrete around corroded material to a depth of 12 mm behind the steel and 50 mm beyond the corroded area, after taking load off the element being repaired by jacking.

2 Cleaning reinforcement of all corroded deposits by mechanical blasting and welding in new steels if the degree of corrosion reduces primary reinforcing members by 10% in their diameter.

3 Restoration of a passive environment to the steel by either barriers to aggressive agents or by raising the alkalinity of the immediate environment to the steel.

4 Incorporating a bonding agent to prevent subsequent spalling.

5 Application of the new repair material to match the strength required of the existing mix, to be chloride free, and to be installed in thin layers. It is generally recommended to use a Portland cement modified by a polymer latex for ease of handling and reliable performance. Epoxy resin mortars and grouts as well as polyester resin mortars and grouts are more difficult to use. Epoxy resins have lower shrinkage rates than polyester resins but are more expensive.

6 For information on surface coatings, BRE Digest 265 gives a comprehensive table of types and their performance. When carrying out repair work and relying on a coating finish, supervising officers should note that paints can only bridge over crack widths up to 0.2 mm maximum.

Dense mixtures help protect steel, but in dealing with the scale of ions that are causing these reactions, we should be limiting their movement by controlling the *permeability* of concrete. Coatings offer a very different order of permeability due to the nature of their close chemical bonding. Taking a polymer coating of 100 microns in thickness, it can be from 20 to 200 times more effective in terms of resistance to movement of CO_2 than a 50 mm thickness of concrete. With regard to the protection of concrete from water, although the differences in the passage of water vapour is less dramatic, paint films will not absorb water although concrete will. Consequently paint films do offer a high degree of protection from externally absorbed water which may contain chlorides and other gases in solution. *Permeability and protection of reinforced concrete* by C D Lawrence. Cement and Concrete Association reprint 6/86 from symposium 'Concrete structures—the need for protection' Wakefield 1984. See figure 3.19.

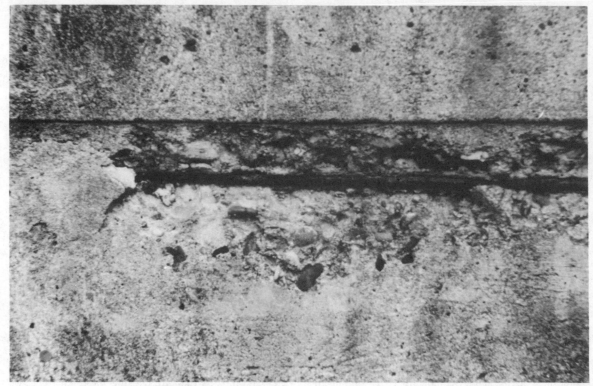

3.19 *Carbonation and its effects. This exposed reinforcing rod is the result of carbon dioxide diffusing through the concrete matrix and changing the ph of the porewater in concrete from an alkaline ph of about 13.6 to the more acid ph value of 3. In this new acid environment the reinforcing steel has a greater potential to corrode, with subsequent expansion, fracturing adjacent concrete and causing eventual spalling. It results from inade-* *quate concrete cover to steel. At this stage the steel way have to be cut out and new welded in, with priming and keying to take a matched new mix. Testing for carbonation can be carried out on site with phenolphtalein which will show healthy alkaline concrete to be pink. Cracking due to carbonation takes place parallel to the reinforcement*

PANELS

Concrete panels are more vulnerable to deterioration from carbonation as they are usually exposed on both sides to the atmosphere.

Moulds for panels are expensive and if possible, the design should be standardised to reduce the number of different panel types. Steel moulds are the longest lasting but also the most expensive to make. GRP has a longer life than timber but less than steel. Handling on site is important to consider and panels should not be made over 7 tonnes, otherwise there will be problems in delivery and cranage.

The actual thickness of concrete panels could be slimmer structurally than designed at present. Thickness is governed by cover to steel. Glass reinforced cement panels have become an acceptable alternative

for cladding, with the advantages of being far lighter in weight. Panels can be cast over trays of selected aggregate bedded in sand as an alternative to casting into moulds.

The decision to use panels takes the designer into the realms of concrete joinery where not only the cast finish needs consideration, but the method of fixing, setting out and the design of weatherproof junctions all needs specifying. It is advisable to work with a cladding manufacturer from an early stage.

Finishing treatments on hardened concrete

Abrasive blasting
Surface finish and degree of texture are dependent on the size and type of particle used in a stream of air or water, which varies from using sand, grit or shot. It is

now common practice to use water in preference to air which is safer for operatives.

Tooling
Mechanically operated tools are used for bush hammering but have to be handled carefully to avoid shattering the aggregates. This kind of heavy treatment should not be carried out until the concrete has hardened for at least three weeks.

Grinding and polishing
Finer work can be achieved by joint tooling or by grinding and polishing two to three days after casting. The greater the labour needed, the more expensive the finish and this provides an additional argument for making sure that the formwork details are precise enough to minimise time consuming hand finishing.

3.3 RENDERS

There are great similarities between plastering and rendering except that renders are usually used for external work and their final mix is dependent on prevailing weather and microclimatic conditions.

The cementitious materials used, set by hydration and so water is needed for the chemical reaction. This is why the materials in their powdered form should be properly cared for on site, away from moisture, and kept under cover and off the ground. They can also be regarded as particle composites with aggregates acting as crack stopping mechanisms.

Renders are now associated with failure in many instances despite a long history of a successful usage in traditional building. This is due to a complete change in the materials used to achieve a homogenous but relatively thin coating over the years, and also a lack of rigour with regard to creating exactly the right conditions for applying render. There is also a change in expectations with regard to the standard of finish required, and the optimisation of physical dimensions. The surface area to be covered may be so large that problems of movement, whether by stress or by thermal response and flexure must be catered for in a way which will show on a building façade, in the setting out of expansion and contraction joints. These lines will be

3.20 *Villa La Roche-Jeanneret 1925 by Le Corbusier* (photograph taken 1986). *Reinforced concrete pilotis with cement rendered breeze block walls. A well maintained façade but note that the windows have clear cill details and horizontal surfaces are weathered*

very apparent and are strongly resisted by architects to the detriment of the final finish. There is also a preference for smooth finishes which are not as reliable in terms of overall performance as the more textured finishes.

Render is also expected to be successful on a variety of substrates, from concrete to brick, to block and even over framing systems. Render is often erroneously thought of as a material in its own right which is simply applied over all these different types of construction. Every time the substrate changes, the nature of the render coating used must also change. Render and substrate must be thought of as a unified composite material and compatible in terms of its likely physical behaviour under stress and after all, both skins must behave as one.

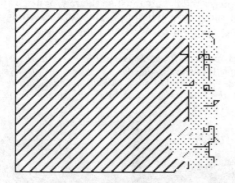

3.21 *Render and substrate thought of as a composite. The outer skin will deform as a result of inner stress*

The main Code of Practice for render is BS 5262:1976 *Code for external rendered finishes.* The Code does exclude special advice on renders for tanking and catering for liquid retaining structures. The Cement and Concrete Association also published a booklet on *External Rendering* (7th edition) which gives practical advice well illustrated with photographs.

Definitions relating to *bond, suction, adhesion* are the same as for plaster. All materials should be pure and conform to British Standards ie:
Cements to BS 12:1978 146:1973 915:1983 4027:1980 5224:1976
Lime to BS 890:1972
Sand to BS 1199:1976
Coarse aggregate to BS 882:1983
Ready mixed material to BS 4721:1986

There are other components to the mix, such as waterproofers, workability agents, bonding agents, and water retaining agents.

SPECIFICATION

The exact specification depends on the background and also the degree of exposure of the building. This could be in a category ranging from sheltered through to moderate and severe. As the work being considered is external, the range of temperatures and also the amount of wetting requires a specification which can cope with all seasonal variations and not show deterioration. Over rigid mixes are not to be advocated as they can crack under stress and water will penetrate through hairline fractures at a fast rate due to capillary action. Open porous textures and rough textures seem to weather the best. There is also evidence to suggest that a larger scale of porosity is not so vulnerable to freezing conditions. (See Section 3.05 Frost and freezing mechanisms.)

The design of buildings has sometimes sought for a crispness and precision 'reminiscent' of the modern movement without proper research. Some buildings by Le Corbusier and Frank Lloyd Wright have details that can only be appreciated if the working drawings have been inspected or the buildings visited. Parapet details were sometimes curved to give adequate run off of water. Render details by de Koninck still incorporated methods for water run off around openings. The detailing of all edges should be a paramount consideration when render techniques are used, and details should be designed at an early stage for:
Parapets, copings
Openings around windows and doors with drips over details that abut damp proof courses
Arrises
Eaves details

The principal aim being to get rid of water and stopping it from flowing back into the building.
See figures 3.22 to 3.31 pages 100 to 101.

3.22–3.25 *Edgar J Kaufmann House Bear Run Penna, 1936 Frank Lloyd Wright. All the rendered surfaces are curved (adobe fashion) helping water to flow off the building but with an absence of drips it can follow the curve around. Drainage has to be carefully detailed, if the outlet does not throw the ater clear the deterioration can occur. In 3.23 water intrusion and rusting of the inadequately clad nearby mesh reinforcement has caused cracking and spalling. Small-scale stalactites have formed of calcium carbonate as free lime is exposed to carbon dioxide*

3.22

3.23

3.24

3.22–3.25 *Edgar J Kaufmann House Bear Run Penna, 1936 Frank Lloyd Wright. All the rendered surfaces are curved (adobe fashion) helping water to flow off the building but with an absence of drips it can follow the curve around. Drainage has to be carefully detailed, if the outlet does not throw the water clear the deterioration can occur.*

3.25

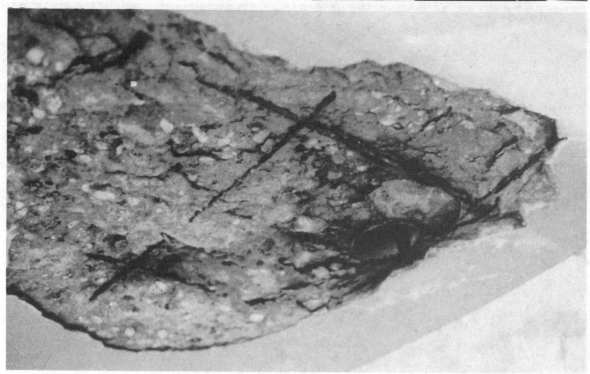

3.26–3.31 *Sanatorium 'Zonnestraal' by J Duicker, B Bijvoet and J G Wiebenga (Engineer) 1926–1931 in Hilversum, Holland* (photographs taken in 1985). *This classic modern movement building shows the tenuous early detailing of mesh reinforced walling infill to a reinforced concrete frame. Figures 3.24–3.26 show the disused wing of the hospital and progressive deterioration through carbonisation and penetration of the building fabric by water. The infill panels show the lightweight sandwich of render over steel mesh (3.26). Rusting metal bulges and puts stress on these light infills. These buildings need good maintenance, as deterioration of their finishes has severe repercussions. Figures 3.27–3.29 show other parts of the same complex when good maintenance is provided and the original intention of the buildings is clearly expressed*

3.27

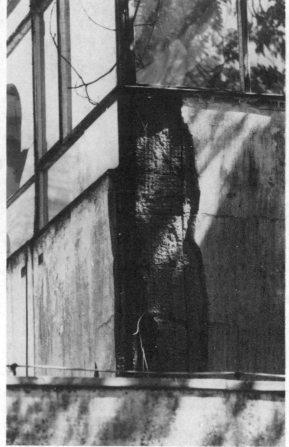

3.28

3.26–3.31 *Sanatorium 'Zonnestraal' by J Duicker, B Bijvoet and J G Wiebenga (Engineer) 1926–1931 in Hilversum, Holland (photographs taken in 1985). This classic modern movement building shows the tenuous early detailing of mesh reinforced walling infill to a reinforced concrete frame. Figures 3.24–3.26 show the disused wing of the hospital and progressive deterioration through carbonisation and penetration of the building fabric by water. The infill panels show the lightweight sandwich of render over steel mesh (3.26). Rusting metal bulges and puts stress on these light infills. These buildings need good maintenance, as deterioration of their finishes has severe repercussions. Figures 3.27–3.29 show other parts of the same complex when good maintenance is provided and the original intention of the buildings is clearly expressed*

3.30

3.31

BACKGROUNDS AND SURFACE TREATMENTS

In BS 5262:1976 the backgrounds are categorised in a similar way to plasters and this standard should be used as a source for detailed reference, although the following gives an outline.

SOLID

High density clay, concrete bricks, blocks, dense concrete or low density concrete with a sealed surface
These are low porosity surfaces which are difficult for render to adhere to. In these situations keying surfaces should be provided wherever possible, either by using keyed bricks and blocks, metal lathing, bush hammering, other physical or chemical methods to expose the aggregation or spatterdash coats to provide an initial roughened surface for further coats. Retarders can be used in concrete to delay the setting of the outer face of the cement so when the framework is struck, the unset slurry can be brushed over to provide a mechanical key. If retarders have been used the surface should be well washed afterwards to provide a clean surface.

Bonding treatments are mentioned but not advocating in the British Standard due to the lack of long-term use of the materials and the vulnerability of some polymers in below freezing conditions.

3.32 and 3.33 *House and detail for Mr Dotremont Brussels 1931–2 by L H de Koninck (photograph taken 1983). The building is in reinforced concrete with rendered walls. Mesh reinforcement is on a 200 mm grid. Formwork is boarded (approx 100 mm wide) prior to rendering with a rough aggregate finish. This is still in a reasonable condition*

3.33

Moderate strength but porous
This category relates mostly to clay, calcium silicate bricks and porous lightweight concrete. The materials have some key and also show good adhesion as the surface topography is sufficiently structured to generate good capillary action.

In materials that are jointed the joints should be well raked out and all debris removed from the surface, including efflorescence. Depth of raked joints in old brickwork should not be less than 13 mm. If the mortar is too hard to be raked out, alternative treatment may mean hard scoring of the brickwork, or the application of metal lathing. Metal lathing may be needed over brickwork which is deteriorating to such an extent it will not support a render.

Calcium silicate bricks and concrete blocks may be sufficiently porous without any extra treatment needed.

SLABS
This relates to woodwool which might be used as permanent formwork and then needs a finishing surface.

The joints are usually the greatest problem in this material and should be reinforced and bridged over with expanded metal, unless it is intended to use metal lathing over the whole surface. Fixing is very difficult into woodwool and methods of clipping will be more successful than nailing even at an angle. For channel reinforced woodwool slabs the junction should be covered with 250 mm wide expanded metal. A spatter-dash coat is advised as the first of a three coat application thrown on with frequent damping in warm weather to assist full hydration.

METAL LATHING
It is critical that the corrosion resistance of the lathing is adequate. As a method it is used over framing systems which may cover insulation on external masonry façades. Three coat work is mentioned on the standard as being the minimum required on metal lathing to provide a coat adequate to reist weather penetration. However, the depth of render required must also be sufficient to provide a rigid matrix that is less susceptible to cracking by also preventing bending of the lathing.

The fixing of metal lathing should be adequate for the gauge and type of lathing used. As a general rule, ordinary expanded metal lathing will need supports at 350 centres minimum. Lath with metal ribbing, or welded mesh, is stiffer and can span further. Individual manufacturers' instructions should be followed for centres. Mesh sheets should always properly lap over each other and be tied together at the edges to prevent movement through the render.

All metal lathing should be galvanised at a very minimum and preferably made from stainless steel. See the related British Standard 1369: *Steel Lathing for internal plastering and external rendering*, and also BS 405 *Specification for uncoated expanded metal carbon steel sheets for general purposes* for expanded metal. Welded wire mesh should be made of squares between 25 mm and 50 mm in size and form not less than 1.02 mm gauge steel and should be galvanised or stainless steel.

There will be far greater movement of expanded metal over timber and metal studding constructions. Metal lathing in these circumstances is not normally stiff enough to cater for the dimensional movement of timber or the thermal movement of metals, and additional restraint fixings have to be designed. There is probably a need for a special type of lathing in these circumstances which has a cross braced pattern. Metal lathing should be fixed over building paper if applied to timber construction.

MIXES FOR RENDERING

As a general principle mixes should become weaker towards the outer face of the building. This also allows for greater flexure on the outer skin.

See Table 1 of BS 5262:1976 on which table 3.7 is based. Type mix 1 is extremely strong and can only be used as a first coat on very stable surfaces ie concrete, or as a stiff first coat giving rigidity to expanded metal. The other mixes (2, 3, 4) are not so hard and are less likely to crack.

Table 2 of BS 5262:1976 gives a complete guide for renderings related not just to their degree of exposure but also to their background condition. In all cases only the preferred mix is given here in table 3.15. See BS 5262 for alternative mixes if required. Categories for exposure are as follows:

Severe These relate to completely exposed conditions for buildings which may be in the countryside or on the edges of towns, or at some height above surrounding buildings.

Moderate Protection from the elements may be given by other buildings or adequate eaves details. Buildings in towns or suburbs come into this category.

Sheltered Buildings that are well protected by other buildings close by and in areas of low rainfall.

When organising render work it is advisable to use contractors with a knowledge of conditions and successful specifications in a particular area.

Where possible it is preferable to use the lime/cement mixes which have greater flexibility. If there is concern over the durability of these mixes, then a stronger cement mix should be used for bases, dados, mouldings, etc.

Descriptions of type of finish in the table:

Wood float
This will give a smooth and flat coat. If the surface is raised by a felt-coated float or treated afterwards with a lambswool roller the sand aggregate is slightly raised to give a softer surface texture which is better at resisting crazing.

Scraped or textured
After initial hardening the surface is scraped hard with thin metal giving a coarser texture than the wood float finish. This is even better at resisting crazing than the textured wood float technique.

Roughcast
Aggregate is thrown on the wall which has already been rolled in a slurry of cement. This gives a very coarse texture, the size of which can be varied according to the aggregate specified.

Drydash
Small aggregates or crushed rock chips are thrown on to the wet render giving a close textured rough surface of natural material. A good hardwearing finish.

See figure 3.34.

Mix type	Cement:lime:sand	Cement:ready-mixed lime:sand		Cement:sand (using plasticiser)	Masonry cement:sand
		Ready-mixed lime:sand	Cement:ready-mixed material		
I	1:¼:3	1:12	1:3	—	—
II	1:½:4 to 4½	1:8 to 9	1:4 to 4½	1:3 to 4	1:2½ to 3½
III	1:1:5 to 6	1:6	1:5 to 6	1:5 to 6	1:4 to 5
IV	1:2:8 to 9	1:4½	1:8 to 9	1:7 to 8	1:5½ to 6½

Note. In special circumstances, for example where soluble salts in the background are likely to cause problems, mixes based on sulphate-resisting Portland cement or high alumina cement may be employed. High alumina cement should not be mixed with lime, ground limestone, ground chalk, silica flour or other suitable inert filler should be employed instead.

Table 3.7 *Mixes suitable for rendering.*
Based on Table 1 of BS 5262:1976

Background material	Type of finish	First and subsequent undercoats			Final coat		
		Severe	Moderate	Sheltered	Severe	Moderate	Sheltered
(1) Dense, strong, smooth	Wood float	II	II	II	III	III	III
	Scraped or textured	II	II	II	III	III	III
	Roughcast		II	II		II	II
	Dry dash		II	II		II	
(2) Moderately strong, porous	Wood float	III	III	III	III	IV	IV
	Scraped or textured	III	III	III	III	IV	IV
	Roughcast	II	II	II	as undercoats		
	Dry dash	II	II	II			
(3) Moderately weak, porous*	Wood float	III	IV	IV			
	Scraped or textured	III	IV	IV			
	Dry dash	III	III	III	as undercoats		
(4) No fines concrete†	Wood float	II	III	III	III	IV	IV
	Scraped or textured	II	III	III	III	IV	IV
	Roughcast	II	II	II	II	II	II
	Dry dash	II	II	II	II	II	II
(5) Woodwool slabs*	Wood float	III	IV	IV		IV	IV
	Scraped or textured	III	IV	IV	IV	IV	IV
(6) Metal lathing	Wood float	II	II	II	III	III	III
	Scraped or textured	II	II	II	III	III	III
	Roughcast	II	II	II	II	II	II
	Dry dash	II	II	II	II	II	II

*Finishes such as roughcast and dry dash requires strong mixes and hence are not advisable on weak backgrounds.
†If proprietary lightweight aggregates are used, it may be desirable to use the mix weaker than the recommended type.

Table 3.8 *Recommended mixes for external renderings in relation to background materials, exposure conditions and finish required. Based on Table 2 of BS 5262:1976. Clause 22 in this standard gives guidance as to the relevance of choosing mixes types I to IV. Type I mixes are the strongest and to be avoided for risk of cracking unless used on absolutely rigid backgrounds. Wherever possible the weakest mix should be specified unless exceptional resistance is needed to physical damage. In this table only the preferred mixes are given, for a wider range of alternatives the British Standard should be checked*

3.34 *Prototype housing 1936 Berrylands, Surbiton (home of author 1985). The render is applied over a one brick thick wall and uses white cement in the mix with dry dashed white aggregate chippings, and is in excellent condition. These finishes should not be painted which lead to moisture retention and commit an owner to constant maintainence. There are substantial tiled cill details and the render is bellmouthed over window heads*

PROBLEMS WITH RENDERS

To avoid cracking, the substructure should be properly designed for the loads and ground conditions prevalent. The substrate to which the render is applied should be firm and unlikely to move *or* movement is catered for properly by dividing the work up into panels with separating movement joints. As the renders are mostly cement based there will be shrinkage overall which will transfer tensile stresses to the material and may cause cracking. If adhesion is good, cracking will be resisted. Successive layers should be allowed to harden thoroughly to minimise any cracking due to shrinkage of earlier undercoats.

Rendering over mixed backgrounds should be tackled in a similar way to plaster but using 300 mm wide strips of expanding metal over building paper or polythene sheeting. If possible, visible joints should be made at these junctions and a proprietary filler/sealant used to act as a movement joint.

There may be salts in the backgrounds to be rendered that could give rise to efflorescence. If possible, the substrate behind (especially if prone to dampness), should have used sulphate resisting mortars, cements, etc. If repairing or coating old buildings, the use of a sulphate resistant cement will not prevent salts present in the substrate from causing damage by 'subfluorescence'.

Sulphate attack refers to the combination of tricalcium aluminate (present in cement and lime) from mortars, renders or cement in concrete, with magnesium sulphate, sodium sulphate or potassium sulphate in wet conditions to form calcium sulpho-aluminate. This compound is twice the volume of the original material and so causes expansion locally. If there is any suspicion of sulphate salts being present that could be activated, then sulphate resisting cements should be used. This is the reason why calcium sulphate (gypsum plaster) should not be added to lime as it will cause swelling by expansion on cement that has already hardened.

3.35 *Rendering de-bonding from a brickwork wall. There are no raked joints in the brickwork and no satisfactory head detail to the render showing that this in an old wall with no original detailed provision for render. A sloping fillet detail would be inadequate although a traditional tile creasing detail would be more pleasing and effective*

3.36 *A detail of 3.35. This show that when de-bonding occurs due to water penetration and in this case, encouraging plant growth between the two materials, the load of the render tilts forward inducing a horizontal brittle fracture before falling as one piece of material*

PROTECTION

If possible, it is better to avoid painting to allow free movement of water vapour through the material. Once painted, an owner is committed to lifelong building maintenance. If this has to be done then moisture permeable paints should be used. It is preferable to use a render specification with a natural aggregate finish that needs no further attention.

3.37 *Cinema, Isle of Sheppey, Sheerness. Three-dimensional render detailing on a cinema. Although a powerful feature, access is needed for maintenance and a specification for natural aggregates and cement that did not require painting would be more appropriate*

3.4 PLASTERS

Although plaster falls loosely into the category of a ceramic by being inorganic and nonmetallic, it should be thought of as a composite material. This is because various components in a mix will give configurations recognisable as either being that of a particle composite or a fibre composite. Whether fibres or particles are used as strengthening or crack stopping elements, they must reflect the need for a particular range of properties depending on the situation. The nature of the composite used has also changed historically, according to the materials available or economically viable at a particular time.

Definitions

The definitions of plaster are set out in BS 4049:1966 and are as follows:

Plaster

1   Gypsum plaster in the dry form.
2   A mix based on lime, cement or gypsum plaster with or without the addition of aggregate, hair or other materials, which is applied while plastic to *internal building surfaces* and which hardens after application
3   The material in its hardened form.

Plastering

The range of operations involved in the application of plaster to internal surfaces.

Adhesion

The bond between the two coats or to a background secured other than by localised mechanical keys.

Bond

The interface strength resulting from adhesion, a mechanical key or both.

Suction

That property of a background which determines its rate of absorption of water.

(**Note**   Care must always be taken that water needed for the correct mixing/setting ratio is not unduly absorbed by the background hence the practice of wetting walls prior to plastering. In order that the wetting is not excessive the use of a bonding agent is sometimes more satisfactory if only to seal some of the voids.)

Perlite aggregate

A lightweight aggregate produced from a siliceous volcanic glass when expanded by heat. (Particles of which can be easily squeezed between the fingers.)

Vermiculite

A lightweight aggregate produced from vermiculite (a micaceous material) when exfoliated by heat. (Small shimmering particles of this material can be detected close up.)

Plaster as a composite

Early particle composites would include those mixes which contained varying aggregates (sand or ground brick) in a matrix of gypsum or lime. Early fibre composites would include the use of straw, hair, or on a much larger scale, a backing of woven wattle construction or timber lathing on stud frames.

Our common particle composites today still include sand but are more likely to include particles from blast furnace waste, or lightweight aggregates such as perlite or vermiculite. Our own fibre composites may include glass fibres and organic fibres which may be modern polymers or natural cellulose fibres. On a larger scale we have replaced light timber woven or lapping systems with expanded metal and ribbed constructions. Plasterboard is also a true lamellar composite of gypsum and thick paper.

All of these plaster composites make for a stable plaster finish that can resist some movement and certainly take up a higher degree of applied stress than neat plaster.

Particle composites have crack stopping capabilities, and fibre composites have directional strength. It is worth pointing out that early wattle systems as well as lathe backing on timber studding have a configuration of fibre reinforcement running in two directions, which will then stabilise an applied matrix. Grid systems with directional reinforcement in two or more directions give added rigidity by equal and opposite support. This is why care should be taken that modern expanded metal backings have adequate restraint in two directions, normally achieved by calculated centres of fixings. Ribbed expanded metal is preferable and should be used wherever possible. Early hyrib expanded metal lathing products recommended Portland cement mixes which still contained a measure of small-scale fibre reinforcement in the form of ox hair, recognising that additional reinforcement was necessary.

Specification

Although the physical parameters may be clear for making a decision about what type of plaster to use taking into account:

Internal or external exposure,
Degree of moisture present,

Special requirements for sound, fire, hardness, thermal insulation and type of background.

There are situations where a decision must be made on an appropriate solution for the work. As the use of lightweight plasters becomes more widespread and it is expedient to use plasterboard it becomes more difficult to consider automatically the use of sand, lime, cement mixes, and also the method of compositional reinforcement. In restoration work, wherever possible, plaster specifications should match the original, behaviour will then be similar and stress cracking between old and new controlled to some extent.

The above principles apply to internal and external situations. The chief difference between internal and external finishes relates to exposure and will determine the matrix used. All calcium sulphate minerals (gypsum) tend to dissolve very slightly in water and, in effect, undergo hydration reverting to the original chemistry of the gypsum mineral with a consequent increase in volume. They are not suitable then for use externally where it is then more appropriate to use cement:sand and cement:lime:sand mixes. (See following section on *Renders*.) As cement goes through an irreversible chemical reaction with water and is generally regarded as insoluble and more stable.

Gypsum: mineral origin
The origin of plaster is in the mineral gypsum which comes in several different colours white, grey, red, or yellowish brown and is a naturally occurring hydrated calcium sulphate. (Chemical formula of $CaSO_4\ 2H_2O$.) There is also a colourless version. It has a low Mohs hardness of 2.0 and can be scratched with a fingernail.

For advice on the detailed application of plasters it is necessary to use the Codes of Practice. In the case of internal plastering use BS 5492:1977 and for external plastering use BS 5262:1976. Both codes deal with the materials available, the properties of the backgrounds, and how specific plasters should be related to them.

Although the British Standard (BS 1191 Parts 1 and 2) sets out four classes of plaster, A B C and D, these options are difficult to achieve in practice. The different classes are based on the extent to which the gypsum is heated and the amount of water that is released. It must not be forgotten that when water is driven off in heating, it involves the breaking of chemical bonds and the release of constituents that make up a stable compound. When water is reintroduced at a later stage in mixing, it immediately re-combines with the dehydrated plaster in an exothermic reaction which gives off heat.

If not very much water is driven off in the manufacture of a plaster, then the addition of water will give a fast re-set to the material. This is the case for plaster of Paris, a class A plaster which has only been part dehydrated in the manufacturing process. To be workable for site conditions this plaster must have an added retarder to delay the hardening process. When a class A plaster is modified in this way it becomes a class B plaster.

The greater the amount of water driven off in the calcining of gypsum, the slower the reaction when remixed with water. Class C plasters are characterised by all the water of crystallisation being driven off. When remixed with water the reaction may be so slow that it is impractical to use the material unless an accelerator is added to speed up the reaction.

SUMMARY OF PLASTER CLASSES

Commonly used products that comply with these classes and are also mentioned in BS 1191 Part 1: 1973 are given after the classes in **bold type.**

Class A   Plaster of Paris
(Hemi-hydrate with no retarder of the setting of the material.) This plaster is commonly used for casting running moulds or small areas of filling, etc. In running moulds a pattern is made up in zinc with a stiffening profile board set behind, and the plaster detail is built up gradually with plaster and scrim, with the final details run in neat plaster.

Class B   Retarded hemi-hydrate gypsum plaster
(Retarded hemi hydrate contains a retarder that controls the set.) These plaster types are used as matrices for lightweight aggregates.

Undercoat		
Browning	a1	**Thistle browning**
		Thistle slow set
		Thistle fibred
Metal lathe	a2	**Thistle metal lathing**
Final Coat	b1	**Thistle finish**
		Sirapite B
		British gypsum
	b2	**Thistle board finish**

Class C   Anhydrous gypsum plaster
(Completely dehydrated gypsum, which incorporates an accelerator to achieve a setting of gypsum in a reasonable time.) Because of its hardness this plaster is often used as a final setting coat, originally referred to as 'sirapite' but no longer easily available.

Class D   Keene's plaster
Completely dehydrated plaster which has a very slow
set but a high workability to achieve a good finish.)
This plaster, previously used for arrises, dados, skirtings, squash courts and surfaces where a very hard
surface was required, is no longer made in quantity.
There are cement substitutes on the market which are
often reinforced with glass fibre.

Standard Keene's
Polar White Cement (fine)
Polar White Cement (standard)

The British Standard 1191:1973 is split into two parts,
the Part 1 dealing with pure gypsum based products,
the Part 2 dealing with pre-mixed lightweight plasters
which contain lightweight aggregates such as vermiculite or expanded perlite. These lightweight plasters are
the most commonly used plasters today and have the
following categories:

Type (a)   Undercoat plasters
1   Browning
    Carlite browning
2   Metal Lathing
    Carlite metal lathing
3   Bonding
    Carlite bonding
    Carlite welterweight bonding coat plaster

Type (b)   Final coat plaster
1   Finish plaster
    Carlite finish
    Limelite finishing plaster

Cement plasters that are now used instead of class D
plasters:
Undercoat premixed: **Limelite**
Resinous for squash courts: **Proderite formula S base
screed and finish.**

   The browning and metal lathing plasters have some
control over the soluble magnesium and salt contents,
the bonding plaster does not. This is worth noting
where there is a possibility of plasters being used in
damp conditions which could encourage efflorescence.
   One coat plasters are becoming more popular especially when they are white in colour. There is a trend
towards the production of a greater range of plasters
that introduce many more components in the traditional gypsum matrix. Although these can cope with a
great variety of situations it means that the basis for
specification is becoming more product based. Specifiers will not be able to quote the British Standards but

should satisfy themselves that a chosen product will
comply in terms of background compatibility, durability, fire resistance and acoustic control to their requirements.

Using the British Standard (BS 1191:1973)
The standard gives a good checklist for approaching
plastering and also for making sure that points of
detailed design are considered, eg with regard to walls/
frames, etc, and corners, coves, openings and archi-
traves. The sequence of trades is critical with regard to
the programming of plaster, as all services should have
had their first fix and all openings should be properly
framed up to provide an edge for finished work.
Depending on the plaster mix used, care must be taken
in ensuring the programming allows for full drying/
hardening prior to final decoration.
   There are additional categories of plaster for use in
specific situations mentioned by the standard which
consider the following:

1   *Thin wall plasters* (skim and fillers). These often
    contain organic binders and may not be compatible
    with the substate particularly if *damp*. They should
    always be checked for compatibility and the manu-
    facturers' instructions carefully followed.

2   *Projection plasters.* These refer to sprayed finishes.

3   *X-ray protection plasters.* Barium sulphate is used as
    an aggregate. (Barium is a heavy metallic element
    and its salts are used for protection against radia-
    tion hence barium meals for patients whose alimen-
    tary tract is under investigation it shows up on X-
    rays.)

4   *Acoustic plasters.* These have sound absorbent
    aggregate which are effective by their porosity. Care
    should be taken that the acoustic properties are not
    ruined by indiscriminate painting that may clog up
    the fissures and holes which affect the distribution
    of sound.

5   *Cement plasters.* These refer to cement and lime and
    lightweight aggregate.

   When cements are referred to in the standard it
should be noted that Portland cement is to BS 12:1978,
Portland blastfurnace cement to BS 146:1973, and
Masonry cement to BS 524:1964. There are references
to high alumina cement which must be used strictly in
accordance with the building regulations and with users
well aware of problems in wider applications. (See BRE
Information Paper 22, 1981 *Assessment of chemical*

attack of high alumina cement concrete.) Normal aggregates used, ie sand should be to BS 1198:1976.

The importance of specifying all components to British Standards is that they do ensure a basic quality and hence purity of the material. There are many unknowns in terms of the exact chemical composition/ contamination in backgrounds, and there must be known components to give assurance in terms of chemical and physical stability. Problems can arise involving efflorescence, staining, unpredictable setting, etc. Even water should be specified to BS 3148:1980. Bonding agents referred to are to BS 5270:1976. As they coat porous material and tend to diminish the size of pores at the same time they will also reduce the effects of suction, the take up of moisture by capillary action. Scrim (a loose weave hessian strip) is used to reinforce corners and joints as needed. It is normal practice to plaster up corners first and then plaster walls up to the junction to minimise the problem of cracking.

Characteristics of different mixes of plaster
Plastering can use, a variety of components, but they all have specific characteristics related to the mix.

Cement/lime/sand
These mixes are highly workable due to the lime component but develop their strength slowly, often forming a hard outer skin which increases over the years. (This is why it is so difficult to match exactly old plaster specifications with these mixes, as hardening is by carbonation.) Each coat has to be allowed to harden first and should be laid on with a wooden float; metal trowelling will produce fine cracks as surface crazing occurs on a cement slurry. The wood float slightly raises the texture and the sand particles act as crack stoppers to surface cracking.

Lime and gypsum plasters
These are highly workable mixes and they are relatively stable. As the lime component shrinks it is compensated slightly by the expansion of gypsum. The presence of lime gives an alkaline environment which inhibits the corrosion of metals.

Lightweight cements
These are similar to using ordinary cement and they can be finished with a lightweight finishing coat of cement or a coat of gypsum.

Gypsum plasters
These are all workable plasters and are probably mostly class B. They all expand on setting, and this is more critical for work, for example, in running cornices

(which normally use class A plaster), etc, where if the work is not carried out quickly, the running mould will snag and cause unevenness. If very smooth surface finishes are wanted then plasters equivalent to class C and D should be used. If worked on, a finish similar to polished marble can be achieved.

Some gypsum plasters contain accelerators or frost proofing additives. These compounds tend to be salts (see section 3.02 *Glossary*) with active ions which can initiate corrosion in metals.

General properties
Gypsum plasters generally, have an insignificant effect on thermal transmittance, condensation, sound absorption (unless acoustic plasters) or sound insulation (which is a function of mass). They are important with regard to fire protection and are classified as class 0 (non-combustible). As a material, gypsum plaster cannot degrade until all the water of crystallisation is driven off, and the temperature of the material remains at about 100°C until this happens. As paper ignites spontaneously at about 300 degrees, this is a safe operating temperature in a fire.

BACKGROUNDS

The British Standard identifies the following problems in plastering:

(a) *Backgrounds: inadequate key/ weakness/ contamination with dirt and grease or water*
This will give failures in bonding between plaster and substrate, and the plaster will move, fall off, or flake.

(b) *Unset by premature drying*
Early hardening before being applied to the background will result in attempting to cover with a material that has already partly set, has insufficient moisture left for adhesion, and will fall away.

(c) *Salt formation and interference*
It is likely that salts will be present in backgrounds, particularly in brickwork and mortar joints. If water is still present in backgrounds, the salts will continually leach out until the source of moisture disappears, or the salt content is exhausted. Purity of components in substrates is essential here, as well as careful programming of work.

(d) *Structural movement, moisture movement, thermal movement*
Movement will cause cracking and could lead eventually to total bond failure, and the plaster will shear away from the substrate. A substrate which is still

hardening, especially if cementitious materials are being used, will still be shrinking, and this will be a cause of failure.

(e) Inadequate suction control

If a great deal of water is lost from a mix during plastering then the outer surface will be embrittled and more likely to fracture with hairline crazing. Sometimes differential moisture loss can be seen by patterning of surfaces behind the plaster 'grinning' through. This shows hydration discolouration quite clearly where a different amount of moisture may be lost from the mix into different adjacent backgrounds, for example brickwork against mortar joints. The amount of water used in the hydration reaction will affect the final tone of the set plaster.

(f) Any combination of (a) to (e)

It is quite common if a failure occurs to try and look for one factor which is easily identifiable, and that will of course then lead to one clear remedy. In fact gypsum can take a good deal of stress and it is probably more common to find there are several factors involved in failure.

SPECIFICATION

In choosing a specification for plastering the BRE Information Paper 213 May 1978 should be referred to for advice. The exact specification will depend on the background to be plastered and the final finish needed.

TYPES OF BACKGROUNDS

Backgrounds will vary from concrete to polystyrene and from rough to smooth. The successful bonding of plaster on to a background relies on some degree of absorption, and not just mechanical keying (see section 3.03 *Bonding*) and cannot be based on visual estimation. If there is any doubt as to the mix specified and to the background to be treated (especially if it involves a departure from the combined experience of contractor/specifier) then a sample panel should be built. If there is trouble with adhesion then bonding agents may well be needed. This is particularly true with regard to concrete, where the density of mix/aggregates is such that there is no absorbency.

SOLID BACKGROUNDS

Dense, strong, smooth backgrounds include:
High density concrete, brickwork and blockwork

As density relates to strength it should be expected that the strongest materials with high compressive strengths will be difficult to plaster successfully.

Moderately strong and porous materials include:
Most bricks and blocks

The increase in porosity will give reasonable adhesion as well as mechanical keys.

Weak and porous materials include:
Lightweight concrete, blocks

The adhesion is increasingly good although plaster may lose so much water into the body of the material that bonding agents may be applied for their properties in closing pore sizes.

No fines concrete includes:
Concrete which shows gap grading where the fine aggregate is partly omitted

The porosity of this material is so high that mechanical adhesion is a greater factor than all the other materials in keeping the plaster on the surface.

Sometimes the plaster will have to bridge over different materials. There could be junctions between concrete and brick, brick and blockwork, or over studding. These are referred to as *mixed backgrounds* and will need a reinforcing bridge, usually of expanded metal. The expanded metal should be fixed over building paper before plastering, and this lack of adhesion to the real substrate behind the expanded metal will minimise cracking.

It used to be common practice to make straight cuts on some junctions, particularly in corners, and this makes better sense than attempting to bridge over dissimilar materials. When walls were more commonly papered it didn't matter so much and was an obvious solution for butting a lathe and studding wall at right angles against brickwork. For junctions where a studding wall is running with a brick wall it was an easy matter to carry over the timber lathes onto the brickwork.

SLAB BACKGROUNDS

These include:
Woodwool and compressed straw boards

BOARDS

These include:
Plasterboard and expanded polystyrene
The Greater London Council Bulletin 100 gave specific advice on plastering over polystyrene. It is a material

that appears to be unsuitable as a background, because it is smooth with no porosity and presents no surface topography that would give adequate mechanical key. The only way of plastering successfully is to use a plaster designed to supply its own means of adhesion.

This bulletin discusses *Carlite* metal lathing plasters, *Carlite* welterweight bonding coat and *Thistle* projection plaster. It is not advised to used PVA bonding agents. After all, the plasters have been designed on the assumption of no bonding capability of the background, and to ignore that fact will lead to a poorer specification, not a better one. See table 3.9.

METAL LATHING

METAL DECKING

PAINTED AND TILED BACKGROUNDS

Although the standard advises on the use of a bonding agent before plastering, it is not a practice to be advocated. The finish will rely on the structural strength of the interface between paint and wall or tile and wall. There may also be problems with compatibility between bonding agents and paint films.

BONDING AGENTS

The use of bonding agents is well known and consists of organic polymer-based materials containing styrene butadiene, polyvinyl acetate or acrylic resins. Polyvinyl acetate is often shortened to PVA. Using the recommendations by 'Febond' for their market bonding agent it should be used as a two-part process. The wall to be prepared for plastering should first be sealed to reduce porosity, and then the coat that assists bonding is applied. The use of PVA in wet conditions is not encouraged and the material should also be protected from frost.

For cement and plaster work:

	Porous surfaces	*Semi-non-porous*
Seal	1:4	1:6
Bond	1:2	1:2

There is also an Agrément Certificate for PVA (Unibond 1986 1741). It is described as a modified one-part ethylene-vinyl acetate emulsion. It is for use with gypsum plasters 'in dry service conditions only', but can be used with sand/cement mixes in wet service conditions. It does not 'significantly' alter water vapour transmissions. It contains 55% solids and can be mixed with water or with ordinary Portland cement and water. Durability is given as 'not less than 10 years'. Long service conditions for estimating the real performance of these bonding agents has not yet been reached. It should be remembered that the service operating temperatures for many polymers is critical, and in extreme cold, the polymer may be able to transform into a glassy state and become embrittled.

Instructions for using bonding agents should be followed carefully. They should not be used neat and the background is normally primed with a diluted solution.

Recommended thicknesses for plastering on polystyrene:

	Ceilings		Walls	
	Undercoat	Finish	Undercoat	Finish
Carlite Bonding	8 mm	2 mm	11 mm	2 mm
Carlite Welterweight	8 mm	2 mm	11 mm	2 mm
Thistle	10 mm		13 mm	

Table 3.9 *Recommended thicknesses for plastering on polystyrene*

For ethylene-vinyl acetate (EVA):

Dry conditions
A first priming coat should be diluted 1:5 with water and allowed to dry. The second coat should be 3:1.

Wet conditions
A priming coat of 1:5 should be used with water and allowed to dry followed by a slurry of 1 part EVA, 2 parts OPC applied while coat is wet.

PLASTER THICKNESSES
Walls
Two coat work is now common practice for cement or gypsum and will work out at 13 mm for brick or block and also on metal lathing. On concrete the maximum thickness should be 10 mm unless the surface is treated to give a deep mechanical key. As the adhesion on concrete is relatively low compared to brickwork, the load of plaster that can be supported is less. Three-coat work will give thicknesses approaching 19 mm and used to be even greater when the type of background warranted a build up of coats to take out great differences in level. Thick coats were more common where the degree of mechanical interlocking was deeper, ie on timber lathes.

Ceilings
On soffits there are more acute problems in connection with defying gravity. Old methods for plastering ceilings worked well with initial coats drawn at 45 degrees over lathes so the plaster would curl over like miniature waves and mechanically key over the timber. Thicknesses could then build up to 25 mm. Today with the lack of mechanical adhesion, plastering on soffits cannot go over 10 mm in thickness.

Plasterboard
On gypsum plasterboard the basic thickness should not be less than 5 mm although there is a tendency for skim coats to mean just that, ie inadequate. Plaster can be applied up to 10 mm thick on plasterboard as the adhesion with the card face is excellent. (*Note* The surface must not be wetted prior to plastering.)

APPLICATION
Backgrounds with large voids or uneven surfaces should be dubbed out before a first coat of plaster. The first coat or undercoat should be applied over a background that may need preparation by wetting, or treatment with a bonding agent. After surface preparation the undercoat should be scratch keyed with a downward action to harden. Second coats should also be scratch keyed for the final coat if a three-coat system is to be used.

Plasters of interest

Artex
A one-coat treatment with a possibility of many different textures.

Snowplast by Blue Circle
Also a projection plaster, gypsum based with resin build, allowing one-coat work with integral undercoat and finishing coat, with a white finish ready for decoration.

Thistle Universal
One-coat plaster. It is a calcium sulphate hemi-hydrate with lightweight aggregate.

Thistle Hardwall
A plaster designed with special resistance to efflorescence. A retarded hemi-hydrate with perlite and vermiculite aggregates.

Thistle renovating plaster
This plaster is designed for old buildings with damp conditions. This is a lightweight undercoat plaster, gypsum with perlite and vermiculite aggregates. Additives promote early surface drying, development of strength although there may be a residual moisture content and contains a fungicide. It should not be used below ground level.

Pyrok
There are three main products giving a textured one-coat finish:
1 Cementitious, for internal and external/wet and humid conditions
2 Plaster, for internal use but not wet/humid conditions
3 Foamed as an insulation product.

Lafarge building products are available from France. Specifiers should check that their plasters conform to British Standards. The plasterboard is stated as being produced to BS 1230:1985.

CARE OF THE MATERIAL ON SITE
Gypsum plaster and cements are both vulnerable to the absorption of moisture. After all, in their bagged and powdered state, they are artificial and will readily recombine with water. Once this happens and moisture is

taken up by the materials prior to plastering they succumb to being part of the 'flash set', probably termed by the speed at which a plasterer has to move to the wall before the mass hardens fully. In this case plaster would be described as having 'gone off' and should not be used (and is probably impossible to use anyway). This explains the need to keep all these materials tightly bagged, under cover, off the ground, and used in strict order of delivery to site. For the same reason, when working on site, fresh plaster should not be added to earlier mixed batches that have been left standing. Plasterers' tools should be cleaned with every new batch being made up, otherwise the plaster mix will go off as hardening is accelerated.

CEMENT AND GYPSUM

These should not be used together, wet in the same mix, there will be great expansion due to initiating sulphate attack on the cement. There are also some proprietary skin treatments which are cementitious and can give unusual chemical reactions and sometimes not set properly if applied to gypsum bonding coats that are still damp. More rarely, trace iron sulphides in cement mixes may give off hydrogen sulphide (pungent smelling) if used in combination with slightly acid preparations. Compatibility between plastering components must be checked and adhered to.

STUCCO

Original definitions of stucco were very general but common stucco for external use consisted of three parts clean sharp sand to one part of hydraulic lime. If a coarser appearance was needed to imitate stone then a larger grained sand would be used. This mix would be spread thinly over the backing coat (which was not fully wet) with a felt covered hand float which lifted the particles up to give the final texture.

ORNAMENTAL PLASTERS

These plasters were intended to imitate marbles. The following descriptions of Scagiola and Marezzo Marble are quoted in full from Rivington's *Notes on Building Construction* 1901 (Longman Green & Co) and is from volume III page 250.

'**Scagiola** is a coating applied to walls, columns etc, to imitate marble. It is made of plaster of Paris, mixed with various colouring matters dissolved in glue or ising glass; also with fragments of alabaster or coloured cement interspersed through the body of the plaster.'

(*Note* Ising glass is a chemical term for fishglue, and is prepared from fish bladders, originally used as an adhesive, but now used more widely today in the food and drink industries.)

This mixture would be applied over an initial coat of lime and hair mortar which is described as having been 'pricked up' and allowed to harden fully. This first coat would be set over traditional lathe construction on timber framing that might make up a pilaster detail. The scagiola surface application would be finished by rubbing with a wet pumice stone when dry, rubbed over with tripoli and charcoal and polished with a felt rubber of tripoli and oil. It would be finally wiped with oil. Tripoli probably refers to the mineral tripolite which is a variety of opaline silica, and must have been used as a fine finishing abrasive.

'**Marezzo marble** is also a kind of plaster made to imitate marble.
'A sheet of plate glass is first procured, upon which are placed threads of floss silk, which have been dipped into the veining colours previously mixed to a semi-fluid state with plaster of Paris. Upon the experience and skill of the workman in placing this coloured silk the success of the material produced depends. When the various tints and shades required have been put on the glass, the body colour of the marble to be imitated is put on by hand. At this stage the silk is withdrawn, and leaves behind sufficient of the colouring matter with which it was saturated to form the veinings and the makings of the marble. Dry plaster of Paris is now sprinkled over to take up the excess of moisture, and to give the plaster the proper consistence. A canvas backing is applied to strengthen the thin coat of plaster, which is followed by cement to any desired thickness; the slab is then removed from the glass and polished.'

PLASTERBOARDS

Plasterboard is used for timber and metal studding construction systems as well as a fast finishing wall technique on masonry, giving an air space which improves thermal insulation.

The British Standard for *Plasterboard* (BS 1230 Part 1:1985) also includes procedures for tests. It consists of a core bonded to paper liners which can be different grades depending on whether the surface is to be plastered or decorated. Most boards are made with a grey side for plastering and an ivory side for decoration. Boards are usually delivered in pairs with the protected internal sides ready for decoration.

Plasterboards are also made with backings of foil and polystyrene or polyurethane for thermal insulation and vapour checks.

Plasterboard is a true composite. The strength of plasterboard relies on the card surfaces being intact to resist stress, so damage incurred in fixing will weaken the material. Nails should pierce but the heads should just touch the surface and not puncture the paper.

Dimensions				
+ or − 5 mm	600	900	1200	− or + 5 mm
Lengths + or − 6 mm	1800	1829	2286	2350
	2438	3000	3300	3600
Thickness	9.5 mm	12.5 mm	15 mm	19 mm 25 mm

Tolerances on thickness are +/− 0.5 mm for 9.5 mm and +/− 0.6 mm over 9.5 mm.

3.10 *Basic dimensions of plasterboard.* From BS 1230:1985

Plasterboard has to conform to specified breaking loads and this strength is not equal in both directions, ie the paper has directional strength in its manufacture.

Water absorption should not be less than 5% and should comply with a class 1 surface spread of flame.

Board thickness	Transverse	Longitudinal
9.5 mm	170	405
12.5 mm	230	535
15 mm	260	620
19 mm	305	765
25 mm	380	1000

Minimum breaking load of gypsum wallboard in newtons (from BS 1230 Part 1:1985)

Table 3.11 *Breaking loads: Wallboards.* From BS 1230:1985

Board thickness	Transverse	Longitudinal
9.5 mm	125	180
12.5 mm	165	235

Minimum breaking load of gypsum baseboard in newtons (from BS 1230 Part 1:1985)

Table 3.12 *Breaking loads: Baseboards.* From BS 1230:1985

Type		Application
Type 1	Gypsum wallboard	Walls/ceilings (decoration)
2	Gypsum base wallboard	For veneers
3	Gypsum MR wallboard	Moisture risk (general)
4	Gypsum MR wallboard	Moisture risk (surface)
5	Gypsum F	As in 1 but improved FR
6	Gypsum baseboard	For plastering
7	Gypsum baseboard F	As 6 but improved FR

The different types as coded in the standard are as follows:
Note: MR = Moisture resistant
FR = Fire resistant (Class 1)

Table 3.13 *Applications.* From BS 1230:1985

	Board thickness	Centres mm
Vertical	9.5 lath	450
	9.5 baseboard	450
	12.7 lath	600
	19 plank	800
Horizontal	9.5 lath	400
	9.5 baseboard	400
	12.7 lath	450
	19 plank	750

Table 3.14 *Framing*

118

JOINTS

There are proprietary joint fillers and tapes for the pre-formed edges of plasterboard which are sponged over after being filled ready for decoration. If edges are to be cut they should be chamfered first to allow for filling; using a knife is more likely to take chunks out of the edge than using a surform blade.

FIXINGS

Nails for fixing plasterboard should be galvanised and preferably have a profiled shank to prevent 'pull-out'. Centres for fixing should be every 150 mm for ceilings and every 200 mm for walls. Nails should be positioned at least 13 mm into the board otherwise the plaster-board will shear at the edge.

Sources of materials

In England the most extensive resources for gypsum are in the North of England. Hydrous (gypsum) and anhydrous (Anhydrite) forms of calcium sulphate are found in West Cumberland, the Vale of Eden and South West Durham. Gypsum is usually found close to the surface with anhydrite lower down. Although anhydrite is used to make ammonium sulphate fertiliser and sulphuric acid, there is a cement by-product. In the *British Regional Geology* series (HMSO 1971) it was estimated that two million tons of anhydrite and gyp-sum was produced annually from this region. There are other minor deposits in East Leake, Leicestershire, and Chellaston, Derbyshire, also Fauld near Tetbury in Staffordshire. The gypsum of Chellaston and Fauld is known for its ornamental alabaster.

Mix type	Cement : lime : sand	Cement : ready-mixed lime : sand		Cement : sand (using air entraining)	Masonry cement : sand
		Ready-mixed lime : sand	Cement : ready-mixed material		
I	1:¼:3	1:12	1:3	—	—
II	1:½:4 to 4½	1:8 to 9	1:4 to 4½	1:3 to 4	1:2½ to 3½
III	1:1:5 to 6	1:6	1:5 to 6	1:5 to 6	1:4 to 5
IV	1:2:8 to 9	1:4½	1:8 to 9	1:7 to 8	1:5½ to 6½

Table 3.15 *Cement based plaster mixes.* Based on Table 5 of BS 5492:1977

119

BACKGROUND					SUITABLE ALTERNATIVE UNDERCOAT PLASTERS		
Class	Type	Suction	Key or bond	Drying shrinkage	Type of finish (see note)		Gypsum
Solid	Normal clay brickwork and blockwork	Moderate to high	Good if joints well raked or bricks keyed	Negligible	I	Gypsum/lime	—
					II	Weak lime	—
					III	Lightweight	Browning
					IV	Cement	—
					V	Projection	—
	Dense clay brickwork (other than engineering brickwork) and calcium silicate blockwork or concrete blockwork or brickwork	Low to moderate	Variable, bonding treatments may be required for cement-based undercoats	Low to high for materials other than clay brickwork	I	Gypsum/lime	—
					II	Weak lime	—
					III	Lightweight	Browning or bonding
					IV	Cement	—
					V	Projection	—
	Clay engineering brickwork, dense concrete	Low	Hacking, spatterdash or bonding treatment may be needed	Negligible for clay brickwork, low to high for dense concrete	I	Gypsum/lime	—
					II	Weak lime	—
					III	Lightweight	Bonding
					IV	Cement	—
					V	Projection	—
	No-fines concrete	Low	Good	Low to moderate	I	Gypsum/lime	—
					II	Weak lime	—
					III	Lightweight	Browning
					IV	Cement	—
					V	Projection	—
	Close textured lightweight aggregate concrete blocks	Low	Poor: bonding treatments may be necessary	Moderate to high	I	Gypsum/lime	—
					II	Weak lime	—
					III	Lightweight	Bonding
					IV	Cement	—
					V	Projection	—
	Open textured lightweight aggregate concrete blocks	Low to moderate	Good	Moderate to high	I	Gypsum/lime	—
					II	Weak lime	—
					III	Lightweight	Browning
					IV	Cement	—
					V	Projection	—
	Aerated concrete slabs and blockwork	Moderate to very high	Poor: bonding treatments may be necessary	Moderate to high	I	Gypsum/lime	—
					II	Weak lime	—
					III	Lightweight	Browning or HSB Browning
					IV	Cement	—
					V	Projection	—

Table 3.16 *Characteristics of suitable plastering systems*

	Sanded browning plasters (proportions by volume)	Undercoats based on cement (proportions by volume)	Remarks	Single-coat work (excluding projection, plaster)
Cement				
—	1:3	1:1:6	Background should be dry to	Not suitable for this type of
Backing	1:3	1:1:6 or 1:2:9	minimise efflorescence	background
Backing		—		
—		1:¼:3, 1:1:6 or 1:2:9		
—		—		
—	1:2	1:1:6	Background should be dry to	Not suitable for this type of
Backing	1:2	1:1:6 or 1:2:9	minimise shrinkage except	background
Backing	—	—	for dense clay brickwork	
—	—	1:¼:3, 1:1:6 or 1:2:9		
—	1:1½	1:1:6		Sufficiently level concrete surfaces may be plastered with thin-wall plasters or board finish plasters: a bonding treatment may be necessary
—	1:1½	1:1:6 or 1:2:9		
—	—	—		
—	—	1:¼:3, 1:1:6 or 1:2:9		
—	—	—		
—	1:2	1:1:6		Not suitable for this type of background
Backing	1:2	1:1:6 or 1:2:9		
Backing	—	—		
—	—	1:¼:3, 1:1:6 or 1:2:9		
—	1:1½	Not normally suitable for this type of background	Background should be dry to minimise shrinkage movement	Sufficient level surfaces may be plastered with thin-wall plasters or board finish plasters: a bonding treatment may be necessary
Backing	1:1½			
Backing	—			
—	—			
—	1:2	1:1:6	Background should be dry to	Not suitable for this type of
Bonding	1:2	1:1:6 or 1:2:9	minimise shrinkage	background
Bonding	—	—	movement	
—	—	Not suitable		
—	—	—		
—	1:2	1:1:6	Very high suction: blocks may require special plasters of high water retentivity or sealing with a bonding agent	Sufficiently level surfaces may be plastered with thin-wall plasters or board finish plasters: a bonding treatment may be necessary
Backing	1:2	1:1:6 or 1:2:9		
Backing	—	—		
—	—	1:1:6 or 1:2:9		
—	—	—		

continued . . .

BACKGROUND					SUITABLE ALTERNATIVE UNDERCOAT PLASTERS		
Class	Type	Suction	Key or bond	Drying shrinkage	Type of finish (see note)		
					Gypsum		
continued ...	Any surface treated with a bonding agent: for example glazed bricks, tiled or sound painted surfaces all treated with bonding agents	Low	Poor: bonding treatments necessary	Usually negligible	I Gypsum/lime II Weak lime III Lightweight IV Cement V Projection	— — Bonding — —	
Slab	Wood wool slabs	Low	Good	Usually fixed dry, but may be high when used as permanent shuttering	I Gypsum/lime II Weak lime III Lightweight IV Cement V Projection	— — Metal lathing — —	
Board	Plasterboard	Low	Adequate with suitable plasters	Fixed dry	I Gypsum/lime II Weak lime III Lightweight IV Cement V Projection	— — Bonding — —	
	Expanded plastics boards	Low	Adequate with suitable plasters	Fixed dry	I Gypsum/lime II Weak lime III Lightweight IV Cement V Projection	— — Bonding or metal lathing — —	
Lathing	Metal lathing	Low	Good	None	I Gypsum/lime II Weak lime III Lightweight IV Cement V Projection	— — Metal lathing — —	

Note   Types of finish (final coats)

I Gypsum and moderately strong lime finishes

(a) *Gypsum*. Any class B or class C gypsum plaster, neat or gauged with not more than $\frac{1}{4}$ volume of lime. Keene's plaster final coats are not included in this category since they are stronger than other gypsum finishes and require stronger undercoats. Traditionally, a 1:3 Portland cement:sand undercoat is used, but this is only suitable for strong backgrounds with good mechanical key, eg brickwork or no-fines concrete. A1:1 class B hemihydrate gypsum plaster:sand undercoat may be used on some other backgrounds, but manufacturers of the plaster should be consulted as to its suitability for this purpose.

(b) *Moderately strong lime*. A final coat of lime putty gauged with more than half its volume of gypsum plaster. Fine sand may be added to this up to an amount equal to the volume of lime putty.

Table 3.16   *Backgrounds: characteristics and suitable plastering systems.* Based on Table 2 of BS 5492:1977

	Sanded browning plasters (proportions by volume)	Undercoats based on cement (proportions by volume)	Remarks	Single-coat work (excluding projection, plaster)
Cement				
	1:1½	Not suitable for this background		Sufficiently level surfaces may be plastered with thin-wall plasters: a bonding treatment may be necessary
	1:1½			
	—			
	—			
—	1:2	—		Not suitable for this type of background
Backing	1:2	1:2:9		
Backing	—	—		
—	—	1:2:9		
	1:1½	Not suitable for this background		Sufficiently level surfaces may be plastered with board finish plasters
	1:1½			
	—			
	—			
	1:1½	Not suitable for this background	Not suitable for paper-faced laminates	If the boards are fully bonded to a firm background sufficiently level surfaces may be plastered with board finish plasters
	1:1½			
	—			
	—			
—	1:1½ followed by 1:2	1:1:6	Three coats required. Metal lathing should be well braced. Mixes for first undercoat should contain hair or fibre. Lathing to receive spray application available	Not suitable for this type of background
Backing	—	1:1:6 or 1:2:9		
Backing	—	—		
—	—	1:1:6 or 1:2:9		
—	—	—		

II Weak lime. This category is restricted to the weaker finishes of lime putty gauged with up to half of its volume of gypsum plaster, to which up to 1 volume of fine sand may be added. The stronger lime finishes, of lime putty gauges with ½ to 1 volume of gypsum plaster, should be used only with the stronger undercoats recommended for neat gypsum final coats.

III Lightweight. Any of the proprietary finishes usually recommended for use on lightweight gypsum plaster undercoats.

IV Cement. Final coats as for cement-based undercoats. The cement:lime:sand mixes are normally somewhat easier to float to an acceptable finish than are the corresponding aerated mixes.
In all cases mixes should not be stronger than the backing to which they are applied.

V Gypsum projection plasters. Gypsum projection plasters are spray applied in one coat which replaces the need for undercoat and finish coats. The multipurpose grade is suitable for application to the background shown.

Plasters	Shrinkage or expansion	Strength and hardness	Remarks
Lime:sand 1:2 to 3	All shrink on drying. Too much clay or fine material or sands of uniform particle size make for high shrinkage.	Weak and soft	Takes a long time to harden and is not recommended for present-day practice
Cement-based undercoats Cement:sand 1:3 to 4	Contents of clay or fine material should not exceed 5%. Strong mixes tend to develop a few large cracks; weaker mixes develop finer and distributed cracks	Strong and hard	Hardens fairly quickly. Undercoats should be allowed to dry thoroughly before applying the next coat. A workability aid or the addition of one-quarter to one-third volume of lime helps application
Aerated cement:sand 1:6 1:8 Cement:lime:sand 1:1:6 1:2:9 Masonry cement:sand 1:4½ 1:6		Sufficiently strong and hard for most purposes, although neither the 1:8 aerated cement:sand, the 1:2:9 cement:lime:sand or the 1:6 masonry cement:sand mixes are sufficiently strong to receive neat gypsum plaster finishes	Hardens slowly. Undercoats should be allowed to dry as above. The aerated mixes do not develop high suction on drying, and they are more effective barriers to the passage of moisture and efflorescent salts
Premixed lightweight cement undercoat	Shrinks on drying	Sufficiently strong and hard for most purposes but the manufacturers should be consulted as to its suitability for use with particular gypsum final coats	Hardens slowly. Undercoats should be allowed to dry as above
Gypsum plaster undercoats Class B plaster: 1:1 to 3	The addition of sand reduces expansion	Strength falls off steeply with increase in sand content. Proportion of sand should be related to suction of background, quality of sand and density of plaster	Sets quickly
Premixed lightweight gypsum undercoats	Their relatively small movement is easily restrained by the backings	Varies with the type of undercoat. Although they are more liable to indentation than sanded gypsum plasters their resilience tends to prevent more serious damage	Sets quickly. It is essential to use the undercoat appropriate to the background. On high suction backgrounds HSB Browning grade will assist application
Gypsum projection plasters	Their relatively small movement is easily restrained by the backings	Sufficiently strong and hard for most purposes	Offers the advantages of an equivalent two-coat plaster system on suitable substrates

Table 3.17 *Characteristics of plaster undercoats.* Based on Table 3 of BS 5492:1977

3.5 STONE

For the use of stone generally as a material, its composition, characteristics and sources, see *MBS: Materials* chapter 4.

Stone is not regarded today as a major structural building material. The winning of stone from quarries is largely to supply aggregate material for concrete or hardcore for the refining of steel, and for the chemical industry. Many quarries have fallen into disuse, and when masonry is designed and detailed in walling and columnar structures, it is often to repair existing buildings. Consequently, in new work, stone is now far more commonly used as a cladding material. The technology of using stone in this way is entirely dependent on adequate methods of fixing, and careful detailing to ensure that weather resistant joints are achieved. In detailing and dimensioning on working drawings, care should be taken in setting out with realistic dimensional tolerances.

The material will vary depending on its geological source. Any mineral suddenly exposed to the atmosphere could be altered. After all, they were formed in the earth's crust in a situation probably devoid of oxygen. Any new face presented to the air after quarrying will change, and so the need for 'seasoning' before use. Some stones once quarried are released from a sideways pressure, the actual crystal lattices of minerals in this situation can sometimes expand. Feldspars and ferromagnesian silicates absorb water and over a long period of time can decay into clays, although this can take hundreds of years. Carbonate and sulphate minerals dissolve very slightly in water and this is a continual although slow process. In rain, (which is slightly acid) calcium carbonate will convert to the more soluble calcium bicarbonate, hence the rate of renewal on all stone buildings. This rate of renewal has been accelerated by the more corrosive nature of our own atmosphere in a post industrial society, where the solvent action of water combined with dissolved sulphur dioxide and carbon dioxide inflicts faster damage through acid corrosion.

Even chlorides from the sea as well as industrial atmospheres, can convert to weak solutions of hydrochloric acid and dissolve carbonate rocks. Nitric acid is produced from oxides or nitrogen, a natural product from the combustion of fossil fuel with a major source from internal combustion engines. Carbonic acid is produced from carbon dioxide dissolving in rainwater. All of these products form powerful corrosive solutions contributing to decay. Even salt used on roads and pavements in winters is a large source of chlorides that can attack the stone bases of buildings. Sandstone is more resistant to this kind of direct chemical attack due to its pure silicate structures, but limestones and clays are vulnerable. Given the worst conditions, stone can decay as fast as steel.

All of these corrosive mediums depend on a supply of water which is plentiful in temperate climates. This brings home the need for catering for corrosion by minimising the amount of water that will lie on surfaces, or be retained in walling systems behind panels and in joints, producing efflorescence on stone faces which, in their expansion, can apply pressure on rock crystals causing fracture. Any mechanical pressure causes fissures which open up the stone, exposing new and unseasoned areas to further deterioration. Soils and biological elements are also sources of decay. Architects in the 1950s and 1960s sometimes indulged in the practice of spraying brick and stone walls in the country with diluted cow manure so that creepers and other life forms would take a hold to etablish the picturesque. The weak acids from lichens roughen stone surfaces which are more prone to hold moisture. Root systems from plant life will disrupt mortar, weaken stonework and accelerate decay. As a particular flora becomes fully established with a full range of insects and birds, not only can bird droppings be added to the list of aggressive agents speeding up the process of disintegration, but also mechanical erosion by physical wear from this new community has an effect.

As a broad summary the chief minerals present in rocks are as follows. For greater detail on particular stones read through the relevant categories.

As stone is not a homogenous material and has a variety of pore structures, the take up of water will vary, and this is relevant for any treatment to stone as well, explaining the patchiness of solutions applied as remedies and for this reason they should be avoided if at all possible.

Rock types and their minerals

Rock type Density kg/m³	Minerals
Granite 2600–2800	Feldspar, quartz micas
Slate 2700–2800	Biotite and or muscovite quartz feldspar
Sandstone 2600–2650 2000–2600 (without quartz bonding)	Quartz with traces of mica and feldspar
Limestone 2650–2850 (dense) 1700–2600 (other types)	Calcite

The deterioration of stone can be minimised by laying the stone correctly, with the natural grain horizontal, if a sedimentary stone is being used, so the load taken is perpendicular to the bedding planes. Avoid rough surfaces which can collect water and sooty deposits, and choose smooth even polished surfaces to allow for fast water run off. Although dense stones are advocated for greater wearability, the ability to resist freezing and spalling fracture may not necessarily be improved by always specifying dense materials. (See section 3.05 Frost and freezing mechanisms.)

Recognition of stone types is usually a problem so the following short guide is included.

GUIDE TO STONE

Stone can first be classified according to its structure which will be as a result of its geological origin. There are three main categories, *igneous, sedimentary and metamorphic*. As all rocks are also a conglomerate of minerals, if the minerals can be clearly identified, then a more precise classification can be given. This often requires microscope work with techniques that involve identification under polarised light.

STONE CLASSIFICATION

Igneous

These stones are formed from molten material beneath the earth's crust. When this material cools depending on the rate of cooling, different minerals are precipitated in order, and the differing proportions of minerals so formed will determine the exact rock type. This process is known as *fractional crystallisation*. The rate of cooling will also determine the size of the crystals. A fine grained crystal structure (eg basalt) will indicate fast cooling, and a large-scale crystalline structure (eg granite) will show slow cooling, giving time for crystals to grow. Although there is a great variety of minerals in igneous rocks, they are chiefly silicates (salts of silicic acids). Igneous rocks have been classified according to the amount of silica present. If they had over 65% SiO_2 present, they were classified as *acidic*, between 52 and 65%, as *intermediate* and less then 45% *ultrabasic*. As rocks do not relate to measures of pH as to whether they are acid or basic in this way, it is now a misleading classification and should be avoided. The broad division relative to silica content has been kept by geologists but the terms replaced by the notion of being *silicic* or *mafic* or *ultramafic*.

EXAMPLES used in building

Granite   (mottled white pink, grey and red). The mottled appearance is to the large crystal structures that can be seen with the naked eye which include silica (white), feldspar (cream or pink) and mica (black). There are also other minerals such as biotite, muscovite and hornblende. The large amounts of feldspar are due to the low density of the mineral which has risen through the molten magma and because of its concenration near the surface of the earth is in abundance and is also early to crystallise.

Gabbro   (grey, black, dark grey). The major minerals are bytownite and pyroxene, quartz, olivine and hornblende.

Serpentine   (green, grey-green and black) is composed of olivine, pyroxene, hornblende mica, garnet and iron oxide.

Sedimentary

As the earth's crust weathers, major outcrops of rocks are worn down by wind and rain. Debris is carried down fast flowing rivers. As the flow of the water decreases the size of the rocks that can be carried also becomes smaller. When rivers flow sluggishly into esturial plains the particle size becomes very small and silt beds and mud banks build up. This continual deposition increases until gradually under self weight, layers of material become compacted. This whole process takes millions of years, but eventually the compacted material becomes hard, and when water recedes, the material left is known as a *sedimentary* rock. Subsequently, these depositions may be compressed into hill or mountain formations and erode again. This whole process is sometimes referred to as the *rock cycle*. On inspection the side of the rock is layered and this records the annual variation in the material laid down. (The laying down of this deposited material is usually referred to as *bedding* and the successive layers of bedding materials as *bedding planes*.) There may also be *graded bedding* and within one layer it may be possible to detect the deposition of larger grained material (laid down in winter and the spring by heavier rivers), as against smaller grained material laid down in summer. If the stone is split, sometimes the fossilised action of wind creating small ridges on an originally exposed sand is revealed. The whorls and patterns in some York sandstones are very clear. If the composition of the rock is studied closely with a hand lens, it should be apparent that the individual particles are slightly rounded, showing the result of abrasive action against other stones when moved by wind, rain, and water.

See figure 3.38.

Sedimentary rocks can also be classified according to their age by fossilised material that may be present. As evolution progresses from fish to amphibia, reptiles can

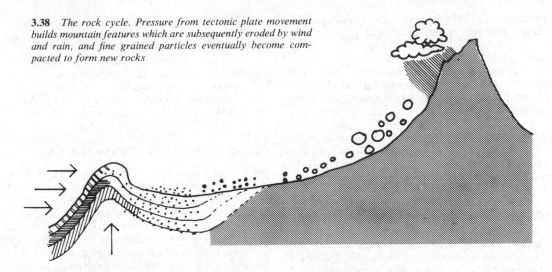

3.38 *The rock cycle. Pressure from tectonic plate movement builds mountain features which are subsequently eroded by wind and rain, and fine grained particles eventually become compacted to form new rocks*

be identified and dated. This kind of classification is known as establishing a *stratigraphic column*.

EXAMPLES used in building

Limestone (white, grey, yellow and cream, red and brown varieties have iron impurities, black has organic components). These are calcareous rocks with fossil fragments that may be so extensive that the material is unsuitable for building. Oolitic limestone has calcareous grains (spherical structures) and other fossil fragments. Travertine is principally calcite produced from precipitation, after water evaporation in caves and springs. Magnesium limestone is a general name for magnesium carbonate. Chalk is a pure variety of limestone, and can be white, cream or light grey.

Sandstone (brown, red, yellow, grey, white). These stones are known as *arenaceous* rocks (Latin for sand or quartz grained materials) with a grain size classified internationally as being above is then chiefly quartz, but if the grains are angular, the rock is often categorised as 'grit'. Sandstone can be cemented by calcite or iron oxide.

Arkose (red pink, grey) usually composed of more than 25% feldspar, the rest being quartz with some biotite and muscovite in a cementitious matrix of calcite and iron oxide. It is often derived from the erosion of early granitic material.

Greywacke (grey, black) has angular grains and is derived from coarse grained feldspar and large-scale rock fragments.

Metamorphic
Metamorphic rocks have been subjected to great heat and pressure, which has consequently changed the state of the original material. Metamorphic rocks can often record particular signs of stress very clearly. The original crystal structures in rocks can be deformed and flattened giving a characteristic directional pattern. Minerals can be subjected to such great heat that they re-crystallise and form entirely new mineral phases. The origin of this pressure is from large-scale crustal movements generated by tectonic plate movement. In the most active regions on earth around the pacific, oceanic plates slip below continental plates forming destructive plate margins. There is enormous friction generated at these points and massive mountain ranges can be built up as in the mountain ranges on the East coasts of North and South America, with accompanying earthquake activity, for example on the St Andreas fault in California. Crustal movement and consequential compression where two blocks of continental crust collide was sufficient to cause deformation on a scale to produce the mountain building of the Himalayas. This process is known as *oregeny*.

The kind of metamorphic activity which is associated with the building of mountain ranges, is known as *regional metamorphism*.

Examples are found in the metamorphosis of shales and mudstones to slates and from limestone to marble. The cleavage of slate is unusual. It does not relate to the bedding planes but occurs at right angles to the bedding planes. This is due to the re-crystallisation of material which takes place with new crystal growth perpendicular to the pressure imposed and elongated parallel to

127

the pressure zone. Hence the crystals are not equiaxed but have directionality and are aligned.

EXAMPLES

Marble (from limestone), **slate/phyllite** (from mudstones and shales. These are consolidated clays and vary from black, grey to dark blue green, red, brown and white).

Contact metamorphism is another category of metamorphic activity where hot igneous material intrudes up through the earth's crust affecting adjacent rocks. Marble, and spotted slate are more common examples of this type of metamorphism.

Marble is a result of the re-crystallisation of limestone to calcite. As the degree of metamorphosis increases relative to the amount of heat small features such as marine fossils are progressively altered until they are eliminated altogether. The original sedimentary bedding planes are often still distinguishable.

EXAMPLES

Marble (from limestone-white, yellow, pink, red, green, black and strongly veined). Marble is chiefly composed of calcite with some dolomite and fossilised remains.

Quartzite (from quartz sandstone-white, red, grey). Interlocking quartz grains can be clearly seen.

Schist (from Greywacke-type of sandstone -whites, browns- red, grey). Schists are all formed by metamorphosis from former sedimentary structures and the particular schist is usually prefaced by the name of the chief mineral present. Characteristically all schists have some flakey minerals present such as mica, or chlorite which can cause splitting.

Slates (from mudstones and shales giving a variety of colours from blacks to blues and greens, even light to dark browns). They are a group of very fine grained materials. They exhibit perfect cleavage which is always perpendicular to the original bedding planes (due to the minerals re-orientating themselves after re-crystallisation).

Identification

One of the easiest field tests in identification is in estimating hardness. Using a Moh's scale of hardness and just a small penknife (see *Glossary* section 3.02).

1	Talc	Can be scratched by fingernail
2	Gypsum	Can be scratched by fingernail
3	Calcite	Can be scratched with copper coin
4	Fluorite	Can be scratched by steel
5	Apatite	Can be scratched by steel
6	Feldspar	Scratches steel with difficulty
7	Quartz	Scratches steel with ease
8	Topaz	Scratches steel with ease
9	Corundum	Scratches steel with ease
10	Diamond	Scratches steel with ease

STONE AND ITS SELECTION FOR USE

Within each category of stone, ie whether igneous, sedimentary or metamorphic, there are great variations in density and strength and consequently, usage. With each category there is also enormous variation in colour. If it is necessary to try and establish the range of stone that might be available in the British Isles for building, there is an extensive range in the Geological Museum in London which can be checked for availability. The publication *Specification* also keeps an up to date list of stone types, their chief characteristics and possible source. See also the *Natural Stone Directory* produced by the Stone Federation, 82 New Cavendish Street, London WM1 8AD, for up-to-date information about quarries.

Igneous

Granites are the major building stones we use in this category and are easily recognisable with their large-scale interlocking crystal structure. They are commonly used for cobbles or sets, kerbstones, bollards, and often the base stone courses in buildings. In large blocks (often weighing as much as ten tonnes) they are used as breakers for sea wall protection on eroded coasts, ie Devon. When polished they make excellent cladding materials.

In deterioration they exhibit individual decay of minerals. The black mica is often the most vulnerable mineral and can be softened by the weak sulphuric acids in the atmosphere decay, or fall out, leaving a pockmarked appearance. Feldspar and ferro-magnesium silicate minerals can hydrate (slowly absorb water) and over hundreds of years decay into clays. This is really the reverse process of the original metamorphic sequence.

See figure 3.39.

Granites are available from Devon and Cornwall, Scotland in general, and the Channel Isles. We also import granite from Sweden, Norway and Portugal. Basalt is available from Scotland and Ireland, and gabbro from Scotland.

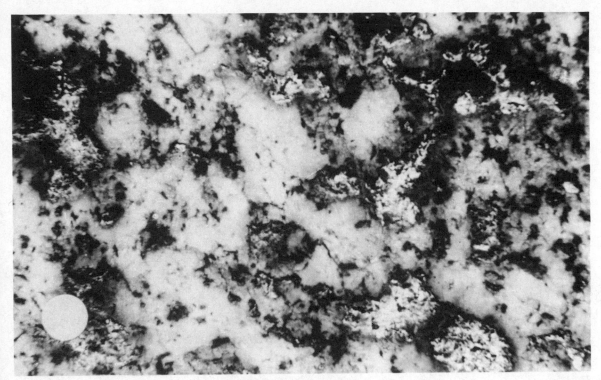

3.39 *Erosion of granite horse trough in front of St Bartholomew's Hospital, London. This shows the erosion of individual crystals of mica leaving small cavities*

Sedimentary

These rocks are the most common used in buildings and include sandstone and limestone for walls, claddings, mouldings, etc. Because of their sedimentary nature with clear bedding planes, they can be easily split into sections. Some fine grained limestones are so homogenous in their structure, the bedding planes have to be indicated by *kerf marks* to avoid laying incorrectly. Some sedimentary stones can be split so thinly they have been used in the past as a traditional roofing material. Splitting these stones for such purposes used to be seasonal, relying on freeze thaw cycles. The perfection of large-scale refrigeration techniques may make it economic to once again use this traditional form of roofing material. Sandstones and limestones can be used for cladding panels but limestones are more likely to decay. This is due to the fact that carbonate and sulphate minerals are more likely to dissolve as a result of weak acid corrosion. Chlorides from the sea can form weak acid hydrochloric acids and sulphur dioxide dissolved in rain water will form weak sul-

phuric acids. Sedimentary stones are more vulnerable to attack, not only because of their own chemical composition, but also because they have a cementitious matrix with minute pores. This degree of porosity is more likely to hold moisture and possibly harbour harmful salts. The largest resources of sandstone are found along the boundary of central southern England and Wales. Limestones are more widespread and include Devonian beds with a grey range found in Southern England as well as the extensive carboniferous beds in the North of England with colour ranges from cream, to red, to light brown, (Durham, Derbyshire and Yorkshire). Around Yorkshire and Nottingham are the Permian limestones which will yield rich yellow-brown and cream colours. In middle England are the Jurassic beds, from Lincolnshire, through Oxfordshire to Wiltshire with colours varying from cream to light brown and green-grey. In South East England are the Cretaceous stones, characteristically coarse textured from Kentish ragstone or to the fine calcite structures in the chalks of Sussex and Devon.

3.40 *St Pancras Station 1987. The erosion of limestone showing deterioration of successive sedimentary layers*

3.41 *Camden Town Hall, London 1987. The erosion of soft sedimentary stone by water movement*

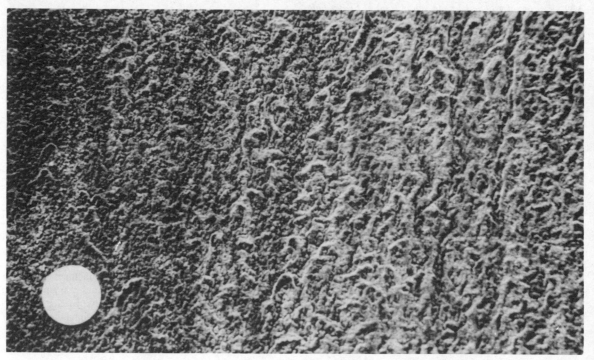

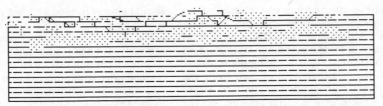

3.42 *Subfluorescence in stone. Salts from ground water or impurities in mortars can be carried through the building fabric in a soluble state before crystallising with a great increase in volume just below the surface. This is partly due to the early evaporation of water from inside pores before it has had time to reach the surface. Different salts will also have different phase transition points and will solidify at different relative humidities. This internal crystallisation puts internal stress on stone and can cause severe spalling. When the crystallisation of salts takes place on the face of materials where accelerated drying can take place, it is then commonly known as efflorescence*

Metamorphic

As these rocks have been subjected to heat and pressure they are normally stronger and more resistant to deterioration. Marbles and slates are our largest categories of metamorphic rocks in use. Slate is easily split because of its natural cleavage which is always at right angles to its original bedding plane. Marbles are also in use as flooring and as a decorative cladding material. Because of its homogeneity and ease in working, it is an ideal carving medium for sculpture. It can however decay almost as rapidly as its source material, limestone.

Marbles are from the most Northern parts of the British Isles, in Scotland and Ireland from the Isles of Skye and Iona and County Galway. Carrera in Italy is still the largest marble producing region in the world (Italy) and there is a great reliance on the Italian technologies developed for handling and finishing stone.

Sources for slate are the Lake District (green) and North Wales (grey, black and blue). There has been a decline in slate mining as seams are worked out or become uneconomic to pursue. The waste heaps are an unfortunate reminder of a highly selective choice of building materials.

Cast stone

This is usually Portland stone in a matrix of Portland cement.

Fixings

As the technology of fixing stone relies more and more on the use of metal accessories a successful stone cladding system is dependent on the construction of these thick veneer finishes and not, necessarily, the material itself. Stone varies considerably in its composition and the connection of the metal fixing into the actual stone is critical. The self weight of a panel, if transferred completely to a small fixing point can put a great deal of localised stress on the panel and initiate fracture. This problem is often thought to be solved by increasing the number of fixing points to distribute the load. In fact the possibility of failure may not always be improved. As the number of fixing points increases, so does the number of components. As the system becomes more complex, a greater number of components can potentially fail. Sometimes stone is backed ie with pre-cast concrete to lighten the panelling system. This can simply introduce more problems, eg the nature of the adhesion between the two materials, and the longevity of the bond, which could degrade unpredictably over time.

Pollution

The chief causes of pollution are rainwater in conjunction with carbon dioxide and sulphur dioxide. Weak acids can form of carbonic acid and sulphuric acid respectively and these can both dissolve calcium carbonate affecting not just limestones but also the calcareous deposits in sandstones. Further reactions between calcium carbonate and weak sulphuric acid solutions can cause transformations of material into calcium sulphate which are then more easily dissolved in rainwater, and crumble away leaving new surfaces of stone open to environmental attack. Pollution is often in the form of very small particles measured in from individual molecules to a maximum size of 20 microns. These airborne particles then fall into the definition of *aerosols* (solid and liquid substances dissipated in air) and have great penetrating power into the body of porous material. Particles over 20 microns are those likely to settle as depositions on surfaces.

The black crusts of material on buildings in London are usually a combination of organic compounds and sulphates (mostly calcium sulphate). The origin of the calcium sulphate skin is by a reaction between sulphur dioxide and the calcium carbonate of limestone, the

131

skin conceals another repercussion of the reaction, an increasingly porous outer surface of the stone as material migrates. Although these reactions provide an outer skin, it does not form a protective layer as more advanced deterioration of stone is taking place underneath. There is also a progressive change from the initial formation of small gypsum crystals to larger more expansive structures which put pressure on the new skin and can cause crumbling of the fabric. The black crusts are porous and act as a bridge for further contamination by gases and water vapour of the existing weakened stone; they can also retain this damaging mixture of dissolved gases and liquids which are now too remote to be washed away.

This explains why buildings that appear to need thorough cleaning, turn into projects requiring substantial restoration. Before outlining a schedule of work, samples of stone should be taken from a façade to establish the real extent of damage by pollution.

Organic

Some lichens can exude weak organic acids that can decay stone. Any kind of growth, of any size whether it varies from lichens or mosses, to plants or ivy can entrap moisture which can be problematic in frosty conditions.

Pigeons

Pigeons will contribute an amount of droppings that are chemically aggressive and façades should be designed so they cannot live comfortably on ledges. They find difficulty in standing on surfaces raking at 70 degrees or more. They are also carriers of disease although a prime cause of their own mortality in central London is cancer rather than death from natural causes.

Cleaning

Cleaning is now a large part of the specification work with which an architect or designer might have to cope. Cleaning is not just for aesthetic reasons. Quantities of grime can retain moisture and itself be made up largely of sooty particles which after falling into solution, will themselves be initiators of decay.

Cleaning can be carried out by extensive surface wetting (which can substantially saturate wall surfaces and construction, creating even more problems, possibly in the corrosion of remote metal fixings). Blast cleaning can use air, water or abrasives, or a combination. Care must be taken in specifying the particle size of abrasive to be used, and fine grades must be used for delicate cleaning. For guidance see BS 6270 Part 1:1982. Stone can be cleaned chemically but these

should always be used as a last resort and with specialist advice as they usually contain aggressive alkalis or acids. Although these are used *in solution* they can seriously damage facing material and should be used with great caution. All surfaces should be very carefully washed after application. Again, care must be taken in case there are adjacent metal fixings which could be vulnerable to electrochemical corrosion.

Introducing large amounts of water could also encourage latent effloresence from trace salts present in the stone or, more likely, in any adjacent mortar. The

3.43 *St Bartholomew's Hospital, London 1987. Comparison between clean and uncleaned Portland stone. Note the shadow effects from blast cleaning. The cleaned surfaces have lost sharpness on their arrises. In cleaning stone over use of abrasives will remove the 'seasoned' skin which is slightly harder, and future decay can then happen at a faster rate. The deterioration of the existing base course emphasises the need for a denser material in this position*

whole of the building fabric should be carefully protected while cleaning is carried out, and glass must be protected from accidental 'sandblasting'. The following list gives basic cleaning methods:

Water   By spray, washing, steaming

Blast cleaning   wet and dry abrasives

Chemical   acids, acid salts, alkalis, organic solvents

Poulticing/dusting: absorbency of contaminants and of aggressive cleaning agents after use.

Method	Process	Relative speed	Relative cost	Advantages	Disadvantages	Used on
Washing	Water spray	Slow	Low	No risk of damage to sound masonry except in frosty weather. No danger to operatives. Quiet	Limestone may develop brown patchy stains. Water penetration may damage interior finishes. Possible nuisance from spray and saturation of surrounding ground. Often requires supplementing with an abrasive method of high pressure water lance	Limestone Cast stone Brick
	Steam	Slow	High	Good for paint stripping (with chemicals)	As water spray but with less risk of moisture penetration. Not easy to obtain uniformly clean appearance	Any surface
	High pressure water	Medium	Medium	Useful where there are no complex profiles and water should be kept to minimum	As water spray	Limestone Cast stone Brick
	Poulticing, used after softening with mist sprays	Very slow	High	On vulnerable and valuable detail, considerable dirt may be removed by successive poultices without any abrasion	Slow method only suitable for high quality work	Polished marble
Abrasion	Dry air	Fast	High	No water to cause staining or internal damage. Can be used in any season	Risk of damage to surface being cleaned and to adjacent surfaces, including glass. Cannot be used on soft masonry. Possible noise and dust nuisance. Risk of drain blockage. Injurious dust from siliceous materials. For best results, needs to be followed by vigorous water washing. Can produce gun shading or mottled finish if operatives are unskilled	All except glazed brickwork and polished surfaces

Table 3.18   *Comparison of cleaning methods*

continued . . .

Method	Process	Relative speed	Relative cost	Advantages	Disadvantages	Used on
Abrasion continued . . .	Wet air	Medium	High	Minimal amount of water. Less visible dust than with dry air abrasion. Uses less abrasive material than dry abrasion	Similar to dry air abrasion but greater risk of drain blockage. Some risk of staining limestone. Can result in mottled finish and gun shading if operatives are unskilled	All except glazed brickwork and polished surfaces
	High pressure water	Medium/ slow	High	Similar to high pressure water washing but with abrasive added. Less abrasive than wet air abrasion	Similar to dry air abrasion but greater risk of drain blockage. Some risk of staining limestone. Can result in mottled finish and gun shading if operatives are unskilled	All except glazed brickwork and polished surfaces
Mechanical	Carborundum disc	Slow	High	No water to cause staining or internal damage. Can be used in any season	Considerable risk of damage to surface, especially mouldings. Injurious dust from siliceous materials. Hand rubbing may be necessary for acceptable finish	Any surface
Chemical	Hydrofluoric acid (HF) based	Medium	Medium	Quiet. Will not damage painted surfaces	Needs extreme care in handling: can cause serious skin burns, and instant damage to unprotected glazing and polished surfaces. Scaffold pole ends need to be plugged and boards carefully rinsed	Sandstone Unpolished granite Brick
	Hydrochloric acid (HCl) based	Medium	Medium	Quiet. Will not damage painted surfaces	Needs extreme care in handling. Any residue on stone will risk formation of soluble salts	Calcium carbonate stains
	Alkali based	Fast	Medium	Quiet. In exceptionally dirty conditions as a preliminary to other methods they may be used to soften deposits	Needs extreme care in use: can cause serious skin burns and damage to stained glass, metal surfaces and paint	Restricted areas Limestone

Table 3.18 *Comparison of cleaning methods*

continued . . .

Method	Process	Relative speed	Relative cost	Advantages	Disadvantages	Used on
Chemical *continued* . . .					Incorrect use can cause serious progressive damage to masonry. The material may lodge in joints and care should be taken to point open joints and to wash the stonework thoroughly after cleaning	
	Liquid detergent	Fast	Low	Quiet. Causes less damage than other chemical methods	May not remove heavier deposits	Glazed brickwork

Table 3.18 *Comparison of cleaning methods. From Table 2 BS 6270 Part I: 1982*

Chemical	Use	Remarks
Liquid detergent	Removing material with organic binders. Cleaning clay brickwork or glazed brickwork	
Alkali-based agent (agent based on sodium hydroxide* (NaOH) or potassium hydroxide† (KOH))	Cleaning limestone	Should only be used in certain cases, eg removal of graffiti and softening up of heavy deposits prior to using other cleaning methods Can leave deposits of harmful salts
Hydrochloric acid‡ (HCI) based agent	Removing cement splashes and calcium carbonate deposits. Cleaning newly erected brickwork.	
Hydrofluoric acid (HF) based agent	Cleaning sandstone, rough granite and clay and calcium silicate brickwork	Only chemical agent that does not leave soluble salts. However, long contact between it and any masonry surface and subsequent rinsing by water is likely to cause the deposition of white silica crystals in the surface pores. These crystals will be very difficult to eliminate For safety reasons it is essential that these agents should be applied only by trained workers

*Commonly known as 'caustic soda'.
†Commonly known as 'caustic potash'.
‡Commonly known as 'spirits of salts'.

Table 3.19 *Chemical cleaning agents. From Table 3 BS 6270 Part I: 1982*

STABILISATION

After cleaning a surface it is very tempting to attempt to stabilise the surface and so extend the life of the finish that has just been achieved. It should be remembered that stone weathers naturally to some extent in the atmosphere and there is a certain degree of case hardening on a fresh stone surface that could be degraded by aggressive cleaning. Some solutions that have been applied to stone surfaces have proved harmful. As stone varies across its surface with respect to its porosity, there will be an uneven distribution of any applied coating. At a later date treatments can appear blotchy and unsightly. Some silicon treatments attract dust particles electrostatically and this debris will be an unwelcome source of contamination. If in doubt over a particular specification it is worth checking with the manufacturer of the solution and inspecting treated stonework where it has already had several years' weathering. Advice should also be taken from the BRE over particular systems and applications. The Society for the Protection of Ancient Buildings have also built up expertise on this subject and both owe a great deal to the expertise of John Ashurst RIBA. (See *Cleaning Stone and Brick* by John Ashurst. Technical pamphlet 4, from The Society for the Protection of Ancient Buildings, 37 Spital Square, London E1.)

For a detailed study on all aspects of stone durability in the environment with reactions from the different types of pollution and methods for protection and consolidation, refer to *Stone decay and conservation* by Giovanni G. Amoroso (Materials Science Monograph 11, published by Elsevier 1983).

Treatments include use of the following:

Organic treatments
Acrylic resins
Epoxy resins
Silicones
Vinyl polymers and co-polymers
Waxes
Unsaturated polyesters

It should be noted that all the organic treatments will be subject to the same problems of environmental degradation discussed in section 2.04 and will have a limited life.

Inorganic treatments
Alkali silicates
Fluoro silicates

Mortars
Mortar repairs should be well specified. As usual, mortar strength should not exceed the compressive strength of the stone. The use of cement should be minimised, and all lime preparations should be used with care as they are aggressively alkaline and can damage eyes and skin.

The specification of mortar and repointing application should be carefully controlled. There is a popular but unsatisfactory treatment to rubble walling in particular, where the mortar is finished proud. Where possible rubble walling should be finished flush pointed. Inset or proud mortar struck joints not only look terrible but allow debris to collect. Masonry cement should comply with BS 5224:1976 and sand generally with BS 1200:1976.

Typical mixes (Source *Architects' Journal, Stone Handbook*)

Lime:sand 2:5
Cement:lime:sand   1:3:12
                             1:2:9   (exposed details)
                             1:1:6   (most sandstones)
                             1:0:3   (dense granites only)

See tables 3.20–3.22.

General guidance
A first source reference should be BS 5390:1976 for advice on the use of stone, walling types, general work on site, restoration and cleaning. As stone forms, from whatever method initially, it will be placed under some pressure due to general crustal activity. Shrinkage cracks and settlement fissures develop. These natural breaks are sometimes referred to as *joints* and certainly ease the quarrying of material, but can limit the size of blocks to be quarried.

References
To appreciate the use of stone as a building material and to quarry it sensitively with the minimum of waste requires a geological sensibility.

Geological Survey Ten Mile Map published by the British Geological Survey (1979).

Natural Stone Directory, Ealing Publications Ltd, 73a High Street, Maidenhead, Berkshire.

Direction of change in properties is shown by the arrows	Mortar designation (see note 8)	Type of mortar (proportion by volume) (see note 1)					
		Cement:lime:sand (see notes 2 and 7)	Masonry cement:sand (see notes 3 and 7)	Cement:sand with plasticiser (see notes 3 and 7)	Hydraulic lime:sand (see notes 2, 4 and 7)	Lime:pulverised fuel ash:sand (see notes 2, 5 and 7)	Lime:brickdust:sand (see notes 2, 6 and 7)
Increasing strength and durability	(i)	1:0 to ¼:3	—	—	—	—	—
	(ii)	1:½:4 to 4½	1:2½ to 3½	1:3 to 4	—	—	—
	(iii)	1:1:5 to 6	1:4 to 5	1:5 to 6	—	—	—
	(iv)	1:1:2:8 to 9	1:5½ to 6½	1:7 to 8	—	—	—
	(v)	1:3:10 to 11	1:6½ to 7	1:8	—	—	—
	(vi)	—	—	—	2:5	—	—
Increasing ability to accommodate movement, eg due to settlement, temperature and moisture changes	(vii)	—	—	—	1:3	2:1:5	—
	(viii)	—	—	—	—	—	2:2:5
	(ix)	0:1:1	—	—	—	3:1:9	—
	(x)	—	—	—	—	—	1:1:3
	(xi)	0:2:5	—	—	—	—	—

Note 1   The proportions given are by volume and relate to lime putty and dry sand. The range of sand content is to allow for the effects of the differences in grading upon the properties of the mortar. Generally, the higher value is for sand that is well graded and the lower for coarse or uniformly fine sand. The designer should clearly indicate which proportions are required for the particular sand being used.

Note 2   Unless otherwise stated, the term lime refers to non-hydraulic or semi-hydraulic lime. Lime may also be obtained in the form of lump quicklime.

Note 3   The masonry cement mortars and plasticised mortars that are included in a given designation are of approximately equivalent strength to the corresponding cement:lime:sand mortars. These may be used at the discretion of the designer to improve workability and early frost resistance.

Note 4   Hydraulic lime is lime which will set under water.

Note 5   Pulverised fuel ash (PFA) with a low sulphate content assists the lime mortar to harden and enhances the hydraulic set.

Note 6   Very finely ground clay brick reacts with lime to give a slight hydraulic set. The brick powder is generally red, brown or yellow in colour.

Note 7   For the purposes of this table, the term sand includes natural sand, stone dust and other fine aggregates used to match the original material.

Note 8   Designations (i) to (v) correspond to the designations for mortar in other British Standards. Designations (vi) to (xi) are included for the purposes of this standard.

Table 3.20   *Mortar types and designations. From Table 4 BS 6270 Part I: 1982*

Nature of stone	Internal walls	External walls			Paving		
		Sheltered exposure	Moderate exposure	Severe or marine exposure	Internal	External	
Highly durable eg basalt, granite, millstone grit (for flint, see note 3)	(v) (vi) (vii)	(v) (vi)	(iv) (vi)	(iii) (v)	(iii) (iv)	(iii) (iv)	Increase in strength and durability
Moderately durable eg many limestones and sandstones	(v) (vi) (vii) (ix)	(v) (vi) (vii) (ix)	(iv) (v) (vi)	(iii) (iv) (v)	(iii) (iv)	(iii) (iv)	Increase in strength and durability
Poorly durable eg some calcareous sandstones, some fine pored limestones	(vii) (ix) (x) (xi)	(vii) (ix)	(vi) (vii) (vii)	(v) (vi) (vi)	(v) (vi) (vi)	(v) (vi) (vi)	Increase in strength and durability

Note 1   In addition to the recommendations in this table, consideration should be given to the best local practice and to any mixes that have been developed to deal with special conditions.

Note 2   The numbers (i) to (xi) refer to mortar designations given in table 3.20.

Note 3   Designation (vi) or (vii) should be used for repointing flint.

Table 3.21   *Recommended mortar mixes for stoneworks. From Table 5 BS 6270 Part I: 1982*

Base material	Form	Grade and standard to be complied with	Protective measures carried out after fabrication
Copper		BS 6017	
Copper alloys		BS 2870:1980, grades listed in Tables 8 and 12	Material other than phosphor bronze to be formed either:
		BS 2873:1969, grades listed in Tables 4 and 6	(a) by bending at dull red heat and allowing to cool in still air, or (b) by cold forming and subsequently stress relief annealing at 250°C to 300°C for 30 minutes to 1 hour
		BS 2874:1969, grades listed in Tables 6, 8 and 9 *except* CA 106 and PB 104	Effectiveness of stress relieving of cold formed components to be tested by the supplier using the mercurous nitrate test described in clause 11 of BS 2874:1969
Austenitic stainless steel, minimum 18/8 composition and excluding free machining specifications	Strip	BS 1449:Part 2 BS 970:Part 4	
	Tube	BS 3014	
	Wire	BS 1554 BS 3111:Part 2	

Table 3.22 *Materials for metal components in masonry. From Table 6 BS 6270 Part I: 1982*

Quarrying

The quarrying of stone requires a huge investment in labour and machinery. Quite often a large amount of over burden must be removed before the extraction of any usable stone. If there is an inadequate natural system of breaks or 'joints', stone may have to be split by drilling and blasting. The phenomenon of frost action on materials can be used to split stone and, if it can be accelerated artificially under cover, annual and unpredictable cycles of freezing and thawing can be avoided. Most quarries are open although slate is mined. The scale of underground workings has to be seen to be appreciated and those at Blauneau Ffestiniog are worth a visit. Once quarried, the stone is sawn with abrasives under a constant flow of water. Some sedimentary stones can be split if they show very distinct bedding planes or cleavage in the case of slate. Polishing is highly mechanised, again with abrasives and water, although stone can be carved and dressed. It is worth remembering that instead of plain surfaces to the material, surfaces can also be 'punched', picked and tooled with fine ridges, or even 'margined' and 'vermiculated' or rusticated with different patterning.

STONE CLADDING

Principles for fixing cladding panels

Cladding which is remote from the building fabric, whether of precast concrete or stone, must be carried on fixings that are strong enough to support the calculated self load of the panel, and any other maximum applied loads from wind or stress from building movement. Large panels are generally defined as exceeding 40 mm in thickness, and must be fixed at every corner back to the structure. Smaller stone fixings may only require two major structural fixings but should be fixed to adjacent tablets.

The whole building should be dimensionally stable and, for steel framed buildings, allowable deflection and degrees of rigidity should be worked backwards from the known tolerances and likely behaviour of the stone cladding panels. Concrete framed buildings should have hardened fully so that full shrinkage of the frame has taken place. It may be necessary to re-survey before detailed design of the panels takes place.

There should be adequate movement joints to allow for shrinkage which will not be complete even one year after casting structural concrete. Dimensional changes are expected to be shrink approximately 12 mm for every 30 m length of concrete. Concrete can also expand if saturated with water by about 3 mm for every 6 m length. Compression joints of 13 mm should be incorporated on every floor and should be a sealant or a compressible polymer. Vertical movement joints should also be designed at the corners of buildings from 1.5 to 3 mm from the corner where stress from thermal or moisture movements is most apparent.

See CP 298:1972 for detailed advice on using stone cladding. The main points covered in this section are:

Fixing types, load bearing and restraining
Panel thicknesses
Mortar and joints
Sealants
Movement
Fixings:metals
Substrate structure:backing
Cavities
Learning by case studies

Fixings types, load bearing and restraining

All load bearing fixings are characterized by the stone or precast panels beings rebated and bearing directly on nibs or ledges, or that are effectively being corbelled away from the main wall by metal fixings that are set securely into the main structure. A direct fixing through the panel is also acceptable and can be exposed (and allow for water shedding) or concealed with holes being filled with stone pellets. There are additional fixing positions often referred to as *restraint fixings*, which do not take the full structural load of the panel but steady the panel against the additional wind loadings or stresses incurred thermally etc. These restraint fixings are configured like a straightforward metal tie or downward pointing cramp. All metal fixings whether loadbearing or restraint should be mechanically dove-tailed into the backing construction to avoid 'pull-out'.

The degree of accurcy required in this work in setting out the dimensioning for fixings should not be less than Grade 1 in PD 6440 and preferably that of 'Special Grade'.

The exact type of fixings should be designed and detailed in conjunction with a fixings specialist, preferably with the manufacturer of the actual fixings who can then advise on structural strength, exact alloy specification, compatibility with other fixings in terms of electrochemical corrosion and atmospheric corrosion generally.

Panel thicknesses

These will depend on the type of stone used. Sedimen-

tary stones should be used fairly thick, ie between 50–100 mm depending on the nature of the individual stone and its strength, but 75 mm is normally accepted as a minimum to allow for variations in the type of stone available. Marble and granites can be thinner, between 20 and 40 mm depending on their situation. Slates should be at least 40 mm thick, wherever they are used.

When detailing stonework, whatever thickness of stone is used, fixings should not go more than halfway across the stone section. This ratio can be less for granite when used in situations below first floor level, but should be more for marble used in exposed conditions above first floor level.

Mortar and joints

Mortar should not be stronger than the stone as is usually made up from ground dust of the stone to be used. The maximum width of joint should be 13 mm.

Limestone and sandstone	1:5:7 to 1:2:8
Minimum width of joints	5 mm
Granite/slate/riven slate	1:4
Minimum width of joints	5 mm/3 mm/7 mm
Marble	1:4 (check type)
Minimum width of joint	3 mm

Sometimes dry joints may be used. Panels should be designed not to abut (which will not cater for any movement), not to be close (which will encourage water penetration by capillary action) and, if possible, incorporate a rebate which will give some weather protection. Any horizontal rebates should be sloped to allow for drainage.

Sealants

There is a variety of sealants on the market applied mostly by gun, although sometimes with a knife, and include the following compounds:

Acrylic, butyl, oleoresinous, polysulphide, polyurethane, silicons.

Joint widths will vary according to which sealant is used, but are generally between 13 and 25 mm. Their depth should nto be less than 7 mm except in the case of oleoresinous joints which should not be less than 25 mm. A backing material should be provided for sealants. Expanded rubber or polyethylene are compatible materials with the above sealants but should not be located in such a way that cavities will be bridged. Some sealants can last for 20 years now and they can be stripped our and renewed easily.

Movement
There must be adequate allowance for movement in three dimensions for setting out on site. This is difficult to achieve with individual fixing points, and the use of channel systems make it easier to adjust panels. The practice of insulating externally calls for more remote fixings which cantilever the slab further out from the main structure. This -uts far more load on the fixings and, in turn, stress on the individual panel, as the calculable force will be a function of the load of the cladding and its distance from the main structure.

Vertical movement joints should be at least every 6 m and horizontally every 12 mm. These joints will have to cater for possible contraction of a concrete structural frame or cementitious materials as well as expansion.

Fixings: metals
All fixings should be non ferrous except for stainless steel. Differing metals should not be fixed to each other or adjacent to each other. If this is unavoidable in detailing they must be separated from each other with a non-conducting medium, ie PTFE (polytetrafluorethyene), to make up the material for washers or separating layers of material.

Metal fixings described in CP 298:1972 are as follows:

Loadbearing: aluminium bronze, silicon aluminium bronze, stainless steel.

Tying back fixings: copper, phosphor bronze, silicon aluminium bronze, stainless steel. See CP 297 and 298 for non ferrous fixings.

Substrate structure: backing
Load bearing fixings are most effective if set into concrete. Fixings set into brickwork require careful spacing to hit the body of a brick and not the edge detail, or be securely coursed in. The brickwork should be detailed as solid, otherwise great care has to be taken with fixings. Fixings into blockwork (especially lightweight) will probably be unsatisfactory.

Cavities
It is becoming more common to set the stone cladding away from a background for two reasons:

1 To ensure that any soluble salts present in backing materials and mortar are not able to crystallise and cause damage to the stone or its bedding.

2 To eliminate the effect of water penetration by capillary action between the stone and its background.

Cavities are recommended to be a minimum of 20 mm.

Pre-cast cladding and stone
An alternative method of construction is to use pre-cast concrete panels with a stone veneer. The stone thicknesses will be the same but their mounting is different. The stone should be fixed by stainless steels dowels (or equivalent strength non-ferrous material) in the concrete and by epoxy resins back to the stone. There should be rubber grommets and a separating layer between the concrete and the stone. This gives a large scale structural walling component that can be ready to receive glazing. As a composite piece of construction, it should be well detailed and insulated to avoid cold bridges. This method saves time on site and gives a high measure of quality control in the fabrication of the reinforced panels, large and complex sections can be made-up to 24 m long (6 storeys). As individual panels can be many tonnes in weight site handling should be well organised and panels should be craned from delivery, straight to fixing, not stored. This is to avoid double handling and any damage on site. There are long delivery times for such large composite constructions and six months should be allowed at least from the time of ordering.[1]

Learning by case studies
It is better to learn techniques from current practice as publicised and to relate different approaches to basic principles. Quite often sound decision making has to be compromised because of unexpected problems or timescale, and the repercussions should be thought out first The Architectural Press in the *Architects Journal* have published Construction Studies which are invaluable to the student and practitioner. In the 13.5.87 issue Wilfried Dechau discusses the Staatsgalerie by Stirling and Wilford. The gallery is clad with stone panels fixed with open joints, a 40 mm cavity and 60 mm mineral wool insulation on stainless steel brackets. Originally the whole building was to be clad with sandstone but the size of some of the panels was so great it would mean the stone would have to be increased to 60 mm instead of 40 mm. This was unacceptable and so travertine was substituted.

There are some unusual features to this stone cladding. Firstly, of all the mixing of stone could be

[1] Trent Concrete.

problematic,[1] and secondly the stone is cut not only with the bed but also across it. Weathering will intensify the differences and give a pronounced texture, but it could be interesting although it could make the building more vulnerable to damage in freezing conditions.

One of the great problems in having cantilevered stone panelling is the joints. Mortar seems unsatisfactory as it gives a false sense of the monolithic. Stirling

---

[1] Advice on the juxtaposition of stones that differ in their constitution is difficult to obtain. Concern that used to be expressed over putting below sandstones may be diminished, given an overall more aggressive environment in which decay happens at a more rapid rate, and from other factors which are outside the control of an architect. Quartz in sandstone dissolves very slightly over time to give the weak silicic acid $H_4S_iO_4$ and this would have an effect on adjacent limestones in a longlife building.

and Wilford have used open joints which is the honest solution, and the shadow gap conceals the insulation behind. There problems with driving rain, particularly with continuous joints around major openings, and so a different technology to deal with water run off has to be incorporated.

For detailed advice on tolerances, finishing and workmanship, reference should be made to CP 298:1972. This code of practice should not be the only advice sought. Stone cladding cannot be understood well if studied in isolation. The choice of stone, design of fixings, and final jointing methods are very much a team effort between designer, stone supplier, fixings manufacturer and subcontractor and all must be involved early on in a contract as their advice will affect how fixings are cast into reinforced concrete, and to what tolerances an overall structure will be built.

4 COMPOSITES

4.01 INTRODUCTION

We tend to use materials that are in fact formed from perhaps several different materials bonded together. In any current book on materials science these materials will be dealt with under the umbrella heading of *composites*. However good the information given on polymeric, ceramic or metallic materials, it is more realistic to understand that those materials will be combined in such a way as to make a particular product, and other criteria must then be established for predicting such properties as strength and durability.

Definition of a composite

A material made from two or more materials which give a range of properties and behaviour not found in the individual component materials.

There are three characteristic types of composites:

1 Fibre These are directional composites and can be designed to give directional strength to a material. Common examples are GRP (glass reinforced polyester) or GRC (glass reinforced cement) or even RC (reinforced concrete where steel acts as the fibre reinforcement). These composites are said to be anistropic, ie they display different properties in different directions.

2 Particle Due to their nature these composites are isotropic and display the same properties and strengths in all directions. Examples include: concrete with different particle sizes set in a matrix of cement, metals which are often alloyed with other elements/phases to produce a mixed anistropic crystalline structure, cermets which are a mixture of ceramic and metallic phases sintered to give products such as cutting tools, brake pads, and HDPE (high density polyethylene with elastomer particles set in the parent matrix to increase toughness). These composites are designed to maximise crack stopping capabilities.

3 Laminate These composites are made out of thin strips or sheets that are bonded together and increase properties in bending that can be facilitated in one or more directions. Examples include plywood where veneers of timber are bonded together with epoxy resins to produce high grade structural materials, or laminated plastics where resins and fillers are bonded together using pressure and heat to produce new materials.

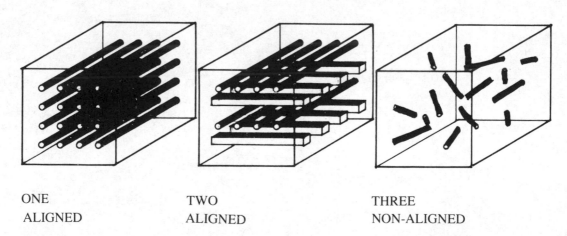

ONE
ALIGNED

TWO
ALIGNED

THREE
NON-ALIGNED

4.01   *Fibre composites and directional reinforcement*

142

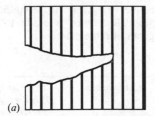 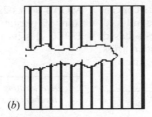 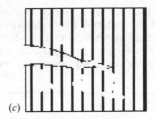

(a) (b) (c)

4.02 *Fibre composites and crack propagation. Fibres can be brittle and set in a brittle matrix (a) or ductile matrix (b). The form of failure will then be influenced by the compositional nature of the matrix and apart from straightforward crack propagation there may be debonding and pull out of fibres (c). The form of failure will then be influenced by the nature of the interface between fibre and matrix. There can also be combinations of ductile fibres set in brittle or ductile matrices (not shown)*

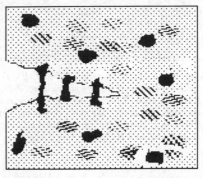

4.04 *Crack stopping with rubbery phases. Rubber particles are used to toughen certain plastics (high density polyethylene for example)*

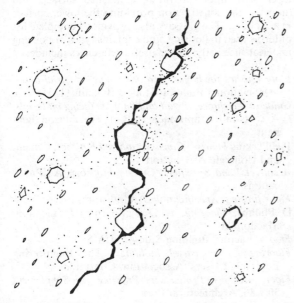

4.03 *Particle composite. A common configuration for particle composites, whether in small-scale flooring systems, concrete or ceramics. Crack stopping occurs as it takes energy to divert a crack around particles.*

Rigid particle composites in flooring

The use of terrazzo finishes and other flooring systems which bed aggregates in a matrix is well tried and tested. There is a growing market for ready made hard particle composites of this nature which arrive in a large tile format. They are made by casting blocks of aggregate material in a cementitious matrix which are then sawn to the right dimensions.

There have been a number of failures in these flooring systems and the first signs are cracking and/or aggregate pullout. These large-scale tiles are often unstable materials to start with. The process of making blocks and then sawing them mechanically is a stress inducer. After the slabs are cut the period of delivery is often fairly short and can be a matter of weeks from manufacture to site. Although it is accepted that rock-like materials should season on exposure to the atmosphere before use, these materials are not making allowances for adjustment the aggregates may make with regard to moisture content. This could affect surface wetting and the proper adhesion of the material. Given that the material is probably in a weakened state on

143

arrival, if the bedding is uneven, placing stress concentrators on the material, then fractures will be induced. Some of these tiles have a matrix which is resin based. This will allow some of these tiles to bend under stress, but the thinly sectioned aggregates will fracture in a brittle manner.

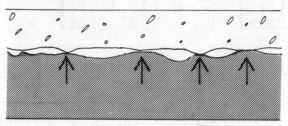

4.05 *Floor tile inadvertantly acting as beam. If a floor tile is not adequately bedded or there are protrusional defects on the tile, it will have to span distances and the stresses incurred will act as point loads. For artificially made conglomerates that are particle composites, there is no directional reinforcement, and cracking is likely on poor backgrounds*

APPLICATIONS

4.1   FLOORINGS

INTRODUCTION

Floor coverings are sections of work that use ceramic and polymeric type materials. They are often composites and the way they adhere properly to their substrate refers back to an understanding in adhesion technology. Problems in their long-term behaviour can be accounted for by careful categorisation and then their use, properties and ultimate degradation can be understood by polymeric or ceramic behaviour.

It should not be forgotten that floor coverings should successfully transfer load to the substrate without distortion or failure. The Japanese term *shiki* refers to the notion of force and the *tatami mat* (often 50 mm in thickness) is seen as a successful spreading of force to the substrate. Concentration of force should be avoided and the concentration of mass on to point loads can transform a human load to elephantine proportions. The effects are seen in concentrations of load by the wearing of stiletto heels, producing pitted surfaces in timber causing permanent damage.

The British Board of Agrément in its MOAT series 2 gives directives for the assessment of floorings. This is an essential reference text listing all types of flooring, and covering the complete range of parameters which assist in choosing the right type of covering material. In MOAT series 23, directives are given for the specification of plastic floorings. Reference is made to the UPEC classification given in table 4.1

Deteriorating mechanism	Classification	Gradings of 'Premises' and 'Performance of floorings'
Walking	U (*usure*)	11 − 5
Indentation and impact wear	P (*poinçonnement*)	1 − 3
Water	E (*eau*)	0 − 3
Chemicals	C (*chemiques*)	0 − 3

Table 4.1 *UPEC classifications*

References

BS 6100 subsection 1.3.3:1987 *Glossary of building and civil engineering terms* defines 'flooring' as the upper layer of a 'floor' providing a finished surface, and 'floor' as the construction providing the lower surface in a building. The glossary also provides a complete list of terms used in flooring, and explains types of flooring material succinctly. Other useful references include:

Floor finishes for houses and other non-industrial buildings, National Building Studies Bulletin 11, HMSO
Guide to the choice of wall and floor surfacing materials. A costs-in-use approach (NBA), Hutchinson Benham
P H Perkins *Floors—Construction and Finishes*, Cement and Concrete Associations
Architects' and Specifiers' Guide—Floorings A4 Publications
Floor finishes, Specification, Architectural Press
D Phillips, *Flooring*, A Design Centre Publication, Macdonald
Floors, Factory Building Study 3, HMSO
Flooring for industrial buildings, The Engineering Equipment Users' Association, Constable
Floor coverings: Products in Practice, AJ Supplement 30.7.86, Architectural Press

Other references, including British Standards and Codes of Practice, are given under the respective headings.

PERFORMANCE CRITERIA

Selection of floorings is facilitated by the *UPEC system* adopted by the Agrément Board which grades *premises*, and gives details of tests for grading the *performance* of various types of floorings under four headings. See table 4.1. A flooring is considered suitable if its grading under each performance heading is not numerically lower than that of the premises in which it is intended to be used.

Other factors which must be taken into account in selecting floorings include: appearance, comfort criteria, and cost.

We now consider in turn: Wear; Cleaning and surface protection; Comfort criteria; Special requirements; and Costs.

Wear

Good resistance to wear caused by pedestrians and vehicles is almost always a primary requirement— surfaces are often deemed to be worn out when quite superficial deterioration mars their appearance.

Wear is greatest where traffic is concentrated, where it starts, stops, and in particular where it turns, and it is an advantage if floorings can be renewed locally in such areas. It is often economical to eliminate causes of serious deterioration such as badly designed legs to furniture and steel tyred trucks. Gravel and other gritty paving should be separated from entrances to buildings by hard paving. Immediately inside buildings grit and moisture, which are particularly damaging to materials such as magnesium oxychloride, should be removed from footwear by doormats wide enough to ensure that both feet make contact with them.

See BS 5385: Part 3: 1988 for *Tile flooring and slab flooring*.

Cleaning and surface protection

The effective lives of most floorings depend very much on how well they are looked after and in selecting materials it is most important to know how much effort and care will be expended in cleaning and maintenance when the building is in use.

The tables of flooring materials on pages 172–189 recommend treatments for each material. It is important that the correct treatments are applied. For example, polishes and seals which contain solvents damage rubber and mastic asphalt, and unsuitable detergents can cause considerable harm to some floorings. Manufacturers' instructions should be carefully followed and tried out on small areas. Instructions should be displayed for the maintenance staff to read.

In deciding upon floorings it should be borne in mind that if too many different treatments are required in one building wrong treatments are more likely to be given to some surfaces.

In design of buildings it is important to realise that it is often difficult to clean and treat floors without scraping and dirtying the lower parts of walls and fixed furniture. These parts should therefore have hard surfaces for easy cleaning.

Smoothness, which makes floorings easier to keep clean, is obtained by fine abrasion; pores can then be filled and the final coating given by a polish or seal. See BRE Digest 25 *Wet cleaning as a cause of Shrinkage of PVC flooring*, Warlow, W J and Pye, P W.

Polishes

Wax polish protects surfaces from abrasion partly by absorbing grit but is too soft for heavy traffic. The finish looks well after buffing. Too many layers of polish darken surfaces and become slippery and require periodic removal and renewal. Solvent wax polishes are not suitable on rubber, mastic asphalt, thermoplastic tiles and similar materials and they may attack the adhesives used for fixing tiles which are themselves resistant to solvents.

Water-wax and/or synthetic resin emulsions can be used on all floorings although water-sensitive materials should be sealed first. They are easy to apply, eg with a mop, and may provide gloss without buffing. Gloss can also be obtained without slipperiness.

Seals

The original seal used on wood flooring was *button polish* (*shellac*) which is fairly easily scratched and stained. Modern seals give good protection for long periods before requiring renewal but they do not penetrate surfaces and are too rigid for application on flexible floorings.

Surfaces to be sealed must be dirt, dust and wax-free. Slow curing, up to forty-eight hours, is a disadvantage in buildings such as hospitals. Regular cleaning with soap or detergent and water is usually sufficient to maintain seals in good condition for long periods. Floor seals include:

Oleoresinous These one-can products, made from a drying oil such as tung oil and a phenolic or other resin, are easily applied, but drying by atmospheric oxidation is rather slow. They are usually yellowish in colour. Being soft they show wear more readily than other seals, but worn patches are easily made good.

Epoxy ester Similar to oleoresinous seals but they are more glossy and harder wearing.

Resin solutions These consist of resins in volatile solvents. They are quick drying but less hard than other seals.

145

One-can urea formaldehyde—self cure These seals are more transparent and wear better than the foregoing. However, like those mentioned below, they tend to stick wood blocks and strips together and cause cumulative movement. One way of stopping this is by waxing floors before they are sanded.

Two-can modified urea formaldehyde—organic solvent An acid hardener is mixed in immediately before use of two-can seals. This finish is of excellent appearance and hard wearing, although difficult to repair if allowed to wear through. Penetration is insufficient on terrazzo, quarries and clay tiles.

One-can polyurethane—moisture curing Humid conditions are necessary to form a hard yet flexible coating which is suitable for timber, cork and magnesium oxychloride. It is too difficult to remove from linoleum and penetration is insufficient on terrazzo, quarries and clay tiles.

Two-can polyurethane (also available pigmented) has excellent resistance to wear and staining but is slow hardening. It is unsuitable on terrazzo, quarries and clay tiles.

Two-can epoxy resin This type is rather slow in hardening and is usually yellowish, but has excellent resistance to wear and staining.

Synthetic rubber seals These are suitable for the same uses but are generally cheaper than two-can polyurethanes and give good all round performance.

Water-based seals usually consist of acrylic polymer resins. They are recommended for use on thermoplastic and vinyl-asbestos tiles, flexible PVC, rubber, porous linoleum, terrazzo, marble and asphalt.

Sodium silicate and silicofluoride dressings are suitable only on concrete floorings. See page 178.

Comfort criteria

Although to some extent subjective, comfort assessments are influenced by the temperature, resilience, colour, pattern and texture of the floor, by the temperature and humidity of the atmosphere and by the footwear and activities of the users.

The properties which affect the 'comfort' of floors are:

1 Sound control
2 Resilience
3 Freedom from slipperiness
4 Warmth
5 Appearance.

Softness, quietness, resilience and warmth tend to go together, for example in cork. At the other extreme, hardness, noisiness and coldness are associated for example in concrete and clay tiles.

1 Sound control

Soft floorings which are not masked by furniture can contribute to the absorption of air-borne sound in a room. Thus at the middle frequency of 500 Hz coefficients for carpets on felt vary from 0.25 to 0.50 according to thickness. (For comparison the absorption of *acoustic* ceiling tiles is 0.70 to 0.90 according to type.)

Soft floorings also absorb impact sound and reduce its transmission through floors. *Floating floors* comprising panels of tongued and grooved strip or boards or heavy screeds on resilient underlays, reduce the transmission of impact sound if they are isolated at their edges from surrounding walls and columns. See *MBS: Environment and Services* chapter 6 *Sound*.

Floor finishes are generally of little value in reducing the transmission of air-borne sound through floors—the extent to which this occurs depending mainly upon the mass of the floor as a whole and that of the surrounding walls.

2 Resilience

'Dead' floors are tiring to walk on and resilience is particularly necessary for dancing, gymnastic and similar activities. Thus, wood is more resilient than concrete and wood strips laid on joists or battens are more comfortable than wood blocks laid on concrete. On the other hand, very deep pile carpet is tiring to the feet.

3 Freedom from slipperiness

The proper evaluation of this important parameter should be with the knowledge that the number of falls and injuries relating to slipping cause serious concern in the UK. In 1979 5,895 fatalities were due to falling and 0.5 million were due to slipping. Such falls account for a great deal of absenteeism and designers must minimise the risk.

The method for establishing how slippery a surface may be relates the measurement of the frictional resistance of a surface (mu). There are few guidelines, and tests on the continent use a subject standing with wet feet on a surface which is gradually increased in its raking angle until slip occurs. From this test a friction coefficients relate to the pairing of surfaces to be measured, and there are great differences between wet feet, rubber soled and leather soled shoes. Low values of a coefficient indicate high 'slip'.

Values range from approximately 0.1 to 1.0. PTFE (polytetrafluoroethylene) has a very low value of about Og 0.04 with many surfaces. Wood on most surfaces has values of approximately 0.4 steel on steel has a value of about 0.6. Rubber on tarmac has a high value of about 1.0 but rubber on ice has a value of 0.1, hence the importance in keeping entrance ways dry and warm. Greasy surfaces can bring value down dangerously to about 0.1 g so correct cleaning and maintenance becomes an important part of flooring technology.

The GLC Development and Materials Bulletin 145 (Item B2 Sheet, *Safety surfaces for floors: Methods for evaluation*) itemise activities and discuss the mechanics of frictional resistance and 'slipping'. They used a TRRL skid resistance tester which had a scale of calibration from 0–150 indicating the degree of resistance to test. Below 20 would be considered dangerous, between 20 and 39 marginal and therefore unacceptable, between 40 and 74 satisfactory, and lastly above 75 excellent and essential for heavy traffic in public areas. The most difficult case of safety they had to evaluate would be standing on tube or railway platforms.

Slipping on floors is a major cause of injuries in buildings, in particular to children, physically handicapped and elderly persons. Accidents are more likely to occur in badly lit conditions, at sharp corners, thresholds and on stairs and ramps, on surfaces made uneven or polished by wear or where the degree of slipperiness suddenly changes. Unexpected conditions are dangerous, eg where polish is transferred on footwear from a polished surface on to materials such as terrazzo and where a floor which is dull in appearance is slippery. Gloss and slipperiness are not related. Moisture dirt and grease reduce friction and are particularly hazardous on rubber, PVC and some clay tiles.

Stair treads of hard stones, terrazzo and timber require non-slip nosings or insets. Resistance to slip is increased by frequent joints, as in mosaic, by embossed surfaces and by the temporary depression of soft materials such as cork. It is important that inherent non-slip properties should not be lost by too liberal application of wax polish, especially on timber and linoleum. Non-slip resin-based floor polishes or seals are preferable.

4 Warmth
Effective 'warmth' depends upon the temperature of a surface, its thermal conductivity, thermal capacity, the temperature of the air near the surface, and whether shoes are worn. Dampness reduces the thermal insulation of porous floorings and increases the transfer of heat from shoe to floor. Parts of the body not in contact with floors are cooled by radiation to cold surfaces. Contrariwise hot floors can be uncomfortable and floor warming should not raise the surface temperature above 25°C.

5 Appearance
Floor coverings are an important factor in determining the 'scale' of a room and whether it is informal or formal, warm or cold and so on.

Floor finishes are often condemned because they have lost a surface pattern, faded or worn unevenly. Monochromes, especially black and white and glossy surfaces show the slightest mark whereas marbled, jaspé and similar patterns help to camouflage even marks made by black rubber soles.

Patterns and colours should be chosen from large samples. To ensure matching throughout a contract the material should be obtained in one batch and a proportion of additional material should be ordered for future repairs.

Special requirements
Industrial floors
Typical requirements are high resistance to impact, trucking, thermal shock and constant wet conditions.

Underfloor warming
Generally underfloor warming which does not cause discomfort to occupants does not present insuperable problems. Stones, ceramics and concrete which have high thermal capacity are ideal but manufacturers of other floor finishes and of adhesives should be consulted. Some organic materials soften, embrittle or shrink, especially if they are overlaid with carpets of similar insulation.

Resistance to water
Where floor surfaces are likely to be constantly wet the choice of floorings excludes magnesite, linoleum, cork carpet, wood products, most composition blocks, and all adhesives.

Floors in shower baths and other wet floors require tanking, usually with mastic asphalt.

Resistance to freezing
External paving must be frostproof, eg mastic asphalt, tarmacadam, fully vitrified ceramics and good quality stones and concrete.

Freedom from dusting
Dust arising from abrasion must be avoided particularly where precision work is performed. Concrete

floorings tend to produce dust. Ceramic tiles do not, but care must be taken in selecting the jointing material.

Resistance to chemicals
No flooring or jointing material can resist all possible combinations of chemical attack, and in buildings such as food processing factories and laboratories spillage should either be avoided or arrangements made for its prompt removal. In such situations paviors and vitrified ceramic tiles with chemical resistant bedding mortars and jointing materials combine high resistance to chemicals with resistance to trucking and thermal shock. Floors should be laid to a fall of 1 in 60, or up to 1 in 40 where dangers of slipping or of trucks rolling do not arise. A chemical resistant membrane, eg of acid resistant mastic asphalt or polythene sheet may be required below the flooring as a second line of defence.

Valuable references are BRE Digest 120 *Corrosion-resistant floors in industrial buildings and Tile flooring and slab flooring*. BS 5385 Part 3:1988 and Parts 17 and 18 Determination of chemical resistance.

Fire properties
Although there are no formal requirements for fire resistance or incombustibility, floor surfaces generally should have the same fire classification as the building where possible. Floor surfaces for escape routes should be non-combustible. At a very minimum they should have the same fire rating classification for the building type. Notice should also be taken of smoke and toxic gases that can be emitted from the burning of polymeric materials. See BS 8203:1987. Standards usually represent a minimum requirement and this is one area of risk where economies should not be made. Buildings exempt from formal regulatory approval should still adhere to these standards.

References
Fire Test Results on Building Products, Fire Propagation RW Fisher, *Fire Test Results on Building Products, Surface Spread of Flame*, published by the Loss Prevention Council.
Flame Resistant Treatments, International Wood Secretariat. BS 3119:1956, *Methods of test for flameproof materials*. See also Draft Document 45459:1987.

Resistance to sparking
This relates to stationary charges (static) and not flowing charge from a supply. Anti-static flooring is advisable in situations where equipment such as magnetic relays, circuitry, data storage can be affected.

Sparks can arise from impact by metals on hard surfaces or from friction on electrically non-conductive

materials such as PVC and rubber. Where gases with a low flash point occur, as in operating theatres, electrically anti-static materials must be used. Expert advise should be sought for specific cases. *Anti-static precautions: flooring in anaesthetising areas* DHSS Hospital Technical Memorandum 2, 1977 deals with the subject (HMSO).

Ordinary grades of ceramic tiles, PVC, rubber, cork and asphalt and some sealing treatments are poor conductors of electricity but conductive grades are available. Terrazzo is often used as an electrically conductive floor. Electrical bonding by copper strips or by a special adhesive or coating on the underside of floorings is required to give uniform conductivity throughout a floor. Floor polishes or seals must not be allowed to reduce anti-static properties.

See BS 3187:1978 *Specification for electrically conducting rubber floor.*

X-ray resistance
Ordinary floorings do not resist X-rays and a lead or other resistant barrier may be needed.

Costs of floorings

Initial costs of floorings vary as much as 50 to 1 and difference in serviceable lives can be of the same order. Low initial cost is often associated with rapid deterioration, high maintenance costs and high *cost-in-use*. The fact that timber, composition blocks, terrazzo, cork and natural stones being homogeneous throughout their thickness can be resurfaced, substantially reduces their cost-in-use.

THE SUBSTRATE

Generally, substrates must be rigid and stable: few, if any, finishes can withstand constant movement. They must be level (see page 152), and for thin floor coverings which mirror the slightest irregularities, they must be smooth.

Substrates for floorings which will transmit or be damaged by moisture must be sufficiently dry. BRE Digest 163 describes a simple apparatus comprising a hygrometer which measures the relative humidity of a small volume of air enclosed so it is in equilibrium with the surface. If the reading taken after at least four hours (preferably 12 hours) is in the range 75 to 80% it is safe to lay all floorings.

This section deals with damp-proofing requirements in 'solid' concrete floors and 'suspended' timber floors at ground level where no water pressure exists.

Solid floors at ground level

References
Protection of buildings against water from the ground
BS 8204:1988 Table 4.3 *In situ floor finishes*
BRE Digest 54 *Damp proofing solid floors.*

Dampness may lead to uncomfortably humid atmospheric conditions, a 'cold floor', surface discolouration, and decay of organic materials in underlays, adhesives and floorings. Rising damp, either as liquid or vapour which penetrates through flooring units or through the joints between them is often only remarked upon when condensation appears on the underside of an impervious mat, or where water which evaporates leaves salts on a surface. Incidentally, perishable materials may remain sound where they are able to 'breathe' but decay rapidly if moisture is trapped by superimposed impervious materials.

Concrete and cement/sand screeds are not vapour-proof even if a waterproofing admixture is included in their composition. Only mastic asphalt and pitch mastic are completely vapour-proof. Table 4.2 gives damp-proofing requirements for floorings on solid floors.

Type	Base	Thickness mm	Bay size
Monolithic	Concrete less than 3 hours old	12–25	—
Bonded	Sound, clean concrete more than 3 hours old but not including water repellent admixture	40† min	10 m² max and length not exceeding 1½ × width for screeds to receive thick finishes and heated screeds only – see page 152
Unbonded	Damp-proof membrane or concrete which is weak, contaminated or includes water repellent admixture	50 min *unheated* 65 min *heated*	
	Resilient quilt for *floating floor*	65 min *unheated* 75 min *heated*	

*Joints must also be provided in monolithic and bonded screeds over movement joints in the structure.
†Where bays are very small, eg for terrazzo, minimum thickness can be 25 mm.

According to their position damp-proofing membranes are called:
(a) sub-base membranes
(b) sandwich membranes or
(c) surface membranes.

(a) Sub-base membranes
Damp-proof films with lapped joints can be laid on a sub-grade blinded with fine material before the base concrete is laid. BS 743:1470 states that polyisobutylene film can provide a vapour seal and polythene film at least 0.13 mm thick with lapped joints is of value under thermoplastic and vinylasbestos tiles, although it does not always afford sufficient protection to water-sensitive materials such as magnesium oxychloride, PVA emulsion-cement, flexible PVC, cork or timber.

The membrane must be below base concrete which includes heating elements but in other cases because it takes about four weeks for every 25 mm thickness of concrete to dry out, it is usually best to place the membrane above the base concrete.

(b) Sandwich membranes
These are laid between a concrete base and a screed. Four examples are:

1 *Hot bitumen or coal-tar pitch* at least 3 mm thick and soft enough to avoid brittleness in cold weather, without being tacky in hot weather. (Softening points should be 50–55°C and 35–45°C respectively.) If the concrete is too damp or dusty, pinholes may develop in the membrane. It should be primed with bitumen solution or emulsion, or with a solution of coal-tar pitch for a hot pitch membrane.

2 Three coats of *bitumen solution, bitumen-rubber emulsion* or *tar-rubber emulsion* at least 0.5 mm thick.

3 *Bitumen sheet* damp-proof course to BS 743:1970 with sealed joints.

4 *Plastics films* as for sub-base membranes.

(c) Surface membranes
Damp-proof underlays or floor finishes of 16 mm mastic asphalt and pitch mastic are water- and vapour-proof and eliminate the need to wait for base concrete and screeds to dry. Pitch-epoxy resin coatings are slightly permeable to water vapour and are not able to 'bridge' cracks which may form in the surface to which they are applied.

◄ **Table 4.2** *Thicknesses and bay sizes for dense concrete screeds*

Floor Finishes	Resistance of Finish to damp	Minimum damp-resisting requirements[1]
16 mm mastic asphalt 16 mm pitch mastic	No material, dimensional or adhesion failure	No additional protection normally required[2]
Concrete including terrazo Clay tiles	No material, dimensional or adhesion failure if sulphates are not present	A sandwich membrane is recommended on wet sites[2]
Cement/rubber latex Cement/bitumen Composition blocks laid in cement mortar	No material or dimensional failure Generally no adhesion failure	
Wood blocks dipped and laid in hot soft bitumen or coal-tar pitch covering whole area	Material, dimensional and adhesion failure may occur in wet conditions.	
Thermoplastic tiles PVC, vinyl-asbestos tiles	In wet conditions dimensional and adhesion failure may occur. Thermoplastic tiles may be attacked by dissolved salts	
Magnesium oxychloride	Softens and disintergrates in wet conditions	A sandwich membrane is essential
PVA emulsion/cement	Expands when damp	
Rubber and flexible PVC Linoleum and cork carpet Cork tiles	Loses adhesion and expands when damp	
Wood blocks laid in cold adhesive Wood strip and boards Chipboard	Expands and may rot	

[1] Damp-proof membranes must be continuous with damp-proof course in walls
[2] A damp-proof membrane is always required below floor warming

Table 4.3 *Damp-proofing requirements for floorings on solid floors*

SUSPENDED TIMBER FLOORS AT GROUND LEVEL

A properly constructed floor comprising tongued and grooved timber boards on joists, supported on sleeper walls or piers with damp-proof courses, built off a concrete slab laid on hardcore can provide a dry floor if there is adequate sub-floor ventilation to remove water vapour which rises through the site concrete (see *MBS: Structure and Fabric* Part 1 chapter 8). However, the thermal insulation provided by the boards must be supplemented by insulating boards or quilt or by reflective foil.

150

Floor screeds

References
BRE Digest 104, *Floor screeds*, HMSO
D of E Advisory Leaflet 5, *Laying floor screeds*, HMSO

Screeds to receive floorings are laid, usually on a concrete base, for one or more of the following purposes.

1 To provide a degree of level and smoothness to suit a particular flooring, where this is not provided by the structural base with or without a *levelling compound* applied to it.

2 To raise levels.

3 To provide falls. To maintain a minimum stipulated thickness most parts of the screeded area will be wastefully thick and where possible it is better to form falls in the structural base.

4 To accommodate services. Ideally services should be readily accessible and cracking is likely to occur where screeds are reduced in thickness above embedded pipes.

5 To accommodate floor warming installations.

6 To provide thermal insulation.

7 To provide insulation against transmission of impact sound, in the form of *floating screeds*.

8 To provide a nailable base for certain floorings.

9 To form part of the structure of certain precast concrete floor systems.

Generally, if floor finishes are liable to be damaged, by damp, a damp-proof membrane is necessary, see page 149.

Screeds on timber bases
Screeds would not normally be laid on timber bases but if they are the timber must be rigid, dry and adequately ventilated below. The upper surface of timber must be protected by bitumen felt or building paper and wire netting or light expanded metal should be fixed at about 200 mm centres and so that no part of the mesh rises more than 6 mm above the surface of the timber.

Screeds are considered in the following order:
Concrete screeds
  cement—dense aggregate
  modified cement and sand screeds
  lightweight concrete screeds
Synthetic anhydrite screeds

Cement: dense aggregate screeds
The thickness of cement—dense aggregate screed must relate to their strength, the degree of bond with the base and where applicable the strength of the base. Screeds which are *monolithic* with sound bases can be very thin. Those which are laid separately must be thicker and *unbonded* screeds, in particular *floating* screeds on compressible layers, must be sufficiently thick to be strong in their own right. They are also more liable to crack and curl upwards at the edges of slabs. Screeds are described under the following headings:

1 *Monolithic screeds* (on green concrete)
2 *Bonded screeds* (on hardened concrete)
3 *Unbonded screeds*

1 *Monolithic screeds*
By laying screeds on green concrete within three hours of placing, differential shrinkage between the screed and base is minimised and success is guaranteed. However, an early decision to lay monolithically must be made and the screed must be protected during subsequent building operations.

2 *Bonded screeds on hardened concrete*
The fact that cement aggregate screeds often fail to bond fully to hardened concrete bases may be acceptable for light duty floors, very thick screeds and where the floor finish is of rigid units such as quarries and in such cases the concrete base need only be brushed with a stiff broom just before it hardens. To obtain maximum bond the aggregate in the base concrete must be exposed without loosening the large particles. This can be done by water spray and brushing the hardened concrete, but after the normal delay before laying the screed the dirty surface is usually very difficult to clean, and mechanical hacking[1] just before laying the screed is preferable.

Whether the surface is prepared to give partial or maximum bond it should be thoroughly cleaned and wetted (preferably overnight), any surplus water removed, and not more than twenty minutes before laying the screed a thin coat of cement grout should be well brushed into the damp surface of the base. Alternatively, a proprietary *bonding agent* can be used, but it remains necessary to remove surface laitance and to

---

[1] It is not practicable to hack precast concrete units and screeds should be considered to be 'partially bonded'.

wet concrete before it is applied. Agents based on polyvinyl acetate, however, are not suitable in persistently damp conditions.

3 Unbonded screeds

These screeds must be at least 50 mm thick as shown in table 4.4. Greater thicknesses are necessary for heated screeds and for those laid on resilient layers. Great care should be taken in the design and laying of screeds which incorporate floor warming installations. For those including electrical cables *The Electric Floor Warming Design Manual*, obtainable from the Electricity Council, 30 Millbank, London, SW1 should be consulted.

'Floating screeds' for sound insulation must be at least 65 mm thick and 75 mm thick if they are heated. Wire mesh will not prevent curling but it may restrain drying shrinkage. Resilient layers with a nominal thickness of 25 mm should not be reduced to less than 10 mm under the dead load of the floor and they must be turned upwards at their edges so the screed is isolated from walls and columns. Adjacent edges of quilts should be closely butted and great care must be taken to prevent mortar from seeping into or bridging the installation at any point.

Materials for cement: dense aggregate screeds

Portland cement to BS 12:1978 *Portland cement (ordinary and rapid hardening)* is usually satisfactory. Aggregate should comply with BS 882:1983 *Aggregates from natural sources for concrete (including granolithic)* and BS 1199:1973 *Building sands from natural sources*, zones 1, 2 or 3.

To minimise drying shrinkage, the most common cause of failure, the cement:aggregate ratio should not exceed 1:3 and the driest mix which can be thoroughly compacted with the means available should be used. A sample squeezed in the hand should ball together

Thickness of screed mm	Cement	Fine aggregate (dry sand or crushed stone graded 5 mm down)	Coarse aggregrate (graded 10 down)
up to 40	1	3*–4½	–
40 to 75			
over 75	1	1½	3

*The richer 1 : 3 mix is preferred for screeds for thin floorings such as PVC (vinyl)-asbestos and flexible vinyl tiles.

Table 4.4 *Suitable mix proportions by weight*

without water being forced out. Low water:cement ratios become practicable by the use of workability aids and mechanical compaction.

Mixes Suitable mix proportions by weight are shown in table 4.4.

Where weight batching is not practicable, cement should be batched by hole bags, accurate gauge boxes should be used for measuring the aggregate and proportions should be adjusted to compensate for *bulking* (see *MBS: Materials* page 167).

Mixing Thorough mixing is most important to obtain optimum strength, and a mechanical mixer is advisable.

Laying It used to be thought preferable to lay all screeds in bays to control shrinkage cracking but drying from the upper surface of screeds often caused bays to curl upwards at their edges and it was necessary either to relay or to grind down the raised parts in order to prevent them showing through thin floorings such as vinyl sheet and tiles. It is now recommended by the PSA that *bonded* screeds for thin floorings (other than heated screeds), should be laid in as large areas as possible. Random cracks can then be easily repaired. However, *bonded* and *unbonded* screeds to receive thick floorings, and those including heating, should be laid alternately in bays 'chess board fashon' with close butt vertical joints. Adjacent bays should be laid at intervals of at least 24 hours, the edges of the first laid bays being wetted and brushed with cement grout. Shrinkage will accommodate local thermal expansion and expansion joints need only be provided to coincide with those which are in the structure.

Screeds must be thoroughly compacted preferably with a beam vibrator, particular attention being paid to edges of bays and especially to the corners. Where trowelling is required to give a true surface it should be delayed for some hours when it will be accompanied by a ringing sound. Premature or excessive trowelling brings laitance to the surface which will craze and dust. For some finishes a screedboarded or a wood floated surface suffices, but a very smooth trowelled surface is necessary for thin floorings such as linoleum and vinyl sheet.

The *tolerances for level* given for floor finishes in BS 8204:1988 would apply to screeds for thin finishes. Acceptable deviations from datum could be ± 15 mm over large open areas and local variations in level ± 3 mm in any 3 m. Differences of level between adjacent bays should not exceed ± 1 mm, and less where thin flexible coverings will be laid.

BS 1134: Part 2: 1972 describes a profilometer which records movements of a wheel over surfaces.

Curing The screed must be kept well above freezing point until it is hard and kept damp for at least seven days until it is strong enough to withstand the stress arising from drying shrinkage.

Drying The slower the rate of drying the lower is the risk of cracking and curling, and the temptation to accelerate drying must be resisted for at least the first four weeks. Water sensitive finishes should not be laid until screeds are sufficiently dry. A rough rule is to allow four weeks for every 25mm of screed (or concrete)—above the damp-proof membrane in normal weather but the test described in BRE Digest 18 and BS 8203:1987 should be used (see page 149). Drying by underfloor warming should not commence for at least four weeks and then only at a reduced temperature. It is important to note that drying will not occur below the elements while the heating is in operation.

Modified cement and sand screeds
Proprietary screeds, which include metallic soaps or other water repellents, dry slowly but those which contain emulsions of bitumen, polyvinyl acetate, acrylic resins and/or synthetic rubbers are usually thinner than cement/sand screeds and dry more quickly. Screeds of this type may set quickly, adhere well and be laid to a feather edge, resist cracking and some are *self smoothing*.

Lightweight concrete screeds
Screeds of aerated, lightweight aggregate or no-fines concretes[1] are particularly useful in saving weight where thick screeds are required to provide falls or to accommodate services. Broadly, thermal insulation improves, strength reduces and shrinkage increases with decreasing density. No-fines concrete, however, has low shrinkage. Table 4.5 gives recommended thickness and other information.

[1] Lightweight concretes are discussed in *MBS: Materials* chapter 8.

Type	Usual minimum thickness mm	Remarks
Aerated	40 plus 14–20 *monolithic* dense topping on screeds less than 1280 kg/m³ and if heavy wear is likely before floor finish is laid	Mixing and laying should be done by specialist firms
Lightweight aggregate **'weak'** eg exfoliated vermiculite, perlite	50 plus 15–20 *monolithic* dense topping*	Mixing and laying should be done in strict accordance with the aggregate manufacons eg: *Bonded* screeds are laid on fresh neat cement grout 'Weak' mixes should not be tamped or vibrated *Note* Absorbent aggregates are slow in drying but pfa *no-fines* mixes dry more quickly than dense mixes
'strong' eg expanded clay, shale or slate, foamed slag, sintered pulverised fuel ash (pfa)	40 including 10 *monolithic* dense topping* if floor finish cannot distribute point loads sufficiently	
No-fines eg 1 Portland cement: 10 sintered pfa (*Lytag*) 6 mm single size (by volume)	25 *bonded* or 51 (including reinforcement) *unbonded* plus 10 dense topping* in each case	

* Not richer than 1 cement : 4 sand to minimise risk of shrinkage cracking

Table 4.5 *Lightweight concrete*

Synthetic anhydrite screeds

Screeds of 1 synthetic anhydrite (anhydrous calcium sulphate: 2½ specially graded aggregate (by volume) can be laid to minimum thicknesses of 25 mm for normal use, 30 mm for electric floor warming and 40 mm on compressible layers. Although more costly for equal thickness than cement/sand screeds:

(a) the base need not be prepared to provide bond
(b) almost all the water used combines as water of crystallisation and moisture-sensitive floorings can sometimes be laid as soon as ten days after the screed is laid
(c) very low drying shrinkage means that screeds can be laid in large areas without cracking or curling.

On the other hand, synthetic anhydrite loses strength in damp conditions and bases must be dry before screeds are laid. If the calcium sulphate dries out before it is thoroughly hydrated dustiness and low strength may result.

Dry underlay systems on concrete bases

A proprietary dry floating floor to receive non-rigid light duty floorings consists of 6 or 8 mm sheets of hardboard with rebated edges which are bonded with PVA adhesive when they are laid mesh side up on 13, 16 or 19 mm heat tempered bitumen insulating fibre building board which is laid loose on the subfloor. 2 mm gaps should be left between adjoining insulating boards, 10 mm gaps around rooms and 3 mm gaps between rooms and at every 10 m in corridors. Joints between hardboards and insulating boards should not coincide. Subfloors should be dry and reasonably smooth, although the insulating board accepts a degree of unevenness. The boards should be stored flat on the site for a few days to allow them to adjust to the ambient humidity.

Alternatively, chipboards with t and g joints to all edges are laid on foamed polystyrene boards, at least 12 mm thick, separated from the base by polythene foil. Chipboards should not be more than 610 mm wide with end joints staggered. If 12 mm gaps are left adjacent to all walls, columns, etc. the system has some value in reducing the transmission of impact sound.

TYPES OF FLOORINGS

The range of floorings includes materials as diverse as wool, cork, plastic, timber, granite and steel with widely differing appearance, performance, and initial and maintenance costs. Common types of materials are either: A *Laid in situ* or B *Preformed*.

A	Floorings laid in situ

A I	Without joints
	1 Mastic asphalt
	2 Pitch mastic
	3 Cement rubber-latex
	4 Cement-bitumen emulsion
	5 Cement resin
	6 Polyurethane resin
	7 Epoxide resin
	8 Polyester resin

A II	With joints
	1 Concrete floorings
	(i) Plain
	(ii) Granolithic
	(iii) Terrazzo
	2 Magnesium oxychloride (magnesite)

B	Preformed floorings

B I	Sheet supplied rolled
	Adhesives
	1 Linoleum
	2 Cork carpet
	3 Printed linoleum
	4 Flexible vinyl
	5 Rubber

B II	Boards (other than timber)
	1 Plywood
	2 Chipboard
	3 Hardboard

B III	Timber floorings
	1 Blocks
	2 Blocks, end grain
	3 Boards
	4 Strip
	5 Overlay strip
	6 Parquet

(Plywood—see **B II Boards**)

B IV	Clay and precast concrete floorings
	1 Bricks
	2 Paviors
	3 Quarries
	4 Vitrified ceramic floor tiles
	5 Fully vitrified ceramic floor tiles
	6 Mosiac
	7 Concrete, precast
	8 Terrazzo, precast

B V	Composition blocks

See table 4.15 pages 178–181

B VI   Stones

    1 Granites
    2 Sandstones
    3 Limestones
    4 Marbles
      (mosaic see B IV *Clay and precast concrete floorings* table 4.14 pages 176–177
    5 Slates
    6 Quartzite

B VII   Other tile and slab floorings

    1 Linoleum
    2 Cork
    3 Rubber
    4 Thermoplastic ('asphalt') tiles
    5 Thermoplastic vinylised tiles
    6 Vinyl-asbestos
    7 Flexible vinyls
    8 Asbestos-cement
    9 Mastic asphalt
   10 Cast iron
   11 Steel

B VIII   Glass mosaic   See table 4.14, pages 176–177

B IX   Carpets and felts   See text page 194

C   Raised floors

A   Flooring laid in situ

A I   Without joints (see table 4.7 page 158)
These floorings are able to move sufficiently at ordinary temperatures to accommodate slight structural movements without cracking. The following notes supplement the information given in table 4.7.

1 Mastic asphalt
Mastic asphalt is an elastic gel in contrast to cement which is a rigid gel. Although the grading of aggregates may be similar in both cases the matrix of the mastic has the ability to move under heat or pressure and so exhibit its polymeric thermoplastic tendencies.
Grades are:

(a) *Special hard*—for ambient temperatures 25 to 35°C, schools, showrooms, etc.
(b) *Light duty*—more liable to indentation.
(c) *Medium industrial*—not resistant to heavy trucking.
(d) *Industrial-factory*—resistant to heavy trucking and thermal shock.

Special grades are: coloured; for use at low and high temperatures, eg over floor warming installations; for chemical and mineral oil resistance; non-slip; anti-static and spark-free grades.

An isolating membrane laid loose with lapped joints is essential for mastic asphalt up to 20 mm thick on bases of: timber; concrete or screeds of open texture or containing fine cracks or which have received a surface treatment, eg sodium silicate. A membrane is also required for any thickness of mastic asphalt on timber, roofs and on bases which would cause 'blowing' or which would cause the mastic to cool too rapidly during laying and where a polished surface is required.

Membranes can be black sheathing felt complying with BS 747:1986 *Roofing felts* (*bitumen and fluxed pitch*), Type 4A (i) or *glass fibre sheathing* where the base concrete is in direct contact with the ground.

Mastic asphalt should be heated to a temperature between 200 and 220°C preferably in a mechanically agitated mixer, as near the point of laying as possible to minimise cooling before it is laid.

Slight shrinkage occurs during cooling and thermal shock causes cracking, particularly of Grade I material. During laying and for three or four days the ambient temperatures should be 5 to 10°C.

2 Pitch mastic   Generally properties and laying are similar to those for asphalt.

3 Cement rubber-latex

4 Cement-bitumen emulsion

5 Cement-resin.

6–8 Resin-based in situ floorings   These recently much developed materials, are characterised by toughness, resistance to abrasion and most chemicals, and give dustless and easily cleaned surfaces. Some products are self-levelling to a degree although their high cost precludes their use in sufficient thickness to make levelling screeds unnecessary; Bright colours and coloured flakes suspended in a clear matrix are available.

A II   Floorings laid in situ with joints
Floorings which shrink or are inflexible and which should be laid with joints to accommodate movement include *concrete* and *magnesium oxychloride*.

1 Concrete floorings
Concrete finishes must be of high quality concrete, the principles for obtaining which are stated in *MBS: Materials* chapter 8. Good appearance, resistance to abrasion and avoidance of cracking, dusting, loss of bond with the base and other defects demand careful

specification and supervision and skilled workmanship by specialist layers. In particular, aggregate should be low, mixing, compaction and curing should be thorough. Resistance to wear depends to a large extent on the skill displayed in trowelling. Over-trowelling brings laitance to the surface leading to *dusting*. Adequate temperature, while maintaining the requisite water content, must be maintained for at least seven days' curing and the flooring must not be brought into use until it is sufficiently strong.

Power floating will provide a good smooth industrial flooring finish and remove the necessity for a finishing screed but is more expensive. Additional costs may be justified by not having to wait until the screed has fully hardened and thus speeding up the time for handover.

Concrete finishes can be classed as either *integral finishes* on concrete clabs or *applied toppings* laid *monolithically* with, *bonded* to, or *unbonded* to the base. Structural slabs, such as domestic garage floors at least 100 mm thick, can be finished by a tamping beam, float, trowel or by mechanical surfacers, as soon as the concrete has been thoroughly compacted and is sufficiently stiff to avoid an excess of laitance being bought to the surface.

Toppings may be of *plain*, *granolithic* or *terrazzo* concrete and will normally be laid on concrete bases. Falls should be formed in the base concrete so the thickness of the finish is uniform. Thicknesses above 40 mm should be laid in two courses, both at least 20 mm thick, the upper course immediately following the first course.

Services should be laid in the base concrete or in ducts, rather than in the concrete topping.

(i) *Plain* concrete toppings with ordinary aggregates provide utilitarian finishes for light and medium duty. They should be laid as recommended for granolithic finishes for best results.

Information concerning granolithic and terrazzo finishes is summarised in table 4.9, page 164.

(ii) **Granolithic** Useful references are *A specification for granolithic floor topping laid in in situ concrete* (Cement and Concrete Association) and BRE Digest 47.

Granolithic is a utilitarian finish in which superior resistance to abrasion is a primary requirement and aggregates must be granite or aggregates with equivalent density and strength. Coarse aggregate should comply with BS 882:1971 *Aggregates for granolithic concrete floor finishes* and the fine aggregate should comply with BS 1199:1200:1976 *Building sands from natural sources*. (Crushed materials may contain dust and it requires more mixing water to give a workable mix). Proportions of topping granolithic should be 1:1:2 (by weight) subject to small adjustments to

compensate for *bulking* of sand and to obtain a satisfactory overall grading from 10 mm down. Mixing should be done by machine.

The methods for laying are similar to those for screeds and thicknesses depend upon similar considerations, although here functional requirements are considerably more exacting.

Monolithic finish As with screeds the best adhesion to the base is obtained by laying granolithic within three hours of the base having been placed or sooner in hot weather. It must be emphasised that the description 'monolithic' cannot apply to finishes laid at a later stage. Although an early decision to adopt the method, and protection during subsequent building operations are essential it should be used wherever possible particularly where granolithic is laid over heating elements.

For floors in contact with the ground a monolithic finish becomes possible if the damp-proof membrane is laid on blinding below the base concrete. For suspended in situ floors the finish can be taken to contribute to the structural thickness. Monolithic finishes need be only 10–25 mm thick.

Bonded finish ('*separate construction*') The rules for obtaining the maximum bond between screeds and concrete bases more than three hours old apply to granolithic finishes and they should be strictly observed. See page 151.

Unbonded finishes Where finishes are laid on concrete bases which are contaminated with oil, or containing a water repellent, or where they are laid on separating membranes a thickness up to 75 mm is needed, but even with prolonged damp curing the possibility of slabs curling upwards at their edges must be accepted.

Joints Granolithic should be laid in bays of the sizes given in table 4.6, the lengths of which should not exceed $1\frac{1}{2}$ × widths. Vertical butt joints should occur over construction joints in the base and movement joints must be provided to correspond with any in the base.

Finishing surfaces After the topping has been levelled and fully compacted, and is set, it must be trowelled at least three times during the next 6 to 10 hours to produce a hard and dense surface free from laitance, and with as much coarse aggregate just below the surface as possible. Usually about two hours after the first trowelling the surface should be retrowelled to close any pores, laitance which arises being removed and not trowelled back into the surface. The final trowelling, usually being the third and sometimes the fourth, is delayed until considerable pressure is needed to make an impression on the surface.

Construction	Thickness mm	Maximum bay size m²
Monolithic	10 – 25 max	30
		on concrete base 150 mm thick
		15
		on concrete base 100 mm thick
Bonded		
floors	40 min	
stairs		15
treads and risers where forms are		and length not exceeding
used	20 min	1½ × width
risers where forms		
are not used	15 min	
Unbonded	up to 75	2

Table 4.6 *Thicknesses and bay sizes for granolithic floorings*

Granolithic must be protected against drying winds and strong sunlight and as soon as it is sufficiently hard it should be protected continuously for seven days, or longer in cold weather, with:

1 Canvas, straw mats or 50 mm of sand kept damp

2 Impervious sheets held in position, lapped 75 mm and overlapping the edges of slabs. This method is necessary for coloured concrete

3 A proprietary curing medium.

Drying should be delayed as long as possible to reduce the likelihood of shrinkage cracking. Artificial heating should not be used for at least six weeks and then temperature should be increased slowly. Steel wheeled trollies should not use floors for at least 28 days.

Non-slip properties can be obtained by trowelling in non-slip granules, or later, surfaces can be mechanically or chemically roughened.

Hard materials such as ferrous aggregate, and surface applications of solution of sofium silicate, magnesium or zinc-fluoride improve resistance to abrasion but oleoresinous seals are more effective. Surface treatments applied in accordance with BS 8204:1988 and the manufacturers' instructions can be effective on newly hardened concrete, or on old floors if they are clean and dry.

(iii) Terrazzo (Properties and requirements are summarised in table 4.9).—In situ terrazzo floor toppings are described in BS 8204:1988.

This 'quality' floor (and wall) finish although initially costly provides a hard wearing washable surface in a very wide range of colour combinations. It consists of white or coloured cement with crushed marble aggregate, laid usually on a screed on a concrete base and later ground and polished. It can be slippery when wet or where floor polish is transferred to it from adjacent floorings. For safety the finish should not be smoother than 'fine grit'. Carborundum or bauxite grit can be incorporated in, or trowelled into, mixes. Non-slip inlays are often included in the front edges of stair treads. If polish is ever used, it should be wax-free.

Terrazzo is often used in entrance halls to public buildings, food shops, lavatories and in hospitals. It is especially suitable for anti-static floors, see page 148.

The principles for obtaining sound granolithic finishes apply generally to terrazzo. It can be laid in three ways, ie *monolithically* on a green concrete base or on a screed which may be either *bonded* or *unbonded* to a concrete base. The thickness of screeds must be greater and panel sizes smaller as bond with the base reduces, see table 4.8

Monolithic construction To ensure complete adhesion and to minimise the likelihood of shrinkage cracking, where possible terrazzo should be laid directly on structural concrete bases within three hours of their having been placed, and after they have been brushed with a stiff broom to remove water and laitance. Panels of monolithically laid terrazzo can be larger than with other methods of laying but difficulties may arise in protecting the finish from following trades and the method is not widely used.

Bonded construction Where terrazzo is not laid directly on green concrete it must be laid on a screed preferably within three hours of its having been laid. If the screed is older (it should not be older than 48 hours), a neat cement slurry should be brushed into the surface immediately before laying the terrazzo.

157

Material, form and references	Base	Properties	Appearance
1 **Mastic asphalt** Binder – natural and/or derivative bitumen Aggregate – 'natural rock' or crushed limestone, or coarse siliceous grit for acid-resisting grade Mineral fillers and grit Pigments – optional *Flooring Handbook*, Mastic Asphalt Council and Employers' Federation BS 988:1973 Table 2 *Limestone aggregate* BS 6577:1985 *Specification for mastic asphalt building (natural rock asphalt aggregate)* BS 988:1973 *Coloured (limestone aggregate)* Bs 8204:1988[1]:Section 4	1 Floated and slightly roughened concrete 2 Wood boards No damp-proof membrane required in an unheated floor	Wear varies with aggregate – good to excellent. Non-dusting Hardness – indented by point loads – special grade required in hot positions, eg over underfloor heating Resilience – low but tolerates slight movement if laid on sheathing felt Slippery – if wet or polished Warmth – moderate Quiet – moderate Water and vapour proof Chemical resistance – damaged by oils, greases, acids, sugar solutions – but special grades available. High resistance to alkalis at normal temperatures	Colours – natural black, dark red and brown. Green is costly Textures – matt, polished (Heavily gritted material is less easily polished)
2 **Pitch mastic** Binder – coal tar-pitch Aggregate – limestone or siliceous grit Chalk – up to 15 per cent Pigments – optional BS 1450:1963 *Black pitch mastic flooring* BS 3672:1963 *Coloured pitch mastic flooring* BS 8204:1988[1]: Section 5	Floated and slightly roughened concrete (not timber) No dpm required	Similar to mastic asphalt but superior resistance to mineral oils and inferior resistance to alkalis More brittle at low temperatures and softer at high temperatures – not suitable over floor warming	As mastic asphalt
3 **Cement rubber-latex** Binder – rubber latex – natural or synthetic and Portland or high alumina cement Pigments Aggregate – cork, rubber, wood and/or stone Mineral fillers BS 8204:1988[1]: Section 6	1 Floated concrete 2 Timber, if strong, rigid and thoroughly seasoned 3 Other firm strong bases	Wear – good resistance Resilience – more comfortable than concrete Non-slip, moderately warm and quiet Water resistance – low to medium Good resistance to burns Resistant to dilute alkalis Resistance to oils and greases: natural rubber – low synthetic rubber – good Suitable over floor warming Good adhesion to base	Colours – wide range Texture – smooth Pattern – with marble aggregate resembles terrazzo if buffed
4 **Cement-bitumen emulsion**	A dpm is required	Wear – good resistance, non-dusting	Colours – black and dark colours

Table 4.7 *A I Flooring laid in situ—without joints*

Thickness mm	Laying	Surface treatment		Average Cost factor[2]
		Initial	Maintenance	
15 min – underlays 15 – 20 – Grades I and II 20 – 30 – Grade III 35 – 50 – Grade IV	Materials must not be over-heated Float in one coat for ordinary thicknesses Metal armouring may be incorporated in mastic asphalt Thicknesses up to 19 mm are laid on black sheathing felt or glass fibre sheeting where the base is in direct contact with the ground	Matt finish – trowel with fine sand or stone dust Polished finish – apply special water-wax emulsion (not polishes which contain solvents)	Sweep – avoid oiled sweeping compounds Wash – warm water and neutral detergent, or small quantity of washing soda for very dirty floors. Rinse Non-solvent polish can be applied Strip occasionally	18
May require to be thicker than mastic asphalt for equivalent uses	An isolating membrane is essential on a timber base and on concrete which contains fine cracks, is porous or of open texture Adequate ventilation is necessary to remove toxic fumes from pitch mastic	As mastic asphalt May be buffed to expose aggregate		18
4 – 12 Can be laid to 'feather edge'	Dampen absorptive concrete Prime with latex and cement for heavy duty. On timber base fix galvanised wire netting. Apply finish by trowel as soon as priming coat has set	May be buffed (in two stages) to remove laitance and expose the aggregate Non-oil or solvent emulsion polish only	Sweep frequently, avoid oiled sweeping compounds Wash – warm water and mild soap. Do not over-scrub Non-solvent polish on natural rubber type flooring	25
13	Prime screed Apply finish by trowel	——	Sweep Wash	14

continued . . .

159

Material, form and references continued . . .	Base	Properties	Appearance

Aggregate – sand and crushed granite	See previous page	Resilience – more comfortable than concrete
		High resistance to burns
		Resistance to:
		  solvents – very low
		  acids and oils – low
		  alkalis – high
		Suitable over floor heating	

5 Cement – resin Binder – cement and polyester resin Aggregate – sand, crushed stone etc		Wear – good resistance Resilience – very low Fairly good resistance to acids, alkalis and oils Non-slip Suitable over floor heating	Texture – slight
6 Polyurethane resin Binder – polyurethane resin Vinyl chips or other fillers One and two-part types	Screed Rigid plywood A dpm is required	Wear – good resistance Non-slip Resilience – good Good resistance to water and oils Moderate resistance to acids and alkalis Low resistance to burns Normally suitable over floor heating	Colours – wide range Texture – 'orange peel' with chips Pattern – plain or chips in transparent binder
7 Epoxide resin Binder – epoxide resin Hardener Aggregate Mineral fillers	Screed – must be level (particularly for self-levelling grades), clean and free from laitance Rigid plywood A dpm is required	Wear – high resistance particularly for trowelled type 'Trucking grades' available Non-dusting Adhesion to base – excellent – good for repairs to existing floors Has chemical set and hardens within 48 hours Excellent resistance to water, acids, alkalis, oils and some solvents Can be resilient and non-slip High resistance to burns Can be suitable over floor heating Some anti-static grades available	Depends upon pigments and aggregates used Self-levelling grades tend to be glossy
8 Polyester resin Binder – polyester resin Catalyst Aggregates, fillers, glass fibres Pigments	Screed – must be level Rigid plywood A dpm is required	Wear – good resistance Resilience – very low Good resistance to water, acids, oils Moderate resistance to alkalis High resistance to burns Not suitable over floor heating Resin may shrink and hair-crack in curing	Colours – wide range

General considerations in selecting, laying and maintenance are discussed on page 155

Table 4.7 *A I Flooring laid in situ—without joints*

Thickness mm	Laying	Surface Treatment		Average cost factor[2]
		Initial	Maintenance	
Can be laid to 'feather edge'			Do not use strong detergents for about six months	
3 – 10	Apply by trowel	—	Sweep Wash	18
2 – 3	Various specialised methods	—	Sweep Wash Wax polish is unnecessary and makes it difficult to 'reglaze' worn parts	35–40
2 self-levelling grades 2 sprayed grades 3 – 6 trowelled grades	Prime surface Fill hollows with epoxy resin – sand Spread or trowel Some grades can be sprayed using specialised equipment	Two coats of wax or silicone polish should be applied on self-levelling grades Surfaces of some grades can be ground to resemble terrazzo	Sweep Wash with soap or detergent Polish to maintain good appearance of self-levelling grades	50–70
2 – 6	Trowel	Surface can be ground to resemble terrazzo	Sweep Wash – warm water and soap or detergent Polish – polyacrylate non-slip emulsion	36–46

[1]General reference: BS 8204:1988 *In situ floor finishes*
[2]Approximate cost relationships for typical floorings 'as laid', based on granolithic = 10

Construction	Thickness[1] minimum mm	Panel size[2] maximum m²
Monolithic	15	dividing strips over all construction joints
Bonded		
floors	15 on 25 mm screed	
stairs		
treads	15	
risers	10	
strings	6	1
walls and skirtings	6 on 12 mm render	
Unbonded		
	15 on 50 mm screed	

[1]thickness should be greater if maximum aggregate size exceeds 10 mm
[2]length of panel should not exceed twice the width. Re-entrant angles must be avoided.

Table 4.8 *Thicknesses and panel sizes for terrazzo finishes*

Unbonded construction Where the base is hard, or bond is prevented by contamination or water repellents, the terrazzo topping must be laid as described for bonded construction but on a screed at least 50 mm thick, reinforced with light mesh reinforcement and laid on a bitumen felt, building paper or polythene separating layer lapped 50 mm at the joints.

Toppings The marble aggregate should be clean, angular—not elongated or flaky, and free from dust. Nominal sizes are:

Italian code		Nominal sizes mm	
$\frac{1}{5}$	3	2– 5	9–19
$\frac{1}{6}$	4	4– 6	12–20
2	5	5– 9	22–25

These sizes can be used individually or in combinations, eg for a fine mix 1 part 3–5 mm:1 to 1½ parts 5–6 mm. The larger the size of aggregate the less risk of cracking and particles less than 3 mm should not be used. The cement:aggregate ratio varies with the grading and maximum size of the aggregate, but should not exceed 1:2 by volume.

Toppings may either be laid as mixes which include all the aggregate or by the *seminar method* as mixes containing only fine aggregate into the upper surfaces of which the larger particles are beaten and rolled in. Metal, ebonite or plastic strips should be securely anchored in the screed to divide toppings into panels, see table 4.8, and wherever cracks are likely to form due to structural movements. Expansion and contractions joints in the main structure must, of course, be carried through the flooring and be suitably finished on the surface. After tamping, compaction with a heavy roller, trowelling, and removal of laitance to achieve a dense surface with a regular distribution of aggregate and minimum of cement matrix visible, the flooring must be damp cured. (See *Granolithic floorings*, page 156.) Canvas, hessian and sawdust curing media are very liable to stain terrazzo and where white or coloured cement is used plastics sheets are essential.

Finishing surfaces Terrazzo is sometimes sufficiently hard for grinding and polishing within four days of laying. It is best done by machine except for small areas, and in the following sequence:

Grind with coarse abrasive stone with water;
Wash the floor;
Clean out voids and fill them with neat cement paste.

Damp cure and keep the floor free from excessive temperature changes for at least three days before polishing with a fine abrasive stone with water.
Where possible artificial heat should not be turned on in the building for 6 to 8 weeks and the temperature should then be increased slowly.
Heavy traffic should not be allowed on the floor for at least two days.

Maintenance and cleaning Before opening to traffic, terrazzo should be scrubbed with an acid and alkali-free soap and allowed to stand overnight. The following day the surface should be scrubbed vigorously with hot water and rinsed. Subsequently surfaces should be kept clean with soft soap and rinsed. Strong detergents should not be used and some disinfectants contain phenols and cresols which stain terrazzo.

A II 2 Magnesium oxychloride

This material is made by taking the mineral *magnesite* (magnesium carbonate) which comes in natural finishes that are colourless, white or greyish white which is then calcined at high temperature to remove carbon dioxide and water, giving magnesium oxide. When combined with magnesium chloride a strong hardsetting cement called magnesium oxychloride is formed. (*Note* Oxychloride cements can in theory be formed with other oxides.) One problem is that chloride ions can be released from this material, especially if the surface is wetted. Chloride ions are particularly aggressive as a species and can attack metals, causing corrosion. Because of this and the possibility of staining from corrosion deposits the flooring should be separated from immediate surface contact with metals and special care should be taken with cleaning and floor sealants.

Properties and requirements are summarised in table 4.9. This comparatively low-cost finish consisting of calcined magnesite, wood or mineral fillers pigments and sometimes silica, talc or powered asbestos, gauged with a solution of magnesium chloride, can be laid in plain colours and in mottled and terrazzo effects. However, colours are dull and the material has been largely supplanted by preformed floorings. If the surface is protected by oil or wax, resistance to wear is moderate to high and the floor is free from dusting. It is slippery if highly polished but abrasive grit can be incorporated in the finish to give a non-slip surface. Wood-fillers make the flooring moderately warm and resilient. Magnesium oxychloride is not seriously affected by alkalis, non-drying oils, fats, grease and organic solvents, but it gradually disintegrates if it is continuously exposed to water or to acids and salts by solubility.

Magnesium chloride absorbs moisture from the air and 'sweating' may occur in humid atmospheres. It corrodes metal by the liberation of aggressive chloride ions separated from them by at least 25 mm of uncracked, dense concrete or by a bituminous coating. It is difficult to ensure that floor warming systems remain fully coated and CP:1970 *In situ floor finishes* does not recommend their inclusion in magnesite.

Magnesium oxychloride can also be used as an underlay for thin sheet and tile floorings.

Concrete bases should be finished reasonably free from ridges and hollows but be slightly roughened with a stiff broom. They should be thoroughly dry when the finish is laid. Galvanised wire netting should be laid on timber bases and fixed at about 200 mm centres with galvanised clout nails. Other nails should be left proud of the base at the same centres.

One-coat work is generally 10 to 25 mm thick, and thicknesses greater than 40 mm are laid in two coats, each being not more than 20 mm thick. BS 8204:1988 recommends that 6 mm plastics or hardwood dividing strips should be incorporated at not more than 7600 mm centres.

Drying must be delayed for at least 24 hours and light traffic should not be permitted for three days, or longer in cold weather. Heavy traffic should not be permitted for some weeks. Maintenance involves sweeping, damp mopping and treatment with a polish or seal.

B Preformed floorings

B 1 Sheet supplied rolled (See table 4.11 page 166.) These preformed materials can be laid rapidly with few joints (and these can be welded in (vinyl) PVC sheets). Being thin, a level and very smooth base is needed, although smoothness is less important with materials which have resilient backings. The wear performance of thin materials depends upon flatness of the base, their thickness, the type and intensity of traffic and on maintenance. Edges of sheets must be protected.

All resilient materials are more flexible and easier to handle and bond to the base when they are warm. The base must be clean, dust-free and dry. Sheet floorings require damp-proof membranes in solid ground floors. Some of them will rot in damp conditions and adhesives will fail. Adhesives prevent sheets curling up at the edges, discourage creep and generally improve performance and appearance of thin floorings.

Adhesives must hold various different materials in place while resisting the stresses imposed by traffic and by movements of the flooring and base. It is important to know that no adhesive can act as a damp-proof membrane.

Water-based adhesives, eg starch, casein and lignin are lowest in cost but their brittleness limits their use to porous materials such as linoleum, cork and fabric-backed PVC in dry conditions. The gum-spirit adhesives are also fairly low in cost and suitable for porous surfaces but although insoluble in water some products are attacked in damp conditions.

Bitumen emulsions and solvent solutions are suitable for thermoplastic and vinyl-asbestos tiles but not for all types of flexible PVC floorings. Synthetic latex adhesives withstand normal damp and alkaline conditions. Natural and synthetic rubber-resin solutions used for laying rubber floorings must be applied to both the base and flooring and allowed an exact drying time before the surfaces are brought together. Although more costly than the aqueous product they have very high immediate and final bond strengths.

Continued on page 190

163

Material, form and references	Base	Properties	Appearance
1 Concrete finishes (i) *Self-finish* (ii) *Plain topping* (iii) *Granolithic* *Cement*: usually Portland cement BS 12: 1971 *Aggregate*: BS 1201:1973 *Aggregates for granolithic concrete floor finishes*; BS 1198–1200:1955 *Building sands from natural sources* BS 8204:1988: Section 2 *In situ floor finishes*	Concrete roughened to receive bonded finishes for which concrete should not contain water proofer (Not timber)	Cold, hard, noisy Subject to 'dusting' Resistant to alkalis, mineral oils and many salts Slippery when wet if abrasive is not incorporated in surface. Rounded aggregate is more slippery than angular aggregate	Grey, utilitarian
(iii) *Terrazzo* *Cement*: usually white or coloured Portland cement *Aggregate*: marble or spar BS 8204:1988: Section 3 *In situ floor finishes*		Cold, hard, noisy Slippery when wet, if machine polished, washed with soap, or if polish is applied Does not 'dust'	Resembles a mosaic of polished marble chippings divided into panels by strips
2 Magnesium oxychloride (Magnesite) Calcined magnesite and magnesium chloride with wood or mineral and asbestos fillers and pigments to comply with: BS 776:1972 *Materials for magnesium oxychloride (magnesite) flooring* and BS 1014:1961 *Pigments for cement, magnesium oxychloride and concrete* BS 8204:1988: Section 7 *In situ floor finishes*	1 Dry and non-porous concrete, tiles, etc 2 Timber flooring with galvanised wire netting fixed to it	Moderately hard, warm and quiet 'Dusts' if not protected Slippery if highly polished but abrasive can be incorporated Deteriorates in damp conditions Tends to 'sweat' Not recommended with underfloor warming	White and plain colours, mottled and terrazzo effects

General considerations in selecting and laying these floorings are discussed on page 152

Table 4.9 *A II Floorings laid while 'plastic'—with joints*

164

Thickness mm	Laying	Surface treatment		Approximate cost factors[1]
		Initial	Maintenance	
10 – 25 *monolithic* 40 *bonded* 75 *unbonded*	(i) Base self-finished with trowel float or tamping board (ii) Plain toppings (iii) Granolithic toppings well compacted in bays defined by dividing strips and trowelled when set Damp cured at least seven days	Surface hardener may be applied eg sodium silicate (see page 157) When flooring is dry polyurethane or synthetic rubber seals	Renew hardener or seal when necessary Sweep and wash	5 (19 mm cement : sand) 10 (19 mm granolithic)
12 min terrazzo* laid *monolithically* on structural concrete base 15 min terrazzo* topping laid *monolithically* on 25 mm screed bonded to base or on lightly reinforced 50 mm screed on isolating membrane * Greater thicknesses needed if aggregate is larger than 10 mm	Trowelled and well compacted in bays defined by dividing strips Damp cured Surface ground, filled, cured and reground	See *Terrazzo tiles* page 176		54 – 60
10 – 65 on concrete 15 – 45 on timber	Isolate from plaster and metals (punch home nails in boards, and fill) Trowelled in one or two coats preferably in bays defined by dividing strips Damp cured	Proprietary dressing	Sweep Damp mop mild alkaline soap may be used occasionally Do not use household cleaning powders or sweeping powders Wax polish or drying oil	15 – 25

[1] Approximate cost relationships for typical floorings 'as laid', based on granolithic = 10

Table 4.10 *Timbers for flooring*—see page 191

Material, form and references[1]	Base	Properties	Appearances
1 Linoleum Powdered cork, fillers, pigments, oxidised linseed oil and resins pressed on jute canvas or cork Also on bitumen felt in 2·5 and 3·2 mm thicknesses only Available sealed with polyurethane and butadiene copolymers BS 810 : 1966 *Sheet linoleum (calendered type) and cork carpet* BS 1863 : 1952 *Felt backed linoleum*	1 *Concrete screed* – with steel trowelled finish and levelling compound if required *hardboard* (with rebated edges on polythene film, on sand) A dpm is essential in solid ground floors 2 *Wood boards* (at ground level protected by dpcs and ventilated below) *existing boards* – if sanded and filled lay flooring on paper felt, or preferably treat as: *new boards* – should be t and g preferably strip	Wear – low to high resistance, increases with thickness. *Hardened grades* have good resistance to sharp point loads and to burns Resilience: high for thicker grades Cannot be bent to small radii Quiet and warm Slippery if highly polished Resists oils and weak acids but deteriorates in damp conditions Attacked by alkalis	Colours – large range Patterns – plain, jaspé, moiré, granite, marble, geometrical Textures – semi-matt
2 Cork carpet Granulated cork, pigments, oxidised linseed oil and resins pressed on jute canvas BS 810 : 1966 *Sheet linoleum (calendered type) and cork carpet*	width. Cover with 4·8 mm standard hardboard or 4 mm resin-bonded plywood in sheets not larger than 1 m² laid breaking joint and fixed with ring nails or self-clinching staples at 150 mm centres over the whole area. Paper felt may prevent nails or staples 'grinning' through flooring	Wear – moderate if well maintained in light domestic use Not suitable where excessive soiling is likely Softer, more resilient, quieter and warmer than linoleum Non-slip even when wet or polished Resists occasional water and weak acids Low resistance to alkalis and burns	Colours – medium to dark cork colour and shades of green, red and brown Texture – open
3 Felt base or **printed 'linoleum'** Paint finish or thin vinyl film on bituminous felt	3 *Chipboards* – as floor finish See table 4.12 4 *Mastic asphalt* – as floor finish See table 4.7 5 *Clay and concrete tiles, stone slabs etc* – If in	Wear – low resistance but sufficient for very light duty or temporary work Cracks at low temperatures Not suitable over underfloor warming	Colours – various Patterns – various Texture – glossy
4 Flexible vinyl – homogeneous Mainly PVC binder with varying contents of fillers, plasticisers and pigments	contact with the ground and there is no dpm, surface with 13 mm mastic asphalt. If dry but irregular, apply levelling compound	Wear – moderate to high. Resistance varies with vinyl content and thickness Resilience – varies similarly	Colours – very wide range Patterns – very wide range including vinyl chips in clear vinyl

Table 4.11 *B I Sheet supplied rolled*

Typical sizes			Laying	Surface treatment		Average cost factors[2]
Thickness mm	Width mm	Length m		Initial	Maintenance	
1·6 jaspé and moiré only			Lay flat and keep at room temperature at least 48 hours before fixing	If not factory-finished with a hard seal, clean with mild soap or detergent (not with abrasives or strongly alkaline soap or detergent). Rinse and dry	Sweep Damp mop with mild soap or neutral detergent Burnish polish and only occasionally renew sparingly, or maintain seal	21 (3·2 mm)
2·0	1830	9	Lay on adhesive and roll			28 (4·5 mm)
2·5 plain and marbled only		27	For cheap work on boards, lay loose with edges lapped. Trim edges and tack down after sheet has expanded	Apply suitable seal (later removing any factory dressing) Apply wax or emulsion polish on unhardened, or emulsion polish on prehardened linoleum		
3·2	2000					
4·5						
6·0 plain only						
6·7						
3·2	1830	15	Keep at room temperature for at least 48 hours	Wash, rinse and dry as linoleum	Generally as for linoleum but removal of grit is very important. Apply polish lightly – 'build-up' is difficult to remove	23 (4·5 mm)
4·5				Suitable seals reduce dirt being ingrained		
6·0			Must be bonded to base and rolled	Wax polishes on unsealed and emulsion polishes on sealed material		
1·0			Normally laid loose	None required	Damp mop	2
			Keep at not less than 18°C for at least 24 hours. Must be bonded to base and rolled	Water-wax emulsion polish (non-solvent type)	Damp mop Burnish polish and renew sparingly, only occasionally	24 – 33 (2 mm)

continued . . .

Material, form and references[1] continued . . .	Base	Properties	Appearances
Non-slip grade contains aluminium oxide grains BS 3261: *Unbacked flexible PVC flooring*: Part 1: 1973 *Homogeneous flooring*	6 *Metal decking*	Moderately warm and quiet High resistance to surface water Tends to shrink More resistant to chemicals, oils, alcohols etc and less easily stained than linoleum and vinyl-asbestos tiles Cigarettes may char	Texture – matt to glossy and embossed simulations of travertine, marble, mosaic, timber, etc
Flexible vinyl – backed Cork, foamed plastics, needled felt or inorganic backings *'Cushion vinyl'* has a thin foam interlayer *'Foam-backed vinyl'* has a thick foam backing		Very quiet with resilient backings but surface may be punctured and backings may lose resilience with age Inorganic fibre felt improves dimensional stability	
5 Rubber Natural or synthetic rubber vulcanised, with fillers and pigments, in some cases on fabric backing Available with foamed-rubber base BS 2050 *Specification for the electrical resistance of conducting and anti-static products made from polymeric material* BS 1711: 1951 *Solid rubber flooring* BS 3187: 1959 *Electrically conducting rubber flooring*		Wear – good resistance increases with thickness. Heavy duty quality (black) Very resilient and quiet especially with foamed-rubber base Smooth types slippery when wet Warm Good resistance to water, weak acids but natural rubber is damaged by oils, fats and solvents Damaged by ultra-violet radiation Emits rubber odour, particularly over underfloor heating Special grade required over underfloor heating	Colours – very wide range and black and white Patterns – plain, marbled, mottled etc Textures – matt to glossy, studded, grooved, rough texture

General considerations in selecting, laying and maintaining sheet floorings are discussed on page 190

Table 4.11 *B I Sheet supplied rolled*

168

Typical sizes			Laying	Surface treatment		Average cost factors[2]
Thickness mm	Width mm	Length m		Initial	Maintenance	
1·5	1200	11	Joints can be welded in situ	Do not seal		
	1500	27				
2·0	1800					
2·5	2000					
3·0	2100					
*{3·0 3·9 4·5}			As above seams should be welded			44 (foam backed)
* with resilient backings						
3·8 light domestic floors 4·8 6·4	910 1370 1830	15 — 30	Must be bonded to minimise creep caused by wheeled traffic Press down	Water-wax emulsion polish applied sparingly (non-solvent type only)	Damp (not wet) mop with mild soap (Not with alkaline or abrasive soap, detergents not having a soap base or 'cleaning agents') Burnish polish and renew sparingly occasionally only Strip polish when 'build-up' becomes excessive	45 (4·8 mm) 56 (6 mm wide-ribbed surface)
12·7 to order						
4·5 with foamed backing						

[1] General reference: BS 8203 : 1987 *Sheet and tile flooring*
[2] Approximate cost relationship for typical floorings 'as laid', based on granolithic = 10

Material, form and references[1]	Base	Properties	Appearance
1 Plywood Resin bonded plies Face-ply at least 3 mm thick T and g boards available BS 6566 Part 1:1985 *Specification for construction of panels and characteristics of plies including making* BS 6566 Part 6:1985 *Limits of defects, classified by appearance*	*Full support* Boarded floor Sand bed Expanded plastics boards *Partial support* thicker boards only on: Joists or battens with noggings to support ends of boards without tongues	Wear – moderate, resistance varies with timber and life is determined by thickness of the top ply Moderately warm and quiet – but thin boards 'drum' if not fixed overall to base	Pattern – Normally rotary cut timber
2 Chipboard Wood chips bonded with synthetic resin and compressed Density not less than 640 kg/m² Sanded or sealed finish Available with edges t and g or grooved for loose tongues BS 5669:1979 *Resin-bonded wood chipboard*	Compressible quilt and t and g boards (only) laid loose as floating floor	Wear – Moderate to good resistance Low resistance to water	Colour – warm yellow Pattern – as wood chips
3 Hardboard Wood fibres compressed Preferably *tempered hardboard* BS 1142 : Part 2 : 1971 *Fibre building boards*	Sub-floors must be dry	Wear – moderate resistance Properties of tempered hardboard similar to plywood	Colours – natural browns and integrally coloured yellow, green or red

Table 4.12 *B II Boards* (Timber boards see table 4.13)

170

Typical sizes[2]			Laying[3]	Surface treatment		Average cost factors[4]
Thickness mm	Width mm	Length mm		Initial	Maintenance	
4 fully supported	1220	2440	Panel pins where appropriate Face grain must be at right angles to main supporting members 50 mm nails should be inserted at 150 mm centres	As wood blocks See page 172		19 (6 mm)
13 supported at 460 mm centres	1220	2440				
16 supported at 610 mm centres	1220	2440				28 (13 mm)
12 fully supported	1220	2440	*On sanded boards* Lost head nails at 400 mm centres punched home and holes filled *On joists or battens* Lost head nails at 400 mm centres punched home or can be glued Fill holes Leave expansion gap below skirtings	Fill open texture of untreated boards and apply plastics seal	Damp mop Renew seal when necessary	21 (12 mm)
18 supported at 400 mm centres	1220	2440				
22 supported at 600 mm centres	1220	2440				23 (18 mm)
4·8 fully supported	1220	1220	Wet backs of boards and store flat for 48 h (72 h for tempered hardboard) *On sanded boards*: nail with 25 mm lost head panel pins at 150 mm centres at edges and at 200 mm centres on lines 400 mm apart *On smooth concrete*: bond with adhesive	Can be sealed	Damp mop Polish regularly (must be non-slip type) Renew seal when necessary	14

[1] General reference: *MBS: Materials* chapter 3
[2] Thicknesses and spans between supports relate to domestic loadings
[3] Edges of boards must be protected. Boards can, in suitable qualities, be used as bases for thin floor finishes, but they are considered here as floorings in their own right
[4] Approximate cost relationships for typical floorings 'as laid', based on granolithic = 10

Form of unit and references[1]	Base	Properties	Appearance
1 Blocks Hardwood and softwood units tongued and grooved or dowelled BS 1187:1959 Amd 1968 *Wood blocks for floors* *(interlocking)*	Floated screed on dry concrete slab	Moderately resilient, warm and quiet Not suitable in damp conditions or where wide variations in atmospheric humidity occur The greater moisture movement of timber across the grain than that along the grain is balanced by alternating lengths and widths of blocks thereby avoiding accumulated movement across a floor	Colours – as timbers; some timbers darken and others fade with age Joint patterns *basket* – square and open *herringbone* – square, single and double *brick bonds*
2 Blocks – end grain Usually softwood, impregnated with preservative for wet conditions of use	Level concrete	Exceptional resistance to wear and impact Brittle objects if dropped are less likely to break than on other industrial floorings	Utilitarian
3 Boards Usually softwood Should be tongued and grooved to increase strength and fire-resistance and for draught proofing	Joists or battens Maximum spans for t and g softwood boards or strip for domestic loadings (1·44 kN/m²) are:	More resilient than blocks At the BS 1297 'normal range' of m.c. (16–22%) marked cupping of and gaps between sawn boards – particularly wide boards – will occur. Kiln dried m.c. 12–15%	Good appearance requires first-class material, laying techniques and maintenance
	Finished thickness mm / Maximum span (c–c) mm: 16 — 505 19 — 600 21 — 635 28 — 790		
BS 1297:1970 *Grading and sizing of softwood flooring*	Building Regulations 1976		
4 Strip Hardwoods and softwoods. Up to 102 mm wide with tongued and grooved edges and ends – long lengths		As t and g boards	Joint pattern – Narrow widths (sometimes random) and long random lengths

Table 4.13 *B III Timber floorings*

Typical sizes			Laying	Surface treatment[2]		Average cost factors[3]
Thickness mm	Width mm	Length mm		Initial	Maintenance	
21	75	229 305	(1) Screed primed and blocks laid in hot bitumen, or (2) blocks laid in cold adhesive 13 mm gaps or cork strips under skirtings 13 mm cork strips sometimes recommended to divide floor into bays	Stop if required, sand, stain or dye if required and seal with oleoresinous solvent-based seal (eg polyurethane) or apply wax polish Floor seal or plastics polish is necessary to protect softwoods Non-slip gymnasium oil for gymnasia (only)	Wipe seal with damp (not wet) cloth or apply wax polish Renew seal (surface must be wax-free). Polyurethane seals can be patch repaired Renew wax polish When badly worn resurface by sanding (Effective wearing surface is determined by depth of tongues or dowels below the surface)	40 (softwood) 43 – 79 (hardwood)
63 — 114	76	102 127 229	Blocks dipped in hot soft pitch and laid with close joints or laid dry and grouted	Usually none but hard grit can be rolled into bituminous dressing	Sweep	33 (63 mm)
min 16 19 21 28 BS 1297:1987 t and g flooring	± 1 65 90 113 137	Random 1800 min 3000 min average in any one delivery	Boards cramped Header joints to bear on joists or battens and be staggered at least two boards' width in both directions *Softwood boards* Fix with brads, punch in and stop one brad per bearer for 65 and 90 mm, two for 113–178 and three for wider boards *Hardwood boards* Secret nail through tongue and nail or screw through face and stop or pellet	As 1 Blocks	As 1 Blocks	22 (25 mm ordinary softwood t and g)
19 25	51 63 76 89 102 less 13 mm as laid	Random	Strips cramped Secret nail at 50° just above tongues to all bearers T and g header joints need be supported by noggings only for heavy duty floor			50 – 80 (25 mm hardwood t and g)

continued . . .

Form of unit and reference[1]	Base	Properties	Appearance
– short lengths – (reduce price slightly) BS 1297 : 1970 *Grading and sizing of softwood flooring*	Floated concrete	Resilience etc as for blocks	Narrow widths and short random lengths
5 **Overlay strip** Hardwood Tongued and grooved edges, ends may be tongued and grooved	Sound, sanded, softwood flooring or softwood flooring with underlay	Suitable for light duty	Joint pattern – as end-matched hardwood strip
6 **Parquet** Selected hardwoods square or t and g edges Units for laying may comprise components glued together at their edges	Thoroughly seasoned and level boards – preferably overlaid with 4 mm resin-bonded plywood or 4·8 mm hardboard	Suitable for light domestic duty only	Exotic and costly woods can be used in parquet thickness Patterns, including elaborate marquetry, are independent of base
7 **Parquet panels** 6 mm hardwood parquet mounted on laminated softwood Tongued and grooved on all edges	1 Joists or battens 2 Screed	Composite construction gives wear properties equivalent to strip	As end-matched hardwood strip
8 **Mosaic** Hardwood butt-edged 'fingers' bonded to a base of scrim, felt or perforated aluminium foil or overlaid with membrane which is stripped off after laying BS 4050 : 1966 *Wood mosaic flooring*	Floated screed, 4 mm resin-bonded plywood or 4·8 mm hardboard	Similar to blocks Smaller units and basket pattern localise moisture movement	Generally supplied in less exotic hardwoods than parquet Joint pattern – Usually basket weave in 114 or 150 mm square units each comprising five or six 'fingers' respectively

Plywood, chipboard and **hardboard** see page 170

General considerations in selecting, laying and maintaining timber floorings are discussed on page 190

Table 4.13–*continued*

Typical sizes			Laying	Surface treatment[2]		Average cost factor[3]
Thickness mm	Width mm	Length mm		Initial	Maintenance	
25	76 less 13 mm as laid	Random 230 — 610	As 1 Blocks	As 1 Blocks	As 1 Blocks	
9 — 16	up to 76	Random	Glued and secret pinned along tongued edges Laid at an angle with boards if no underlay is used			46 – 55
5 — 10	51 76 89	Various	Glued and pinned Pins punched home and holes filled	As 1 Blocks or can be french polished for light duty	As 1 Blocks or revise french polish	90 (6 mm)
25 — 32	305 and 610 squares for laying		1 Glue tongues and nail through tongues if necessary 2 Bedded in hot bitumen 3 Some interlocking products can be laid loose, eg as removable dance floor on carpet	Products without-shop finishes treated as *blocks*	As 1 Blocks	
10 — 16	305 and 457 squares for laying		Bonded with cold adhesive and rolled Any surface overlay removed Gaps below skirtings and cork expansion strips as for wood blocks			34 – 60 (10 mm)

[1] General reference: BS 8201:1987 *Flooring of wood and wood products*
[2] See CP 209: 1963 *Care and maintenance of floor surfaces* Part I: Wooden flooring
[3] Approximate cost relationships for typical floorings 'as laid', based on granolithic = 10

Material, form and references[1]	Base	Properties	Appearance
1 **Bricks** Manufactured from un-refined clays, pressed and burnt Intended primarily for walling BS 3921 : 1969 *Bricks and blocks of fired brickearth, clay or shale*	*Internally* – concrete *Externally* – (i) for vehicular traffic – concrete (ii) for pedestrian traffic – rammed earth or hard-core	Best products (eg *Engineering bricks Classes A and B* (BS 3921) have excellent resist-ance to wear, impact, chemicals and frost) For external use '*Special qual-ity*' (BS 3921) bricks must be specified	Colours – wide range Joint patterns – brick bonds and unbond-ed, with wide joints Texture – usually plain
2 **Paviors (or Pavers)** (i) Manufactured as for *Engineering bricks*	Concrete or screed finished to suit method of laying	As *Engineering bricks* but without frogs	
(ii) Manufactured from refined clay and fired at very high temperature		Most paviors have resistance to chemicals and wear sup-erior to that of quarries	Colours – red, buff, cream, brown Texture – plain, rib-bed, chequered and roughened
3 **Quarries** Manufactured from un-refined clays, pressed and burnt BS 6431 Part 1:1983 Part 2:1984 Parts 3, 4, 5:1986 *Clay tiles for flooring*	A damp-proof mem-brane may be need-ed to prevent water vapour passing through joints and through porous units and to prevent water evapora-ting from the sur-face leaving salt deposits	Similar to equivalent bricks. Some have harder surfaces than interiors Wear resistance good to ex-cellent, especially for red and blue quarries *Slipperiness*: moderate to good *Maximum water absorption* (BS 1286): Class 1 6 per cent Class 2 10 per cent *Size tolerance* (BS 1286): 4 ($\pm$2) per 95 mm 8 ($\pm$4) per 193 mm	Colours – natural clay colours, ie red and in certain sizes, brown, blue and buff. Slight vari-ations are charac-teristic Texture – slightly ir-regular Joint patterns – usu-ally square bond. Wide joints are necessary for less accurate quarries
4 **Vitrified ceramic floor tiles**[2] Manufactured from re-fined clays, of more uni-form composition than used for quarries and which include fluxes to increase vitrifica-tion		More accurate size and shape and more uniform colours than above units Smooth surface Greater resistance to wear, oils, fats and chemicals in-cluding alkalis and to frost than quarries	Colours – black, white and wide range of mono-chromes and min-gled colours Textures – *Matt* de-velops sheen with wear. Available

Table 4.14   *B IV   Clay and precast concrete floorings*

| Sizes[4] | | | Laying | Surface treatment | | Average cost factor[5] |
Thickness mm	Width mm	Length mm		Initial	Maintenance	
65	102·5	215	*Externally:* pedestrian traffic – units may be bedded in sand or weak mortar; heavy traffic – units bedded on 16–19 mm cement : sand mortar on concrete base	Clean off and protect as for quarries	Sweep	30 – 60
19 — 51	95 108 114 124	190 216 241 251	*Internally:* See page 190 Remove cement stains with proprietary fluid	As *Bricks*		60
				Externally as *Bricks* *Internally* as *Vitrified tiles*		70

Preferred Modular co-ordinating sizes:

| 19 | 100 | {100 / 200} |

Modular work sizes

| 19 | 95 | {95 / 193} |

Non-modular work sizes

15	150	150
16	{76}	152
19}	{152}	
22}	{114}	229
32	{229}	

Other BS thicknesses

| 12·5 | — | — |
| 19·0 | — | — |

also diagonal halves, sills, stairtreads, etc

Laying: Methods of laying — See page 190

	Thickness of bedding mm
Mortar on	
– concrete	15–20
– separating layer	15–25
Semi-dry mix	25 min
Cement-based adhesive	5 max

Initial: Clean immediately with sand or sawdust. Wash repeatedly with water until any efflorescence ceases. Protect with whitewood sawdust during works

Maintenance: Wash with warm water and neutral sulphate-free detergent (Soap residues cause slipperiness and hold dirt) Rinse thoroughly with clean water (Do not use oiled sweeping compounds)

Average cost factor: 30 – 50

Polishes, linseed oils and other seals are not absorbed. Use polish sparingly and remove occasionally – a build-up becomes slippery and holds dirt — 60

Preferred Modular co-ordinating sizes

| 9·5 | 100 | {100 / 200} |

Modular work sizes

| 9·5 | 95·5 | {95·5 / 194·0} |

continued . . .

Material, form and references[1] continued . . .	Base	Properties	Appearance
Non-slip tiles contain silicon carbide The clay is ground, pressed and fired at high temperatures BS 6431:1982	As previous page	Electrically conductive grades are available *Slipperiness*: moderate when dry and oil, grease and wax free *Water absorption*: (*BS 1286*) 4 per cent max (Typical products 1–2 per cent) *Size tolerance* (BS 1286): 3 ($\pm$1·5) per 95·5 mm 6 ($\pm$3·0) per 194 mm	with non-slip silicon carbide surface and a glazed tile is textured with sand *Ribbed, studded, panelled and granulated* *Glazed* – not suitable for heavy duty Joint patterns – geometrical. Accurate size and shape of tiles permits narrower joints than quarries
5 **Fully vitrified ceramic tiles**[2] Manufactured to give a higher degree of vitrification than *vitrified ceramic floor tiles Class 2* BS 6431:1982		Similar to vitrified ceramic tiles but are virtually impervious and have excellent resistance to chemicals and staining *Water absorption:* (BS 1286) 0·3 per cent max (Typical products absorb appreciably less)	Colours – wider range than for vitrified ceramic tiles Textures and joint patterns – as for vitrified ceramic tiles
6 **Mosaic** Tesserae, usually of vitrified or fully vitrified ceramic are supplied bonded to paper in sheets up to 800 mm square. (Also available in glass and marble)		Similar to equivalent tiles of equal thickness *Slipperiness:* Rice grain clay tesserae and recessed joints reduce slipperiness for bare feet. Flush joints can be dusted with silicon carbide abrasive Glass suitable only for light pedestrian traffic	Colours – as tiles Texture of tesserae – Glazed, matt rice grain and incorporating abrasive. (The latter can be used as non-slip insets in terrazzo or marble stair treads Joint patterns – Normally regular but special patterns can be ordered
7 **Concrete – precast** Ordinary or coloured cement and aggregate hydraulically pressed Heavy duty tiles have hard stone or metal aggregate and/or abrasive included in surface		Properties vary widely Better products benefit by quality control, hydraulic pressing etc, are 'pre-shrunk' and have high resistance to wear, but inferior products may craze and 'dust' Resistance to chemicals varies with density	Colours – given by natural grey, white and pigmented cements and by aggregates when exposed in manufacture, by wear or by weathering Textures – plain, rib-

Table 4.14 *B IV Clay and precast concrete floorings*

Sizes[4]			Laying	Surface treatment		Average cost factors[5]
Thickness mm	Width mm	Length mm		Initial	Maintenance	
Non-modular work sizes			After bedding mortar has set, completely fill joints with 1 cement:1 fine sand grout[3] and point joints wider than 6 mm with 1 cement:3 fine sand[3]. Remove surplus with dry cement (not sawdust)	As previous page	As previous page	
9·5 }	76 }	152				
12·5 }	152 }					
Other BS thicknesses						
16·0	—	—				
19·0	—	—				
Some non-BS sizes			Joints			
8·5	76	67	See page 192			
10·0	100	100*				80
11·0	102	102	Damp-cure and do not allow even light foot traffic for at least 4 days			
12·7	150	150*				
13·0	60	200*				
15·0	250	240				
17·5		250*				
18·0		254				
22·2						
32·0						
* imported tiles						
also diagonal halves, hexagonal and other shapes, sills, stairtread tiles etc						
			Bed as for ceramic tiles. When the bedding is hard, the paper is stripped and joints are grouted with neat cement			100
4	5 – 13					
—						
10	sided squares, hexagons etc		Joints			
			See page 192			
15	150	150	As for similar clay products see above and page 191 but the backs of concrete tiles or slabs are brushed with neat cement slurry immediately before they are laid	May be sealed to prevent oil stains – see Concrete Finishes page 156	Scrub with detergent in hot water and with mild scouring powder if dirt is engrained (Avoid acidic cleaning agents on Portland cement, and strong alkaline	30 – 50
20	200	200				
20	225	225				
30	300	300				60 (industrial)
35	400	400				
40	500	500				
also hexagons and other shaped *tiles*						

continued . . .

Material, form and references[1]	Base	Properties	Appearance
continued ...			
7 **Concrete** *continued* BS 1217 : 1945 *Cast stone* BS 1197 : 1973 *Concrete flooring tiles and fittings* BS 368 : 1971 *Precast concrete flags*	Flags for pedestrian traffic may be laid on rammed earth or hardcore	Not suitable for chemical-resisting floors Accurate size tolerances: tiles ±1 mm flags ±2 mm on length and breadth	bed and containing abrasives
8 **Terrazzo – precast tiles** Hydraulically pressed concrete tiles, faced with marble aggregate in white or coloured cement matrix about 10 mm thick (abrasive may be incorporated) Surface ground BS 4131 : 1973 *Terrazzo tiles* BS 4357 : 1968 *Precast terrazzo units* (*other than tiles*) eg stair treads and risers	Concrete	Properties generally as for high quality precast concrete units Similar to in situ terrazzo, but tiles benefit from factory production as above Should not be laid for 21–28 days after pressing *Size tolerance* (BS 4131) ±1 mm	Colours – wide range Joint pattern – can be inconspicuous or colours of tiles can be alternated Appearance similar to in situ terrazzo but very large aggregate is sometimes used in a matrix of smaller particles and cement Liable to staining by some timbers, rope and straw

General considerations in selecting, laying and maintenance are discussed on page 190

[1] General references: BS 5385:1988 *Tile flooring and slab flooring*; BRE Digest 79 *Clay tile flooring, MBS: Materials, Ceramics* chapter 5, *Bricks* chapter 6, *Concrete* chapter 8

Table 4.14 *B IV Clay and precast concrete floorings*

Composition blocks	Concrete or screed	Good resistance to wear	Colours – rather dark
Composition blocks Various combinations of cement and drying oil or PVC binder, chalk, sawdust, wood flour, inert aggregate, and pigments pressed into blocks and cured Blocks have dovetailed keys on underside BS 5385 : 1987 *Tile flooring and slab flooring*	Concrete or screed A dpm is recommended on wet sites and is essential below floor warming	Good resistance to wear Heavy duty blocks incorporate white spar chippings Resilience low. Very good resistance to indentation Moderately warm Slippery only if highly polished Very good resistance to vegetable oils Good resistance to water, alkalis, acids, animal and mineral oils	Colours – rather dark Black and four colours on grey cement base Seven colours on white cement base Patterns – basket, herringbone and brick bond

Table 4.15 *B V Composition blocks*

Typical sizes[4]			Laying	Surface treatment		Average cost factors[5]
Thickness mm	Width mm	Length mm		Initial	Maintenance	
50 ⎫ ⎬ 598 63 ⎭ work sizes for *flags*		⎡ 448 ⎨ 598 ⎨ 748 ⎣ 898	Mortar for flags from 1 lime : 3–4 sand (slow setting, not frost proof), PC lime : sand mixes, to 1 Portland cement : 6 sand (strongest) Joints See page 192		cleaners on high alumina cement products) Phenols and cresols in some disinfectants cause indelible pink stains	17 (flags)
15 20 20 30 35 40 max width hexagons	150 200 225 300 400 500 300 and 500	150 200 225 300 400 500	As for clay tiles see page 191 but backs of tiles are brushed with neat cement slurry immediately before they are laid. Dividing strips (see in situ terrazzo) between groups of tiles	Usually ground after laying to remove any lipping edges Protect with non-staining sawdust Scrub with non-alkaline non-acid soap and allow to stand overnight Rinse with hot water Can be protected against staining with suitable water-based seal	Wash with warm water and occasionally fine abrasive powder. Use soap only if it is thoroughly rinsed off Do not apply polish or allow to become contaminated with soap or wax Do not use oiled sweeping compounds or disinfectants containing phenols and cresols	70

[2] Geometrical shapes sometimes called tessellated tiles
[3] Mixes by volume
[4] Subject to specified tolerances
[5] Approximate cost relationships for typical floorings 'as laid', based on granolithic = 10

10 and 16 Also accessories	52 63	157 190	Bed on 13 mm 1 cement : 3 sand Joints grouted with proprietary mortar Cure with wet sawdust	Sand Seal	Sweep with damp sawdust Wash with soap and water Rinse Apply proprietary polish Can be resurfaced by sanding	36 (10 mm) 43 (16 mm)

Material, form and references[1]	Base	Properties	Appearance
1 **Granites** eg Cornish BS 435 : 1931 *Granite and whinstone kerbs, channels, quadrants and setts*	1 *Internally* and for heavy-duty externally – concrete	Excellent resistance to wear, impact, frost and chemicals Slippery when polished, eg by wear Impervious to water and water vapour Resistant to staining	Colours – grey, red, pink, blue, black Pattern – mosaic of crystals Texture – from rock-face to glossy
2 **Sandstones** eg 'York stone' type (usually riven) Darley Dale Forest of Dean BS 435:1976 and BS 1919:1976 *Specification for natural stone kerbs, channels, quadrants and setts*	2 *Externally* for pedestrian traffic only: Sound hardcore or compacted soil	Wide range of density and hardness Some varieties eg 'York stones' have very high resistance to wear and frost and are 'non-slip' More absorbent stones readily stained Sandstones are attacked by sulphates washed from limestones in towns	Colours – grey, buff, brown, pink, red Texture – from rough-sawn to smooth. Riven surfaces may have mica particles
3 **Limestones** eg Portland Hopton Wood Kotah		Some varieties have high resistance to wear and frost Resistant to alkalis but not acids More absorbent varieties readily stained Hard varieties slippery when worn Best laid joint bedded	Colours – grey, buff, white Texture – from sawn to high (integral) polish
4 **Marbles** eg Swedish green Dove Sicilian Travertine and hard limestones commonly called *marbles*	Granite, slate and quartzite are impervious but a dpm in bases at ground level may be needed to prevent salt deposits on joints	Many varieties are very hard but superficial scratching by footwear tends to obscure bright colours and markings Generally darker marbles are harder than lighter ones	Colours and Markings – very wide range Texture – from sanded to very high (integral) polish Pattern – slabs or mosaic
5 **Slates** usually riven and edges sawn eg North Wales Westmorland Lancashire BS 680 : 1971 *Roofing slates*		Very good resistance to abrasion Riven surfaces of coarser slates are non-slip but polished smooth surfaces are slippery when wet Impervious to water and water vapour Stained by oils and greases if not sealed	Colours – green, blue, purple, black, greys (seals intensify colour) Texture – riven, sawn, sanded, rubbed or finely polished

General considerations in selecting, laying and maintenance are discussed on page 190

Table 4.16 *B VI Stones (Cast stone—see Concrete-precast page 178).*

182

Typical sizes		Laying	Surface treatment		Average cost factors[2]
Thickness mm	Length and width mm		Initial	Maintenance	
40 and setts	up to about 1830 × 910	*Internally* and for heavy-duty externally *Granites* Bed on 1 cement : 1 lime : 3 sand	Clean	Scrub with water and neutral sulphate-free detergent Rinse Surface may need to be roughened after many years	310–560
40–75 and setts	up to about 3050 × 1220	*Limestones and sandstones* Bed on 13–76 mm 1 Portland cement : 1 lime : 5–6 sand on concrete base	Clean Seals prevent staining but are not recommended by BS 5385 : Part 3 1988 Polish can make smooth surfaces dangerously slippery	Scrub with water and where necessary, a suitable neutral, sulphate-free pumice powder or detergent Rinse	110
15–40	300–600 squares				110
50	up to about 1500 × 600	*Externally*: for light pedestrian traffic only: bed on 1 lime : 3–4 sand to 1 Portland cement : 1 lime : 5–6 sand on compacted subsoil hardcore. If base is impervious, bed should be drained to prevent frost heave. Hollow bedding may cause cracking of slabs			
15–30 and mosaic – see table 4.13	up to about 1500 × 900			Scrub with warm water and sulphate-free non-caustic detergent Rinse Do not use soap (causes slipperiness), or oiled sweeping compounds	270 – 370 (19 mm)
6–13 19–25 32–40	457 × 229 381 × 381 1500 × 900	*Marbles, slates and quartzites* Bed on 1 cement : 1 lime : 3 sand. Brush backs of slate and quartzite with neat cement slurry			250 – 270 (19 mm)

Due to natural camber, riven slates require to be thicker than sawn slates, and may not be suitable in large sizes

[1] General references: BS 5385 : 1988 *Tile flooring and slab flooring, MBS: Materials* chapter 4
[2] Approximate cost relationships for typical floorings 'as laid', based on granolithic = 10

continued . . .

183

Material, form and references continued . . .	Base	Properties	Appearance
6 **Quartzite** eg Norwegian		Excellent resistance to abrasion and chemicals Riven surfaces are non-slip wet or dry Resistant to staining Dirt is not absorbed but riven surface holds dirt	Colours – grey, green, buff, yellow Texture – riven

Table 4.16   *B VI   Stones*

	Base	Properties	Appearance
1 **Linoleum**	As sheet linoleum page 166		Pattern can be provided by varying sizes and direction of tiles
2 **Cork** Granulated cork (no fillers) bonded by natural or artificial resins under heat and pressure Square, or tongued and grooved edges for tiles 8 mm thick and upwards Available with thin vinyl film surface Common densities: 480 and 560 kg/m³ BS 8203:1987 *Sheet and tile flooring*	Trowelled screed Paper felt underlay on boarding A dpm is essential in solid ground floors	Wear – good resistance especially high density grade tiles, but damaged by stiletto heels or badly designed furniture. Dirt becomes ingrained and cork is readily stained if not protected Resilient Very quiet and warm Non-slip – even when wet or polished Moderate resistance to acids Low resistance to alkalis Not suitable in damp conditions	Colour – honey to dark brown and dyed colours Pattern – cork granules Appearance deteriorates if maintenance is neglected
3 **Rubber** (i) Cut from sheet Some tiles contain fibre reinforcement	As sheet rubber page 168		Colours – as sheet but heavy duty tiles usually black Pattern – can be provided by varying direction and sizes of tiles Texture – smooth, studded bold ribbed, and other anti-slip grooved textures
(ii) Moulded with dovetailed grooves on underside and bold grooves or ribs on upper surface Interlocking or plain edges BS 1711 : 1951 *Solid rubber flooring* BS 8203:1987 *Sheet and tile flooring*	Tiles laid into screed or mastic asphalt on concrete – a dpm is not required	As sheet but non-slip Suitable for heavy duty public circulation areas Grease resistant grade available	

Table 4.17   *B VII   Other tile and slab floorings*

Typical sizes[1]		Laying[2]	Surface treatment		Average cost factors[3]
Thickness mm	Width and length mm		Initial	Maintenance	
10–20	152–229-mm sided squares and oblongs Random sizes up to 900 mm long	Movement joints as *concrete units* page 193			135 (19 mm)
As sheet	229 305 up to 914	As sheet linoleum but must be bonded to base	As sheet linoleum page 167		21 (3·2 mm)
3 5 8 25 stair treads	229 305 —	Keep tiles at room temperature for at least 48 hours Fix with adhesive and headless steel pins If pinning is not practicable 'load' tiles until adhesive has set	After fine sanding ordinary tiles, apply flexible seal or heavy grade solvent wax polish If great care has been taken in laying, sanding of prefinished tiles may not be necessary Water emulsion polish can be applied on sealed tiles, and wax polishes on unsealed tiles	Sweep frequently Damp (not wet) mop with detergent or mild (non-alkaline) soap Revive polish or seal periodically Smooth surface and colour can be restored by sanding	32 (6 mm)
As page 169 6 13 ribbed	229 – 914 914 × 1829	As sheet rubber page 169			44 (5 mm)
10 20	457 914	*On fresh screed:* Sand/cement applied to backs *On old screed or mastic asphalt:* tiles bedded in latex/cement	—	Sweep and vacuum Wash occasionally Can be polished (non-solvent type)	50

continued . . .

COMPOSITES

Material, form and references continued . . .	Base	Properties	Appearance
4 Thermoplastic 'asphalt tiles' standard (not to be confused with 'vinyl' tiles which are also thermoplastic, or with mastic asphalt tiles) Bitumen or non-vinyl resin binder, mineral fillers, asbestos fibres and pigments BS 2592: 1973 *Thermoplastic flooring tiles, sometimes known as asphalt tiles* BS 8203:1987 *Sheet and tile flooring*	As for 'Sheets supplied in rolls' – but not wood boards	Wear – moderate resistance Rather noisy Hard at lower temperatures and crack if not uniformly bedded Surface temperature with floor warming must not exceed 27°C (they soften at higher temperatures) Resistant to alcohol and water Moderate resistance to alkalis May be attacked by dissolved salts Poor resistance to solvents, acids, oils and greases Slippery if highly polished	Colours – limited range of dark colours (darker colours are cheapest) Patterns – plain or marbled
5 Thermoplastic – 'Vinylized' thermoplastic tiles with vinyl content BS 2592: 1973 BS 8203:1987 *Sheet and tile flooring*	A dpm is essential where rising moisture is severe	Slightly flexible and more resistant to wear, oils and greases than ordinary thermoplastic tiles	Colours – wider range than ordinary thermoplastic tiles
6 Vinyl asbestos vinyl (usually PVC) binder, asbestos fibres, fillers and pigments BS 3260: 1969 *PVC (vinyl) asbestos floor tiles* BS 8203:1987 *Sheet and tile flooring*		Properties intermediate between thermoplastic tiles and flexible vinyl tiles	Colours – brighter than thermoplastic tiles Textures – include 'travertine'
7 Flexible vinyl material as flexible vinyl sheet Tiles are not suitable where welded joints are required BS 3261: 1973 *Unbacked flexible PVC flooring* BS 8203:1987 *Sheet and tile flooring*	As for flexible vinyl sheet page 166		Colours – as sheet material Pattern – can be provided by varying direction and size of tiles

Table 4.17   B VII   Other tile and slab floorings

186

Typical sizes[1]		Laying[2]	Surface treatment		Average cost factors[3]
Thickness mm	Width and length mm		Initial	Maintenance	
2·5 or 3·0	250 or 300	Usually warmed to make them more flexible before laying on a suitable adhesive Thermoplastic tiles may crack at low temperatures if not uniformly bedded	Water-wax emulsion polish only (not polish containing solvents) Seals should not be used	After at least two weeks wash with mild soap or neutral detergent (not alkaline cleaners) Remove stains with fine steel wool and cleaning powder Burnish and apply polish sparingly	9 – 14 (3·2 mm)
2·5 3·0	229				21 (3·0 mm)
1·6 2·0 2·5 3·0 or 3·2	225 or 300				24 (3·2 mm)
1·5 2·0 2·5 3·0	225 250 300 457–914 non-BS				24 – 33 (2 mm)

continued . . .

Material, form and references continued . . .	Base	Properties	Appearance
8 **Asbestos-cement** Portland cement and asbestos fibres *Semi-compressed tiles* (BS 690 : 1971) – suitable for roof terraces *Fully-compressed tiles* (BS 690 Part 2 : 1981) (*Not recommended for internal use due to asbestos content*)	Floated concrete or screed on concrete	Wear resistance moderate to good High resistance to water and alkalis Moderate resistance to acids Low resistance to animal and vegetable oils	Light grey – standard
9 **Mastic-asphalt – preformed** as in-situ material but tiles are pressed		Generally as for in-situ flooring but preformed tiles are denser Acid resisting grade available	Colours – black, brown, dark red Texture – plain or chequered
10 **Cast iron** plates and grids	Concrete	Hard, cold and noisy Extremely resistant to metal tyred trucks, impact and molten metal spillage High resistance to acids and alkalis Suitable for heavy duty industrial floors	*Plates* – plain, studded, ribbed
			Grids – with hexagonal holes
11 **Steel** '*Anchor plates*' – trays pressed from 10 swg (3 mm) sheet. Tongues turned down from slots in face form 'anchors'. Available unfilled or filled with concrete	Concrete	As cast iron	Steel plates with bedding mortar exposed in slots

Table 4.17 *B VII Other tile and slab floorings*

Typical sizes[1]		Laying[2]	Surface treatment		Average cost factors[3]
Thickness mm	Width and length mm		Initial	Maintenance	
8 25	305	Flexible bedding compound	Fully compressed tiles can be sealed or polished	Wash and sweep	15
16–51	114 × 229 203 254	Bedded in screed, 13 mm mortar or bitumen Often laid with tight joints	As in situ mastic asphalt page 159		21
6·3 25·4 over flange *Squares* 22·2–25·4 *Triangles*	229 × 229 305 × 152 and 305 mm 305 mm sides	Bedded in 19–76 mm 1 cement : 1½ sand : 3 gravel, 6·3–3·2 mm Damp cure for at least 3 days and delay use for 5 days	—	Sweep and scrub	50
12·7	305 × 152 and 305 mm	Holes filled with 1 cement : 1 granite, 3·2 mm Cure as above			
22–50	305 × 152, 305 and 457 mm	Plates 'buttered' on underside and laid, with anchors downwards in 38 mm bed of stiff 1 cement : 2 sand : 1½ gravel Cure as above	—	Sweep and scrub	74

[1] Preformed skirtings and other fittings are available in some materials
[2] Adhesives should be those recommended by the manufacturer of the flooring and should be used as they advise. (No adhesive is effective as a damp-proof membrane)
[3] Approximate cost relationships for typical floorings 'as laid' based on granolithic = 10

COMPOSITES

Floorings should not be washed until adhesive is thoroughly hard.

B II   Boards (See table 4.12 page 170)
Suitable boards of appropriate thickness can perform the dual function of supporting traffic and other loads between joist or batten or over other supports and providing a wearing surface of good appearance with few joints.

B III   Timber floorings (see table 4.13 page 172)
General references
BS 8201:1987 *Wood flooring (Board, strip, block and mosaic)*
Timber selection by properties Part 1: Windows, doors, cladding and flooring PRL. HMSO
Timber floorings, The Timber Research and Development Association (TRADA)
BRE Digest 18, *Design of timber floors to prevent dry rot*, HMSO
MBS: Materials chapter 2, *Timber*
BS 1187:1959 *Wood blocks*
BS 4050:1968 *Mosaic*
CP 209: Part 1: 1963 *Wooden flooring methods on polished finishes*

Timbers of widely differing properties, appearance and costs can be used in various ways in buildings of almost all types, whether they be residential, educational, industrial or public. Timber is hard wearing (resistance in any one species increases with density), and resilient, more so where fixed on joists or battens rather than a solid base. Resistance to acids and alkalis varies from moderate to high, but polishes and in particular seals, provide protection from them, and also from staining, dirt and water. Timber flooring must be correctly seasoned and also designed to accommodate the moisture movement which is inevitable in service. To prevent fungal attack, timber which is not exclusively heartwood of an inherently durable species must be kept with a sufficiently low moisture content, or be treated with a preservative. Some timbers which are suitable over floor warming are listed in table 4.10, but they are not recommended where carpets with insulating underfelts are to be used.

Quarter sawn timber has less movement in its width, gives better wear and may have more attractive appearance than plain-sawn timber. However, its high cost is unlikely to be justified except in cases such as softwood gymnasium floors, where freedom from splintering is essential. End grain timber is even more resistant to wear than quarter sawn timber.

A notable advantage of timber flooring is that it can be repeatedly resurfaced, provided any tongues or dowels are well below the surface.

190

Moisture content of timber   BS 1297:1970 *Grading and sizing of softwood flooring* specifies a maximum moisture content of 22% for air-dried timber and 15% for kiln-dried timber. BS 8201:1987 gives 18–. If considerable shrinkage is to be avoided, where flooring is installed in modern buildings lower moisture contents requiring kiln seasoning are necessary. Moisture contents likely to occur in service are:

No heating | 14–18%
Intermittent heating | 12–15%
Continuous heating | 11–12%
High degree of central heating | 9%
Over underfloor heating | 6– 9%

Selection of timber   Table 4.10 based on FPRL Bulletin 40 classifies some timbers for uses as strips, boards or blocks (but not end grain blocks) in respect of wear and other properties.
Specialist subcontractors should be consulted, as both availability and cost vary considerably.

The base   Timber must be protected from moisture by damp-proof membranes in solid ground floors, and by damp-proof courses and ventilation below suspended floors (see *MBS: Structure and Fabric* Part 1). Timber fillets embedded in concrete are required to by either treated in accordance with BS 3452:1962 *Copper-chrome water-borne wood preservatives and their application*, or pressure impregnated with copper-chrome-arsenate. Any surfaces which are exposed by cutting must be thoroughly treated with a 10% aqueous solution of the preservative.
The relative humidity of air trapped on the surface of concrete infill between fillets should not exceed 75–80% when wood flooring is laid.

Laying   Good quality flooring should not be delivered to a site, or fixed before windows are completely glazed, the heating installation has been tested and the building has been maintained at its normal temperature with correct ventilation for at least a week.
A gap must be left for expansion between timber flooring and walls and columns. This can be concealed by a skirting which should not be fixed to the flooring. Where underfloor heating is installed the flooring should be laid in contact with the concrete filling between fillets to obtain maximum thermal transmittance.

Surface treatment   See CP 209:1963 *Care and maintenance of floor surfaces* Part 1: *Wooden flooring*.
Good appearance and cleanliness of floors is obtained by fine sanding and filling the pores of the wood to reduce absorption. *Wax polish* gives good

Timber			RS	G	CA	FH	B	D	SM
African mahogany		LP				FH			
African walnut								D	
Afrormosia		NP			CA	FH			SM
Afezelia		NP			CA	FH			SM
Agba		LP				FH			SM
Brush, box	HI		RS		CA				SM
Burma teak		NP				FH			
Douglas fir		LP		G					
East African olive								D	
European beech	LI	HP		G					
European birch		LP							
European oak		HP			CA		B	D	
Greenheart	HI								
Guarea		NP		G		FH	B		
Gurjun		NP		G	CA				
Idigbo		LP							SM
Iroko		NP			CA	FH			SM
Japanese maple	HI		RS	G			B		
Keruing		NP		G	CA				
Loiondo	LI	HP		G		FH	B		SM
Missanda	LI	HP				FH			SM
Muhuhu	HI	HP				FH		D	SM
Muninga		NP		G		FH			
Niangon		LP							
Opepe		NP			CA	FH			
Panga panga		HP				FH		D	SM
Parana pine		LP							
Purpleheat		HP						D	
Redwood		LP							
Rhodesian teak	HI	HP	RS	G	CA	FH	B	D	SM
Rock maple	HI	HP	RS	G			B		
Sapele		NP		G			B	D	
Scots pine		LP							
Utile		NP							
Wallaba	HI								
Western hemlock		LP		G					
Yew								D	

HI   *Heavy duty industrial* including trucking and other impact loads as in factories, mills, workshops and warehouses.

LI   *Light duty, industrial* including trucking of a light nature, eg clothing and food processing establishments.

HP   *Heavy pedestrian* Intensities of more than 2000 persons per day, usually concentrated in traffic lanes, eg in public institutions, barracks and corridors in large schools and colleges.

NP   *Normal pedestrian* Residential and domestic buildings, small classrooms and offices.

RS   *Roller skating rinks.*

G   *Gymnasia (softwoods rift sawn only).*

CA   *High impermeability to chemicals and acid.*

FH   *Suitable over floor heating.*

B   *Ballrooms.*

D   *Decorative.*

SM   *Small movement.*

◀ **Table 4.10**   *Timbers for flooring*

appearance but is soft and requires frequent renewal. *Button polish* (*shellac*) provides a filler coat before wax polishing but is too easily scratched and stained to serve as a durable finish.

Seals (see page 145) are preferable for heavy duty, or where liquids are likely to be splashed. They are very tough and normally only require to be kept clean during a long life which can be prolonged by applications of resin-emulsion polish. Ordinary paste wax polish on sealed floors makes them dangerously slippery.

Penetrating or *dust-allaying* oils hold dirt and are only suitable for heavy duty and where appearance is unimportant.

B IV   Clay and precast concrete floorings
Information concerning these floorings is summarised in table 4.14 page 176. Both clay and concrete products are hard, noisy and 'cold', have high thermal conductivity and capacity and are suitable over under-floor warming installations. Concrete products are lower in cost but the better clay products have the following advantages:

(a) Very high resistance to chemicals, except hydrofluoric acid and strong hot caustic alkaline solutions.

(b) They are harder and more resistant to abrasion than concrete products and are 'non-dusting'.

(c) Colours are permanent and can be very intense and tiles can be glazed.

(d) There is a much wider range of sizes, shapes, textures and colours.

Thermal movement of clay products is about half, and the modulus of elasticity about 1.5 to 3 times that of other products.

Bedding systems BS 5385:1988 *Tile flooring and slab flooring* describes methods for laying various units on different bases and for stated conditions of use.
  (i) *Bedding in cement: sand mortar bonded to the base.* This traditional method is for heavy traffic. Concrete bases should be at least four weeks' old and screeds at least two weeks' old. They should not contain water repellent admixtures. After dipping the

191

COMPOSITES

more absorptive units in clean water, but not soaking them, they are drained and beds should be 15 mm thick for tiles of 10 mm or less and 15 to 20 mm thick for thicker units.

To improve adhesion a light dusting of dry cement can be trowelled into the upper surface of the bedding or either a slurry of neat concrete or a cement-based adhesive can be applied to the backs of the tiles before they are laid. The backs of concrete tiles are usually painted with neat cement slurry.

Unfortunately, where units are bonded rigidly to bases, loss of bond with 'arching' or 'ridging', particularly of the thinner units, sometimes occurs, for one or more of the following reasons:

(a) Shrinkage of the concrete base in drying. (Defects are likely to show in the first twelve months.)

(b) Shrinkage of the concrete base in cold weather. (Thermal movement of concrete is two to three times that of fired clay.)

(c) Rapid local thermal expansion of tiles caused by steam or hot water hosing.

(d) Creep deflection of concrete structural floors.

The expansion of ceramics, particularly the less dense materials, with absorption of moisture which occurs most rapidly in the first weeks after they leave the kiln (see *MBS: Materials* chapter 6) may contribute to compressive stresses in tiling.

The risk of 'arching' and 'ridging' of tiles which are bonded to subfloors can be reduced by providing *movement joints* as described below, and by the following methods of laying, which permit some relative movement between tiles and subfloor.

(ii) *Separating layer method* This method is suitable internally, except on stairs, on true and smooth concrete based. Units can be laid as above but on the bedding mix 15 mm thick and at least as thick as units up to 25 mm thick, separated from the base by polythene film[1], bitumen felt[2] or building paper[3] with 100 mm lapped joints or by damp-proof membranes. See figure 5.06.

[1] 500 grade for most conditions
[2] BS 747 : 1986
[3] BS 1521 : 1980

(iii) *'Thick-bed', semi-dry method* To prevent bond with reasonably level concrete bases damped if necessary to reduce suction, a lean mix, 1 cement: 4 sand containing only sufficient water so it retains its shape when squeezed in the hand is tamped down at least 25 mm thick. For a bedding thicker than 40 mm a 1 cement: 1½ dry. 10 mm 'down' coarse aggregate: 3 dry and mix (by weight) should be used. (If proportions are batched by volume bulking of sand should be allowed for.) A slurry of 1 cement: 1 fine sand of creamy consistency is applied about 3 mm thick immediately before the units are well beaten down. The backs of concrete tiles are painted with a 1:1 slurry. Joints should be grouted within four hours of laying.

(iv) *'Thin-bed', cement based adhesive method* On a sufficiently level, and dry base, dry tiles are well tamped on an adhesive which should comply with BS 5385 : 1976, Part 1 and be not more than 5 mm thick. The method is not recommended on screeds over underfloor heating. This, and the following proprietary products, should be used in strict accordance with the manufacturer's instruction.

(v) *Bedding in rubber-latex cement mortar* This method is practicable on any base, including metal decking. The mortar, which resembles rubber-latex cement flooring, accepts some movement and is resistant to mildly corrosive conditions.

(vi) *Bedding in bitumen emulsion: sand* The base is primed with the compound (BS 3940 *Adhesives based on bitumen or coal tar*) which is spread to a minimum thickness of about 10 mm.

Joints Joints must be sufficiently wide to accommodate some movement and variations in size of units, about 152 mm square and up to about 15 mm for larger and less accurate units. It is important that joints are completely filled in order to prevent penetration of liquids, to support their top edges and evenly distribute stresses between units. When the bedding has set ordinary joints are grouted with 1 cement: 1 fine dry sand, by volume, and those in mosaic with neat cement.

Movement joints should be taken through the tiles and bedding as indicated in figure 4.06. They are topped with an elastic but suitably hard sealant (see BS 5385:1988 and *MBS: Materials* chapter 16). Movement joints should be avoided where there is heavy traffic but if they occur they should be protected with metal angles—see figure 5.06. Compressible back-up

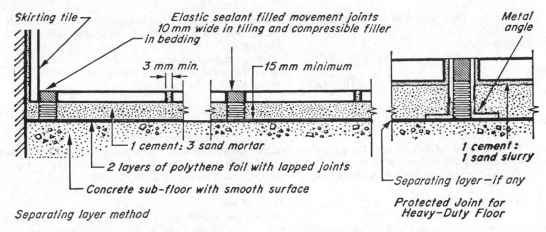

Separating layer method

4.06 *Laying of clay and precast concrete flooring*

materials are used to control the depth of sealant and the way it deforms, and fillers are used to fill the remaining joint. Sometimes one material fulfils both functions. They must be compatible with the sealant. A barrier such as polyethylene film may be needed to prevent elastic sealants sticking to the back-up or filler material. For light duty where a watertight seal is not required, preformed strips such as cork, cork-rubber or rubber-bitumen can be used. They should be keyed into the bedding.

Clay units   BS 5385:1988 recommended that where units are bedded 'solid', movement joints should be provided to perimeters,[1] over supporting beams and walls, over structural movement joints, and at 4.5 m centres. However, units bedded on a semi-dry mix, at ground level and which will not be subjected to large and rapid changes in temperature or humidity. usually do not require perimeter joints in floors which do not exceed 6 m in one direction. In such floors any intermediate joints can be at 9 m centres.

Concrete units   laid by any method, require perimeter joints[1] where floors exceed 15 mm in any direction and intermediate joints at 15 m centres.

B V   Composition blocks (See table 4.15 page 178)

B VI   Stones (See table 4.16 page 182)
Stones are hard, 'cold' and noisy but very suitable for underfloor warming. They have good resistance to oils but may be stained if they are not sealed.

[1]Where movement joints are required to perimeters they should also be provided around columns, machine bases, steps, etc.

B VII   Other tiles and slabs (See table 4.17 page 184)
These units include heavy-duty cast iron slabs, semi-rigid materials such as compressed cork and thermo-plastic tiles and tiles cut from sheet materials which are also provided in rolls.

The durability of floor finishes in small units is heavily dependent on their fixing and hence adhesion. Following on from the flooring case study in section 2.03 attention should be given to compatibility with adhesives. From BRE Digest 212 (Site use of adhesives Part 2) 'Flexible pvc flooring contains plasticisers which tend to migrate into the adhesive causing the flooring to shrink. Reaction between plasticiser and adhesive may sometimes result in the staining of the flooring material.'

One common plasticiser, dibutyl pthalate often has a common compatibility with most solvents in proprietary tile adhesives and will migrate into the adhesive destroying adhesion bonds in the process. It achieves this by depressing the glass transition temperature of the adhesive, keeping it in a viscous state. Vinyl flooring is a complex mixture of co-polymers vinyl chloride and vinyl acetate, with a plasticiser, extender, whiting, fillers, stabilisers, pigments and should be thought of in conjunction with its adhesive as a particle composite. With this range of components it is understandable that there can be a wide range of failure mechanisms. Substrates can also cause problems. Alkaline material from ordinary Portland cement can sometimes cause softening of adhesive. It should be noted that alkaline cleaners are often used to remove oil and grease prior to floor laying and these should be neutralised by further chemical cleaning.

B VIII Glass mosaic (See table 4.14 page 176)

B IX Carpets and felts

References
Product selection for architects: Carpets, RIBA Journal, January 1970
BS 3655:1981 *Code for informative labelling of carpets, carpeting and rugs* deals with size, construction, fibre content and cleansing.
BS 4223:1983 specifies *A method for the determination of constructional details of carpets with a yarn pile.*
BS 5557:1978 *Textile floor coverings* is a useful reference.
British Carpet Technical Centre.

Carpets vary widely in quality, which is generally related to initial cost. Low initial cost is often associated with high *cost-in-use*. It should be noted that durability and deterioration in appearance are not directly related. The materials used for pile, backing and underlay all influence performance. A high pile is not always an advantage in wear but the weight of pile, including that woven into the backing, and the number of tufts per 100 mm^2 are guides to durability.

One easy to perform test is attempting to tear out fibres using teeth; messy, but a good comparative guide to quality.

With correct and regular maintenance the better quality carpets are extremely durable, but all carpets are damaged by grit, by rubber soles and pointed heels to shoes, and by pointed legs to furniture.

Use-category gradings adopted by *The British Carpet Centre* are valuable aids in the selection of carpets.

The BCC system grades Axminster and Wilton woven carpets produced in this country and non-woven carpets manufactured by members of *The Federation of British Carpet Manufacturers* as suitable for:

1 Light domestic, eg bedrooms
2 Light to medium domestic
3 General domestic and/or light 'contract' use
4 Heavy domestic and/or medium 'contract' use
5 Luxury domestic and/or heavy 'contract' use
(Carpets in this category usually have only one stated use.)

Types of carpets
Machine made carpets (hand made carpets are not considered here) are either *woven or tufted:*
Woven carpets In Axminster-type carpets the pile is woven with the backing and is always cut, the method permitting a large number of colours to be used. In Wiltons the pile is wove into the backing: the number of colours is restricted. Plain coloured woven carpets are usually Wiltons and their pile is usually denser than Axminsters.

Woven carpets are made in *body widths* of 457 mm to about 1 m and *broadloom widths* up to 4.572 m in thicknesses of 6 to 9 mm.

Tufted carpets Here the looped or cut pile is stitched into a jute backing and secured with latex. Patch repairs are more easily made than with woven carpets. A good quality carpet may have a PVC primary backing and an expanded PVC secondary backing, both of which include glass fibre reinforcement.

Types of pile
Cut pile has a matt appearance but tends to *shade* and *track*. *Cording* or *loop pile* does not shade and the irregular appearance of *cut loop* minimizes tread marks and shading.

Types of carpet fibres
Fibres which are used alone or in various combinations include:

Wool fibres are resilient and warm and do not soil easily. They do not ignite easily and are self-extinguishing. However, wool is costly and is attacked by moths if it is not specially protected. A '*Woolmark*' is awarded to pure wool carpets of specified quality.

Nylon is strong, tough and very hard wearing, but is less soft and resilient than wool. It soils but is easily cleaned. It melts at high temperatures.

Polypropylene, although cheap, this has comparable durability to nylon and cleans well. It is difficult to dye and tends to flatten quickly.

Acrylic is not as soft as wool but is resilient, wears well and is easily cleaned.

Rayon has low strength and resilience but is cheap and provides bulk in carpets.

Organic fibres can be treated to render them antistatic but:

Stainless steel fibres are included in some carpets to eliminate static electricity which can arise when all animal or synthetic fibres are walked on.

Felts These consist of fibres needled into a jute hessian backing.

Fixing

The base should be smooth, level and without gaps. Good quality resilient underlays, either separate or integral, add considerably to the lives of carpets and reduce the downward transmission of impact noise.

After being well stretched, carpets should be fixed at their edges by tacks or by angled pins on *gripper strips*. Carpet to carpet joins can be made by sewing, or by adhesive strips.

Some felts are stuck to subfloors, but animal hair carpet tiles bind together at their contacting edges and do not require to be stuck down.

Aluminium or brass extrusions are used to protect the edges of carpets at junctions with other floorings.

Maintenance

Stains should be removed immediately. Vacuum cleaning is necessary at intervals varying widely with use, and less frequently, dry cleaning or shampooing, which are best done in situ, are required.

C   Raised floors

C I   Raised floors

Raised floors are becoming standard items in offices where deep servicing is needed for computer rooms, etc. Systems in use allow for the laying of large format tiles on either jacks or continuous plastic/timber runners. The jack system may allow for easier levelling especially in existing premises and is possible on unscreeded floors, although installation may prove more expensive due to the additional time taken. Firebreaks should be checked for in these flooring systems especially where partitions above form compartments. As part of the fire protection system these areas may need to be serviced to provide flooding of halon gas in the event of fire. One unexpected repercussion of deep floor systems is the provision of new warm homes for the City of London's fluctuating rat population. Infestation should be catered for.

5 METALLIC MATERIALS

5.01 INTRODUCTION

Metals are the one group of materials that are at the most risk in our atmosphere. In their natural state they exist normally as oxides and sulphides before extraction into pure elements. Once liberated from their ore body they can be highly reactive in the atmosphere and can recombine with oxygen and in some cases sulphur dioxide to attain more stable compounds, resembling those from which they originated. Metals have a range of order and those metals that are found in a pure state in the earth's crust, such as silver and gold, mercury and copper, are known as *noble metals*, those metals that are more reactive are known as *base metals*, and include all our more commonly used building materials such as lead, iron and aluminium. This division of *base* and *noble* metals is marked by a division in the electrochemical series which rates the *electrode potential* of every metal. This potential is a physical measurement which describes the state of equilibrium between a metal and its ions.

$$M^{n+} + ne \rightleftarrows M$$

Equilibrium for base metals (Tend to dissolve with a loss of electrons)

Equilibrium for noble metals (Tend to stay stable with no loss of electrons)

Electrochemical series: standard electrode potentials for half cell reactions

Metal	Half reaction	E^{o}/V
Gold	$Au^{3+} \rightleftarrows Au$	1.42
Silver	$Ag^{+} + e \rightleftarrows Ag$	0.80
Copper	$Cu^{2+} \rightleftarrows Cu$	0.34
Hydrogen	$H^{+} + e \rightleftarrows 1/2\ H_2$ (reference electrode)	0.00
Lead	$Pb^{2+} + 2e \rightleftarrows Pb$	-0.13
Iron	$Fe^{2+} + 2e \rightleftarrows Fe$	-0.44
Zinc	$Zn^{2+} + 2e \rightleftarrows Zn$	-0.76
Aluminium	$Al^{3+} + 3e \rightleftarrows Al$	-1.66

For a description of corrosion mechanisms see MBS: *Materials* chapter 9.

See figure 5.01.

As the metals we use in the building industry have a tendency to corrode, especially steel as an iron alloy, our effort to keep them stable relies on the effectiveness of coatings and finishes. The only other route open is to specify alloys that are stable, often by their ability to form tenacious oxide coatings that are difficult for water and air to penetrate. One example of this mechanism is the use of chromium with steel to make stainless steel. This alloy works by selective oxidation, the chromium oxidises, first forming a protective chromium oxide coating for the metal below. There should be at least 12% chromium in the alloy for effective protection.

Coatings applied to metals must then do the following:

(a) Protect the metal substrate from initiators of corrosion such as air or water, and be engineered to inhibit corrosion.

(b) Provide effective bonding to the metal.

(c) Be compatible with the metal to an extent that thermal movement can be undertaken by metal and coating together.

In (b) for coatings and structural adhesive bonding to metals the principles of surface preparation treatment are similar for optimising performance. The scrupulous removal of all contaminants is defined by Kozma[1] as providing a 'new chemically active surface of high surface energy'. Mechanically removing oxidised material may be followed by special pretreatments of chemical etching to facilitate strong chemical binding between metal and coating systems.

[1]'Surface pre-treatment of steel for structural adhesive bonding', L Kozma, *Materaisl Science Technology*, volume 3, no 11, Nov 87, pp 954–962.

5.01 *Complete decay of steel. In this steel wheel barrow, the metal is reduced to a paper-thin state and the weight of an adjacent section is sufficient to cause fracture. Once steel is exposed and starts to corrode, the conversion of steel into rust (a hydrated iron oxide) is progressive and continual until all the metal is converted. As the rust deposit forms, it does not provide a layer that can protect the inner unaffected metal, it is so porous that air and water vapour can diffuse through and initiate further conversion*

Coatings systems

The most important part of this process is the cleaning and preparation for the coating. As the metals most commonly coated are irons and steels, cleaning is generally to remove an oxide film (millscale if the section has been rolled). See CP 3012: *Code for cleaning and preparation of metal surfaces*. The quality of surface finish is important and blast cleaned surfaces have to be specified, see BS 4232: *Specification for surface finish of blast cleaned steel*. Swedish standards are often quoted for this work, where 2½ is generally acceptable and quoted for surfaces requiring above average protection. For steels needing a metal finish cast iron grit is recommended to provide a bright surface with an idealised angular 'peaked' surface profile for good adhesion. There are two main methods of blast cleaning sometimes referred to as mechanical blasting using steel shot which will give a rounded profile to the surface topography or grit blasting which will give a more angular profile. One drawback with mechanical blasting (especially when using grit) is that contaminants can be left behind and metal surfaces should then ideally be washed. This is best carried out under factory conditions as for the best results the metal should be heated to 500 degrees centigrade for at least 90 minutes. Angular topography also gives a greater surface area of exposure and a higher topography which is reflected in the greater depth needed in the thickness of the coating system applied. This should be $3 \times$ the average maximum profile, (AMP) according to ISO standards (8503 Parts 1 to 4).[1]

Recommended high performance coating thicknesses
For grit blasting
180 microns for fine profiles
300 microns for medium profiles
450 microns for coarse profiles

For shot blasting
120 microns for fine profiles
210 microns for medium profiles
300 microns for coarse profiles.

Coating systems can be organic or inorganic but are preceded by treatments such as phosphating which act as corrosion inhibitors. These treatments are also useful for stabilising lightly rusted carbon steels. The compounds used are reactive with iron oxide and form new conversion coatings that are not only insoluble but are integral with the steel surface. For example, phosphoric acid reacting with iron oxides will give a stable phosphate coatings that can be between 12–14 microns thick.[1] These products, although water based, will form inorganic and nonmetallic complexes ready to receive the rest of the coating system.[2] (See BS 4382 for simple site check tests. Wherever possible these finishes should be performed in controlled conditions, particularly to enable blast cleaning to be properly carried out. This is not always possible for site work and the very minimum standards for site preparation should allow for cleaning with power tools; wire brushing is not adequate for visible high quality finishes or minimal structural sections; although probably acceptable for well sized industrial structures. See *Painting Steelwork*

[1]'A Paint Manufacturer's Viewpoint: painting for protection, R W Green (Consultant ICI), *Corrosion Prevention and Control*, February 1986.

[1]'Conversion coatings on rusted carbon steel, Ferretti, Ferrarone, Barcano, *Corrosion Prevention and Control*, August 1987.
[2]'Rust conversion coatings', Paul J Des Lauriers, *Materials Performance* volume 26, no. 11, Nov 1987, pp 35–40.

5.02 *Port buildings, Manhattan Island. These metal buildings rely heavily on paint films for their protective coatings and are generated from the technology of bridge building*

by IP Haigh Construction Industry Research and Information Association Report 93, 1982.

Galvanising

This term is commonly given to molten zinc dipped coatings on steel. The steel is cleaned and then dipped in inhibited hydrochloric acid which produces iron chloride on the surface of the metal that can act as a flux. There are inter-metallic layers formed between the zinc and the steel in the process, as the steel is dipped in a bath held at a temperature of 720 K, but these compounds are relatively brittle. See BS 792:1986 *Specification for hot dip galvanised coatings on iron and steel*. Galvanising works by zinc being anodic to steel. If the coating is scratched then the zinc will decay preferentially to the steel and so offer protection.

5.03 and 5.04 *Galvanised crash barrier, Northern Spain. These show giant crystal growths from slow cooling of the zinc deposition on the underlying steel*

Aluminium and tin coatings on steel

Steel can also be dipped in molten tin but this is an expensive process and sometimes dipping in an alloy of lead (88–75%) and tin is used for engineering parts in cars. Steel can also be coated with aluminium by dipping in the molten metal after rigorous cleaning is carried out giving coating thicknesses of 50–75 microns.

Sheradising

This process of applying a zinc coating is different from galvanising, as instead of hot dipping, items to be treated are rotated in a drum with powered metal zinc which at high temperatures (640 K) diffuses into the hot metal items. This gives a harder outer coating than galvanising and is also more porous, providing good adhesion for subsequent painting. In a similar way aluminium (aluminising) and chrome (chromising) can also be applied. See BS 4921:1988 *Specification for sheradised coatings on iron and steel articles.*

5.05 *Empire State Building, Manhattan. The use of gold as a finish can be justified as appropriate especially with lettering in such inaccessible places*

Anodising

This process is applied to aluminium. Although aluminium forms a consistent and strong oxide film which prevents further corrosion, this film can be artificially increased by anodising. Objects to be treated become *anodes* in an electrolyte, and the applied voltage causes aluminium ions to migrate outwards, towards the edge of the existing oxidised layer. Once they reach this point they undergo a reaction with oxygen and spare electrons from the dissociation of water to produce more alumina. This thicker oxidising coating is quite porous and can be dyed to give colour prior to sealing. See BS 1615:1987 *Method for specifying for anodic oxidation coatings on aluminium and its alloys* and BS 3987:1974 *Specification for anodic oxide coatings on wrought aluminium for external architectural applications.*

Controlled patinas

There are a great variety of treatments that can be carried out to copper and its alloys as well as steel. They all involve treating the surface with various acid mixtures or particular compounds and then after the surface has stabilised, (often after wrapping for a period of at least 24 hours) being kept in this condition by waxing or sealing. The nature of the finish is bound

to be experimental and there will be considerable colour variations, although these add to the attraction. Experimental samples should always be made first for approval. Depending on the colours used, pinks, greens, browns and yellows can be made on copper-based alloys. The effects on iron and steel are more limited.

See *Colouring, Bronzing and Patination of Metals*, Richard Hughes and Michael Row, Crafts Council, 1982.

Weathering steels

This is the name given to alloyed steels which have a range of elements that will provide a coating to steel that will corrode no further. Cor-ten is the best example of this and is the USA name for the alloyed combination of iron, carbon, copper and phosphorous which provides a particularly good oxidised coating. This type of alloy was introduced into the UK in 1967 and is known as 50 Grade weathering steel. After a few years the steel weathers to a purplish brown but there are problems. Although the material is widely used in the states for engineering structures and saves on normal maintenance with coatings, different parts of the structure can weather differently according to how they are exposed, and how water runs down sections. Staining can also occur and be unsightly and should be catered for.

5.06   *Entrance to McGraw Hill, New York by Hood, Godley and Fowlhoux 1930–31*

5.07 *Chrysler Building New York by William van Allen 1930
At that time the McGraw Hill building was the largest to use
terra-cotta as a facing material. It had a glazed green finish.
These two entrances are typical of an approach in America in
this period, where entrances had to be maintenance free and
made from materials that were stable. Here was an opportunity
for the use of stainless steels, nickels, chromium, bronzes, glass
and enamels. The Chrysler Building was refurbished in the early
1980s, but little work was needed to the entrance*

Opposite
5.08 and 5.09 *Lloyds of London by Richard Rogers 1986.
Here, the choice of metals is critical. Alloys have to be chosen
that are stable and will not react with each other. Abandonment
of surface coatings places heavier demands on engineering the
right alloys and their connections*

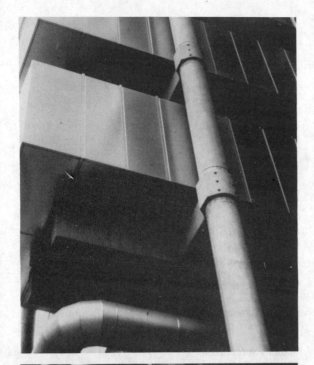

5.10 *Paolozzi sculpture. This small piece is leaning against a wall and belongs to Colin St John Wilson (Cambridge). The piece is rusting but robust enough to give years of pleasure before final decay (nature of metal unknown)*

6 ENDPIECE

Although this book deals with a recognisable range of materials and observes that their choice is generally to do with ultimate performance and minimisation of their degradation, there are some other factors worth considering in making materials choices.

Healthy occupancy

It is now acknowledged that there are fairly high levels of indoor pollution in buildings that can make people unwell by creating a slightly toxic environment. Although articles had been published in the scientific press outlining some major pollutants, ie background radiation, nitrous oxides and gases from formaldehydes (see *New Scientist* 5.12.85 'The Aggressive Environment'[1]) it did not reach the public press until 1987. Poor ventilation rates have been criticised as being a major contributor, and these are partly a repercussion of energy saving in buildings which require a well sealed and highly controlled environment. However, highly controlled environments that minimise air movement and convective forces can endanger health.

We also have to change our approach to the specification of materials. In 1984 Wanner reported at the Third International Conference on Indoor Air Quality and Climate in Stockholm that emission rates of formaldehyde from particle boards in some new buildings, after one year, have been found to exceed admissible limits. His report was based on a research project which concentrated on looking at particular pollutants that, if emitted, would have some effects on health. Materials studied were the group of wood products that were all based on using wood waste to form particle boards and plywoods. His study also included ceiling tiles, fabrics, foam insulation and masonry. Various solvents, including touelene, butanol and isocynate were studied alongside asbestos and radon. Uncoated panels could continually emit formaldehyde which would initially give symptoms of a sore throat, irritation to the eyes and feelings of general discomfort.[2] People are able to detect concentrations of levels below 1 ppm and there have been more cases of dermititis and asthma in UF foam insulated houses in the USA.[3] Long-term exposure can cause severe respiratory failure.

Formaldehyde vapour has for some time been confirmed as an irritant but, in the building industry observations have been confined to the use of urea formaldehyde foam insulation in cavity walls. In BRE Information Paper 25 (1982) observations are made that although it has been in use for over 20 years it is now known that it can cause discomfort through 'irritation to the eyes and respiratory tract'. It is categorically not advised for lightweight timber construction and other systems that have a high level of through ventilation, but only in sealed systems, ie in brickwork cavity walls which consciously minimise the possible leakage of fumes. (See BRE Digest 236 for advice and also BS 5617:1978 which is the relevant British Standard. However, even in brickwork cavities, if the temperature of the walling system is raised to sufficiently high levels, the foam can deteriorate and release formaldehyde.

Indoor contaminants[2]

Asbestos (fire retardants)
Ozone (photocopiers, electrostatic air cleaners, electrical equip)
Nitrogen dioxide (gas cookers)
Respirable sized particulates (dust)
Radon (soil, masonry, concrete, water service)
Formaldehyde (particle boards, plywoods, laminates, carpets)
Carbon monoxide (cigarette smoke, gas, coal)
Urea resins (laminates)
Ions
Asbestos
Mites
Pesticides (timber treatment, eradication generally)
Nitrogen oxides
Microbes
Allergens
Volatile organics
Fibreglass (insulation)

[1] 'The Aggressive Evironment', *New Scientist* 5.12.85
[2] Turiel, I, *Indoor Air Quality and Human Health*, Stanford University Press 1985
[3] Wanner, H U, *Environmental International* v 12 1–4 1986 containing papers from third International Conference on Indoor Air Quality and Climate Stockholm, Sweden 1984 pp 311–315.

Combustion products
Components of tobacco smoke
Lead (paints)
Organic compounds (paint)
Fluorocarbons, odourants (aerosol sprays)

Resources

Specification decisions should also allow for the sensitive use of resources. If materials are available in a form that does not represent a drain on resources for that material, they should be used. If the material is in short supply as it is a finite resource, or it is known that the use of it will in fact represent unacceptable alteration of the environment, then it should not be used. There are some very significant areas of consumption which show a rising use of existing resources. The use of limestone is increasing, not just for cement and lime products but for road stone and railway ballast, powdered for agricultural use (altering the pH of soils to alkaline conditions) and as a flux for the iron and steel works in Consett and Teesside. Although the usable bed thickness of limestone is about 22 m in Weardale, the quality of the very hard carboniferous limestone is in greater demand than the softer and more porous magnesian limestones, and the volume now being excavated is altering the landscape of Britain. The excavation of other bulk materials is also rising. Sand and gravel excavated has risen from 2×10^6 cubic metres in 1965 to 4×10^6 cubic metres in 1975. (British Regional Geology series latest figure.)

If the use of a material represents a high consumption in energy for processing which may mean an accompanying pollution product from the products of combustion, then the material should not be used. There are situations where compromise may be unavoidable but in a world of diminishing and changing resources our decisions should be qualitative and conscientious. After all, we are not only agents but instrumental and powerful decision makers in the large-scale use of materials, and the effects of bad decisions are often irreversible.

6.01 *Summit Plateau, Ben Nevis, Summer 1987* (photographer: Steve Keates)

SI UNITS

All quantities in this volume are given in SI units, which have been adopted by the United Kingdom for use throughout the construction industry as from 1971.

Traditionally, in this and other countries, systems of measurement have grown up employing many different units not rationally related and indeed often in numerical conflict when measuring the same thing. The use of bushels and pecks for volume measurement has declined in this country, but pints and gallons, and cubic feet and cubic yards are still both simultaneously in use as systems of volume measurement, and conversions between the two must often be made. The sub-division of the traditional units vary widely: 8 pints equal 1 gallon, 27 cubic feet equal 1 cubic yard; 12 inches equal 1 foot; 16 ounces equal 1 pound; 14 pounds equal 1 stone, 8 stones equal 1 hundredweight. In more sophisticated fields the same problem existed. Energy could be measured in terms of foot pounds, British Thermal Units, horsepower, kilowatt hour, etc. Conversion between various units of national systems were necessary and complex, and between national systems even more so. Attempts to rationalise units have been made for several centuries. The most significant stages being:

The establishment of the decimal system during the French Revolution.

The adoption of the centimetre and gramme as basic units by the British Association for the Advancement of Science in 1873, which led to CGS system (centimetre, gramme, second).

The use after approximately 1900 of metres, kilograms, and seconds as basic units (MKS system).

The incorporation of electrical units between 1933 and 1950 giving metre, kilograms, seconds and amperes as basic units (MKSA system).

The establishment in 1954 of a rationalised and coherent system of units based on MKSA but also including temperature and light. This was given the title *Système International d'Unites* which is abbreviated to SI units.

The international discussions which have led to the development of the SI system take place under the auspices of the Conference General des Poids et Mesures (CGPM) which meets in Paris. Eleven meetings have been held since its constitution in 1875.

The United Kingdom has formally adopted the SI system and it will become, as in some 25 countries, the only legal system of measurement. Several European countries, while adopting the SI system, will also retain the old metric system as a legal alternative. The USA has not adopted the SI system.

The SI system is based on six basic units:

Quantity	Unit	Symbol
Length	metre	m
Mass	kilogramme	kg
Time	second	s
Electric	ampere	A
Temperature	degree Kelvin	°K
Luminous intensity	candela	cd

The degree Kelvin will be used for absolute temperatures, for customary use the degree Celsius (°C) will still be used and for temperature intervals (difference between two temperatures) degrees Celsius (°C) will also be used. (273.15°K is 0°C and °K and °C are identical in terms of temperature intervals.) In addition to the basic units there are two supplementary units:

Quantity	Unit	Symbol
Plane angle	radian	rad
Solid angle	steradian	sr

Degrees °, minutes ' and seconds " will also be used as part of the system.

From these basic and supplementary units the remainder of the units necessary for measurement are derived, eg:

Area derived from length/m^2.

Volume derived from length/m^3.

Velocity derived from length and time/m/s.

Some derived units have special symbols:

Quantity	Unit	Symbol	Basic units involved
Frequency	hertz	Hz	$1 \text{ Hz} = 1/\text{sec}$ (1 cycle per sec)
Force, energy	newton	N	$1 \text{ N} = 1 \text{ kg m/s}^2$
Work, quantity of heat	joule	J	$1 \text{ J} = 1 \text{ Nm}$
Power	watt	W	$1 \text{ W} = \text{J/s}$
Luminous flux	lumen	lm	$1 \text{ lm} = 1 \text{ cd sr}$
Illumination	lux	lx	$1 \text{ lx} = 1 \text{ lm/m}^2$

Multiples and submultiples of SI are all formed in the same way and all are decimally related to the basic units. It is recommended that the factor 1000 should be consistently employed as the change point from unit to multiple or from one multiple to another. The following table gives the names and symbols of the multiples. When using multiples the description or the symbol is combined with the basic SI unit eg, kilojoule kJ.

Factor		Prefix Name	Symbol
one million million (billion)	10^{12}	tera	T
one thousand million	10^{9}	giga	G
one million	10^{6}	mega	M
one thousand	10^{3}	kilo	k
one thousandth	10^{-3}	milli	m
one millionth	10^{-6}	micro	μ
one thousand millionth	10^{-9}	nano	n
one million millionth	10^{-12}	pico	p

It will be noted that the kilogram departs from the general SI rule with respect to multiples, being already 100 g. Where more than three significant figures are used it has been United Kingdom practice to group the digits into three and separate the groups with commas.

This could lead to confusion with calculation from other countries where the comma is used as a decimal point. It is recommended therefore that groups of three digits should be used separated by spaces, not commas. In the United Kingdom the decimal point can still, however, be represented by a point either on or above the bottom line.

CONVERSION FACTORS

Quantity or application	SI Unit Description	symbol	Present Unit (PU)	Conversion Factor (CF) PU × CF = SI value
SPACE length	metre		foot	0.31
			inch	0.025
area	square metre	m²	square yard	0.84
			square foot	0.09
	square millimetre	mm²	square inch	0.000 65
	square millimetre	mm²	square inch	645
volume	cubic metre	m³	cubic yard	0.76
			cubic foot	0.028
			gallon (UK)	0.0045
			gallon (USA)	0.0038
	litre $\dfrac{m^3}{1000}$		gallon	4.55
			pint	0.57
MASS mass	kilogramme	kg	pound	0.45
			ton	1016
density	kilogramme per cubic metre	kg/m³	pounds per cubic foot	16
			pounds per gallon	99.78

continued . . .

Quantity or application	SI Unit Description symbol		Present Unit (PU)	Conversion Factor (CF) PU × CF = SI value
MOTION	velocity	metre/second	m/s	feet per second	0.31
				feet per minute	0.0051
				miles per hour	0.45
FLOW RATE	volume flow	cubic metre per second	m³/s	cubic foot per second	0.028
		litres per second	l/s	gallons per minute	0.076
PRESSURE	pressure	newtons per square metre	N/m²	foot water gauge	2890
		or Pascal	Pa	millibars mb	10⁵
TEMPERATURE	customary temperature (level)	degree Celsius	°C	degree Fahrenheit	$\frac{(°F-32)}{9}$
	temperature interval (range or difference)	degree Kelvin	K	degrees Fahrenheit	0.56
HEAT	quantity (energy)	joule	J	British Thermal Unit	1.055*
		kilo Joule	kJ	BTU	1.055
		kilo Joule	kJ	kilowatt hr kWH	3600
	flow rate (power)	watt	W	BTU per hour	0.29
				ton of refrigeration	3516
	intensity of heat flow rate	watts per square metre	W/m²	BTU per hour per square foot	3.16
	thermal conductivity	watts per metre degree Celsius	W/m K	BTU inch/hour foot² degree F	0.14†
	thermal conductance U-value	watts per square metre per degree Celsius	W/m² K	BTU per hour per square foot per degree F	5.68
	thermal resistivity	metre degree Celsius per watt	m K/W	square foot hour degree F per BTU inch	6.93†
	thermal resistance	square metre degree Celsius per watt	m²K/W	square foot hour degree F/BTU	0.18
	thermal diffusivity	square metre per second	m²/s	square foot per hour	0.0000 026
	thermal capacity per unit mass (specific heat)	kilojoule per kilogramme degree Celsius	kJ/kg K	BTU/pound °F	4.19
	thermal capacity per unit volume	kilojoule per cubic metre degree Celsius	kJm³ K	BTU/cubic foot deg F	67.1
	calorific value (weight basis)	kilojoules per kilogramme	kJ/kg	BTU per pound	2.32
	calorific value (volume basis)	kilojoules per cubic metre	KJ/m³	BTU per cubic foot	37.26
	latent heat	kilojoules per kilogramme	kJ/kg	BTU per pound	2.32
	refrigeration	watts	W	ton	3516

continued . . .

	Quantity or application	SI Unit		Present Unit (PU)	Conversion Factor (CF)
		Description	symbol		PU × CF = SI value
MOISTURE	moisture content	grammes per kilo-gramme	g/kg	grains per pound	14.28
	vapour permeability	kilogramme metre per newton second	kgm/Ns	pound foot per hour pound force	0.000 008 6
LIGHT	illumination	lux	lx	foot candles lumen per square foot	10.76
	luminance	candela per square metre	cd/m^2	foot lambert	3.43

*In practice 1 BTU is taken as equivalent to 1 kilojoule.
†The apparent discrepancy between imperial and SI units may be made resolved by expressing the SI units in basic terms before cancellation of terms, eg:

Jm/m^{2}s K becomes W/m K($\frac{m}{m^2}$ = m and J/s = W)   m^{2}s K/Jm similarly becomes m K/W

209

SOURCE OF
PROBLEM, INQUIRY
INVESTIGATION FROM
ARCHITECT, CONTRACTOR
DESIGNER, MANUFACTURER
SURVEYOR ENGINEER
TRADE PERSONNEL

ADVISORY BODIES
LEGISLATION
GOVERNMENT DEPTS HMSO
BRITISH STANDARDS
BUILDING RESEARCH STATION

REFERENCE MATERIAL
ENGINEERING INDEX
AND OTHERS
RESEARCH PAPERS
ACADEMIC BOOKS
PATENTS

COMPENDIA
ARCHITECTURAL PRESS
NATIONAL BLDG SPEC
RIBA PUBLICATIONS
DATA
BANKS
BARBOUR
MICROFILE

Route finding for information

An explanation of the diagram

Faced with a problem to solve, the means of obtaining
information and applying it to the source of enquiry is not
always easy. Information retrieval or the collection of
data can be either highly organised, using for example the
CI/SfB classification or completely idiosyncratic. There
are also routes for finding information and a first start will
often be the **compendia** (as illustrated) which take a broad
but well classified view of the field which will lead to more
detailed sources. The compendia take their main material
from three major areas of interest shown as **advisory
bodies, academic reference material** and **associations**.
The advisory bodies which hold the most objective
viewpoint in terms of setting standards are informed by the
established academic sources as well as taking the advice
and experience of industry. The **associations** broadly
represent the interests of the manufacturing and supply
groups and also fund research and development in
particular materials and components. The **academic
reference material** varies from general textbooks to
research papers written at doctoral level. There is often a
long time lag between research and availability of that
knowledge that can be used by practitioners, although
eventually the work done will inform the associations and
the advisory bodies.

ASSOCIATIONS
MANUFACTURERS
LITERATURE
MANUFACTURERS/TRADE
ASSOCIATIONS
PROFESSIONAL INSTITUTIONS
MATERIALS RELATED
RESEARCH CENTRES

Although the diagram appears chaotic it is probably a
more realistic way of looking at the branching out of
information than a normal flow path diagram. The pattern
itself has an affinity for those random geometries generated
by route making, (as seen on maps) cracking patterns,
(seen in ceramics and also in cracking mud) and often in
nature (on the bodies of snakes). It may be necessary to use
information from all the areas and there is genuine
networking between these areas. The most difficult part
will be in deciding between contradictory sets of
information from all these sources and in the end the
arbitier has to be **own experience**, the last major category.

OWN EXPERIENCE
EDUCATION
OBSERVATION
PRACTICAL KNOWLEDGE

CI/SfB CLASSIFICATION

The following information from the *Construction Indexing Manual 1976* is reproduced by courtesy of RIBA Publications Ltd.

Used sensibly and in appropriate detail, as explained in the manual, the CI/SfB system of classification facilitates filing and retrieval of information. It is useful in technical libraries, in specifications and on working drawings. *The National Building Specification* is based on the system, and BRE Digest 172 describes its use for working drawings.

The CI/SfB system comprises tables 0 to 4, tables 1 and 2/3 being the codes in most common use. For libraries, classifications are built up from:

Table 0	Table 1	Tables 2/3	Table 4
-a number code	-a number code in brackets	-upper and lower case letter codes	-upper case letter code in brackets
eg 6	eg (6)	eg Fg	eg (F)

An example for clay brickwork in walls is: (21) Fg2, which for trade literature, would be shown in a reference box as:

CI/SfB 1976 reference by SfB Agency	
(21)	Fg2

The lower space is intended for UDC (Universal decimal classification) codes—see BS 100A 1961. Advice in classification can be obtained from the SfB Agency UK Ltd at 66 Portland Place, London W1N 4AD.

In the following summaries of the five tables, chapter references are made to the seven related volumes and chapters of *Mitchell's Building Series* in which aspects of the classifications are dealt with. The following abbreviations are used:

Introduction to Building	IB
Environment and Services	ES
Materials	M
Structure and Fabric, Part 1	SF (1)
Structure and Fabric, Part 2	SF (2)
Components	C
Finishes	F

Table 0   **Physical Environment**
(main headings only)

Scope: End results of the construction process

0	Planning areas
1	Utilities, civil engineering facilities
2	Industrial facilities
3	Administrative, commercial, protective service facilities
4	Health, welfare facilities
5	Recreational facilities
6	Religious facilities
7	Educational, scientific, information facilities
8	Residential facilities
9	Common facilities, other facilities

Table 1   **Elements**

Scope: Parts with particular functions which combine to make the facilities in table 0

(0-)   Sites, projects
Building plus external works
Building systems C 11

(1-)   Ground, substructure
(11)   Ground *SF (1)* 4, 8, 11; *SF (2)* 2, 3, 11; *IB* 17.3
(12)   Vacant
(13)   Floor beds *SF (1)* 4, 8; *SF (2)* 3
(14), (15)   Vacant
(16)   Retaining walls, foundations *SF (1)* 4; *SF (2)* 3, 4; *IB* 17.4, 17.5
(17)   Pile foundations *SF (1)* 4; *SF (2)* 3, 11
(18)   Other substructure elements
(19)   Parts, accessories, cost summary, etc

(2-)   Structure, primary elements, carcass

(21) Walls, external walls *SF (1)* 1, 5; *SF (2)* 4, 5, 10; *IB* 17.6

(22) Internal walls, partitions *SF (1)* 5; *SF (2)* 4, 10; *C* 9; *IB* 17.7

(23) Floors, galleries *SF (1)* 8; *SF (2)* 6, 10; *IB* 17.8

(24) Stairs, ramps *SF (1)* 10; *SF (2)* 8, 10

(25), (26) Vacant

(27) Roofs *SF (1)* 1, 7; *SF (2)* 9, 10; *IB* 17.9

(28) Building frames, other primary elements *SF (1)* 1, 6; *SF (2)* 5, 10; Chimneys *SF (1)* 9

(29) Parts, accessories, cost summary, etc

(3-) **Secondary elements, completion of structure**

(31) Secondary elements to external walls, including windows, doors *SF (1)* 5; *SF (2)* 10; *C* 3, 4, 5, 7; *IB* 17.6

(32) Secondary elements to internal walls, partitions including borrowed lights and doors *SF (2)* 10; *C* 3, 7; *IB* 17.7

(33) Secondary elements to floors *SF (2)* 10; *IB* 17.8

(34) Secondary elements to stairs including balustrades *C* 8

(35) Suspended ceilings *C* 10

(36) Vacant

(37) Secondary elements to roofs, including roof lights, dormers *SF (1)* 7; *SF (2)* 10; *C* 6

(38) Other secondary elements

(39) Parts, accessories, cost summary, etc.

(4-) **Finishes to structure**

(41) Wall finishes, external *SF (2)* 4, 10; *F* 3, 4, 5; *IB* 17.6, 17.11

(42) Wall finishes, internal *F* 2, 4, 5; *IB* 17.7, 17.11

(43) Floor finishes *F* 1; *IB* 17.5, 17.8, 17.11

(44) Stair finishes *F* 1; *IB* 17.11

(45) Ceiling finishes *F* 2; *IB* 17.11

(46) Vacant

(47) Roof finishes *SF (2)* 10; *F* 7; *IB* 17.9, 17.11

(48) Other finishes; *IB* 17.11

(49) Parts, accessories, cost summary, etc; *IB* 17.11

(5-) **Services** mainly piped and ducted)

(51) Vacant

(52) Waste disposal, drainage *ES* 11, 12, 13; *IB* 17.10

(53) Liquids supply *ES* 9, 10; *SF (1)* 9; *SF (2)* 6, 10; *IB* 17.10

(54) Gases supply; *IB* 17.10

(55) Space cooling; *IB* 17.10

(56) Space heating *ES* 7; *SF (1)* 9; *SF (2)* 6, 10; *IB* 17.10

(57) Air conditioning, ventilation *ES* 7; *SF (2)* 10; *IB* 17.10

(58) Other piped, ducted services; *IB* 17.10

(59) Parts, accessories, cost summary, etc Chimney, shafts, flues, ducts independent *SF (2)* 7; *IB* 17.10

(6-) **Services** (mainly electrical)

(61) Electrical supply; *IB* 17.10

(62) Power *ES* 14; *IB* 17.10

(63) Lighting *ES* 8; *IB* 17.10

(64) Communications *ES* 14; *IB* 17.10

(65) Vacant

(66) Transport *ES* 15

(67) Vacant

(68) Security, control, other services; *IB* 17.10

(69) Parts, accessories, cost summary, etc; *IB* 17.10

(7-) **Fittings** with subdivisions (71) to (79)

(74) Sanitary, hygiene fittings *ES* 10

(8-) **Loose furniture, equipment** with subdivisions (81) to (89)
Used where the distinction between loose and fixed fittings, furniture and equipment is important.

(9-) **External elements, other elements**

(90) External works, with subdivisions (90.1) to (90.8); *IB* 17.12

(98) Other elements

(99) Parts, accessories etc. common to two or more main element divisions (1-) to (7-)
Cost summary

Note: The SfB Agency UK do not use table 1 in classifying manufacturers' literature

Table 2 **Constructions, Forms**

Scope: Parts of particular forms which combine to make the elements in table 1. Each is characterised by the main product of which it is made.

A Constructions, forms—used in specification applications for Preliminaries and General conditions

B Vacant—used in specification applications for demolition, underpinning and shoring work

C Excavation and loose fill work

D Vacant

E Cast in situ work *M* 8; *SF (1)* 4, 7, 8; *SF (2)* 3, 4, 5, 6, 8, 9

Blocks

F   Blockwork, brickwork
Blocks, bricks *M* 6, 12; *SF (1)* 5, 9 *SF (2)* 4, 6, 7

G   Large block, panel work
Large blocks, panels *SF (2)* 4

Sections

H   Section work
Sections *M* 9; *SF (1)* 5, 6, 7, 8; *SF (2)* 5, 6

I   Pipework
Pipes *SF (1)* 9; *SF (2)* 7

J   Wire work, mesh work
Wires, meshes

K   Quilt work
Quilts

L   Flexible sheet work (proofing)
Flexible sheets (proofing) *M* 9, 11

M   Malleable sheet work
Malleable sheets *M* 9

N   Rigid sheet overlap work
Rigid sheets for overlappings *SF (2)* 4; *F* 7

P   Thick coating work *M* 10, 11; *SF (2)* 4; *F* 1, 2, 3, 7

Q   Vacant

R   Rigid sheet work
Rigid sheets *M* 3, 12, 13, *SF (2)* 4; *C* 5

S   Rigid tile work
Rigid tiles *M* 4, 12, 13; *F* 1, 4

T   Flexible sheet and tile work
Flexible sheets eg carpets, veneers, papers, tiles cut from them *M* 3, 9; *F* 1,6

U   Vacant

V   Film coating and impregnation work *F* 6; *M* 2

W   Planting work
Plants

X   Work with components
Components *SF (1)* 5, 6, 7, 8, 10; *SF (2)* 4; *C* 2, 3, 4, 5, 6, 7, 8

Y   Formless work
Products

Z   Joints, where described separately

Table 3 **Materials**

Scope: Materials which combine to form the products in table 2

a   **Materials**

b, c, d Vacant

Formed materials e to o

e   **Natural stone** *M* 4; *SF (1)* 5, 10; *SF (2)* 4
e1   Granite, basalt, other igneous
e2   Marble
e3   Limestone (other than marble)
e4   Sandstone, gritstone
e5   Slate
e9   Other natural stone

f   **Precast with binder** *M* 8; *SF (1)* 5, 7, 8, 9, 10; *SF (2)* 4 to 9; *F* 1
f1   Sand-lime concrete (precast)
     Glass fibre reinforced calcium silicate (gres)
f2   All-in aggregate concrete (precast) *M* 8
     Heavy concrete (precast) *M* 8
     Glass fibre reinforced cement (gre) *M* 10
f3   Terrazzo (precast) *F* 1
     Granolithic (precast)
     Cast/artificial/reconstructed stone
f4   Lightweight cellular concrete (precast) *M* 8
f5   Lightweight aggregate concrete (precast) *M* 8
f6   Asbestos-based materials (preformed) *M* 10
f7   Gypsum (preformed) *C* 2
     Glass fibre reinforced gypsum *M* 10
f8   Magnesia materials (preformed)
f9   Other materials precast with binder

g   **Clay (Dried, Fired)** *M* 5; *SF (1)* 5, 9, 10; *SF (2)* 4, 6, 7
g1   Dried clay eg poisé de terre
g2   Fired clay, vitrified clay, ceramics
     Unglazed fired clay eg terra cotta
g3   Glazed fired clay eg vitreous china
g6   Refractory materials eg fireclay
g9   Other dried or fired clays

h   **Metal** *M* 9; *SF (1)* 6, 7, *SF (2)* 4, 5, 7
h1   Cast iron
     Wrought iron, malleable iron
h2   Steel, mild steel
h3   Steel alloys eg stainless steel
h4   Aluminium, aluminium alloys
h5   Copper
h6   Copper alloys
h7   Zinc
h8   Lead, white metal
h9   Chromium, nickel, gold, other metals, metal alloys

i   **Wood** including wood laminates *M* 2, 3; *SF (1)* 5 to 8, 10; *SF (2)* 4, 9; *C* 2
i1   timber (unwrot)
i2   Softwood (in general, and wrot)
i3   Hardwood (in general, and wrot)

i4 Wood laminates eg plywood
i5 Wood veneers
i9 Other wood materials, except wood fibre-boards, chipboards and wood-wool cement

j **Vegetable and animal materials**—including fibres and particles and materials made from these
j1 Wood fibres eg building board *M* 3
j2 Paper *M* 9, 13
j3 Vegetable fibres other than wood eg flaxboard *M* 3
j5 Bark, cork
j6 Animal fibres eg hair
j7 Wood particles eg chipboard *M* 3
j8 Wood-wool cement *M* 3
j9 Other vegetable and animal materials

k, l Vacant

m **Inorganic fibres**
m1 Mineral wool fibres *M* 10; *SF (2)* 4, 7
Glass wool fibres *M* 10, 12
Ceramic wool fibres
m2 Asbestos wool fibres *M* 10
m9 Other inorganic fibrous materials eg carbon fibres *M* 10

n **Rubber, plastics, etc**
n1 Asphalt (preformed) *M* 11; *F* 1
n2 Impregnated fibre and felt eg bituminous felt *M* 11; *F* 7
n4 Linoleum *F* 1

Synthetic resins n5, n6

n5 Rubbers (elastomers) *M* 13
n6 Plastics, including synthetic fibres *M* 13
Thermoplastics
Thermosets
n7 Cellular plastics
n8 Reinforced plastics eg grp, plastics laminates

o **Glass** *M* 12; *SF (1)* 5; *C* 5
o1 Clear, transparent, plain glass
o2 Translucent glass
o3 Opaque, opal glass
o4 Wired glass
o5 Multiple glazing
o6 Heat absorbing/rejecting glass
X-ray absorbing/rejecting glass
Solar control glass
o7 Mirrored glass, 'one-way' glass
Anti-glare glass

o8 Safety glass, toughened glass
Laminated glass, security glass, alarm glass
o9 Other glass, including cellular glass

Formless materials p to s
p **Aggregates, loose fills** *M* 8
p1 Natural fills, aggregates
p2 Artificial aggregates in general
p3 Artificial granular aggregates (light) eg foamed blast furnace slag
p4 Ash eg pulverised fuel ash
p5 Shavings
p6 Powder
p7 Fibres
p9 Other aggregates, loose fills

q **Lime and cement binders, mortars, concretes**
q1 Lime (calcined limestones), hydrated lime, lime putty, *M* 7
Lime-sand mix (coarse stuff)
q2 Cement, hydraulic cement eg Portland cement *M* 7
q3 Lime-cement binders *M* 15
q4 Lime-cement-aggregate mixes
Mortars (ie with fine aggregates) *M* 15; *SF (2)* 4
Concretes (ie with fine and/or coarse aggregates) *M* 8
q5 Terrazzo mixes and in general *F* 1
q6 Lightweight, cellular, concrete mixes and in general *M* 8
q9 Other lime-cement-aggregate mixes eg asbestos cement mixes *M* 10

r **Clay, gypsum, magnesia and plastics binders, mortars**
r1 Clay mortar mixes, refractory mortar
r2 Gypsum, gypsum plaster mixes
r3 Magnesia, magnesia mixes *F* 1
r4 Plastics binders
Plastics mortar mixes
r9 Other binders and mortar mixes

s **Bituminous materials** *M* 11; *SF (2)* 4
s1 Bitumen including natural and petroleum bitumens, tar, pitch, asphalt, lake asphalt
s4 Mastic asphalt (fine or no aggregate) pitch mastic
s5 Clay-bitumen mixes, stone bitumen mixes (coarse aggregate)
Rolled asphalt, macadams
s9 Other bituminous materials

Functional materials t to w
t **Fixing and jointing materials**
t1 Welding materials *M* 9; *SF (2)* 5
t2 Soldering materials *M* 9
t3 Adhesives, bonding materials *M* 14
t4 Joint fillers eg mastics, gaskets *M* 16 *SF (1)* 2
t6 Fasteners, 'builders ironmongery'
Anchoring devices eg plugs
Attachment devices eg connectors *SF (1)* 6, 7
Fixing devices eg bolts, *SF (1)* 5
t7 'Architectural ironmongery' *C* 7
t9 Other fixing and jointing agents

u **Protective and Process/property modifying materials**
u1 Anti-corrosive materials, treatments *F* 6
Metallic coatings applied by eg electro-plating *M* 9
Non-metallic coatings applied by eg chemical conversion
u2 Modifying agents, admixtures eg curing agents *M* 8
Workability aids *M* 8
u3 Materials resisting special forms of attack such as fungus, insects, condensation *M* 2
u4 Flame retardants if described separately *M* 1
u5 Polishes, seals, surface hardeners *F* 1; *M* 8
u6 Water repellants, if described separately
u9 Other protective and process/property modifying agents eg ultra-violet absorbers

v **Paints** *F* 6
v1 Stopping, fillers, knotting, paint preparation materials including primers
v2 Pigments, dyes, stains
v3 Binders, media eg drying oils
v4 Varnishes, lacquers eg resins
Enamels, glazes
v5 Oil paints, oil-resin paints
Synthetic resin paints
Complete systems including primers
v6 Emulsion paints, where described separately
Synthetic resin-based emulsions
Complete systems including primers
v8 Water paints eg cement paints
v9 Other paints eg metallic paints, paints with aggregates

w **Ancillary materials**
w1 Rust removing agents
w3 Fuels
w4 Water
w5 Acids, alkalis
w6 Fertilisers

w7 Cleaning materials *F* 1
Abrasives
w8 Explosives
w9 Other ancillary materials eg fungicides

x **Vacant**

y **Composite materials**
Composite materials generally *M* 11
See p. 63 *Construction Indexing Manual*

z **Substances**
z1 By state eg fluids
z2 By chemical composition eg organic
z3 By origin eg naturally occurring or manufactured materials
z9 Other substances

Table 4   **Activities, Requirements**
(main headings only)

Scope: Table 4 identifies objects which assist or affect construction but are not incorporated in it, and factors such as activities, requirements, properties, and processes

Activities, aids
(A) Administration and management activities, aids *C* 11; *M* Introduction, *SF (1)* 2; *SF (2)* 1, 2, 3; *IB* 14, 17, 13
(B) Construction plant, tools *SF (1)* 2; *SF (2)* 2, 11
(C) Vacant
(D) Construction operations *SF (1)* 2, 11; *SF (2)* 2, 11

Requirements, properties, building science, construction technology
Factors, describing buildings, elements, materials, etc
(E) Composition, etc *SF (1)* 1, 2; *SF (2)* 1, 2; *IB* 1
(F) Shape, size, etc *SF (1)* 2; *IB* 4
(G) Appearance, etc *M* 1; *F* 6; *IB* 1

Factors relating to surroundings, occupancy
(H) Context, environment *IB* 6

Performance factors
(J) Mechanics *M* 9; *SF (1)* 3, 4; *SF (2)* 3, 4; *IB* 5
(K) Fire, explosion *M* 1; *SF (2)* 10; *IB* 9
(L) Matter *IB* 10
(M) Heat, cold *ES* 1; *IB* 8

(N)   Light, dark *ES* 1; *IB* 10
(P)   Sound, quiet *ES* 1; *IB* 7
(Q)   Electricity, magnetism, radiation *ES* 14
(R)   Energy, other physical factors *ES* 7; *IB* 3
(T)   Application

Other factors
(U)   Users, resources *IB* 11, 12
(V)   Working factors
(W)   Operation, maintenance factors

(X)   Change, movement, stability factors
(Y)   Economic, commercial factors *M* Introduction; *SF (1)* 2; *SF (2)* 3, 4, 5, 6, 9; *IB* 1, 13
(Z)   Peripheral subjects, form of presentation, time, place—may be used for subjects taken from the UDC (*Universal decimal classification*), see BS1000A 1961

Subdivision: All table 4 codes are subdivided mainly by numbers

SELECTED BIBLIOGRAPHY

Adhesion and Adhesives, A J Kinloch, Chapman and Hall 1987

Basic Corrosion and Oxidation, John M West, John Wiley 1980

Ceramic Science for Materials Technologists, I J McColm, Blackie 1983

Chambers Dictionary of Science and Technology, Chambers 1981

Colour Observed, Enid Verity, Macmillan 1980

Elements of Materials Science and Engineering, Lawrence H Van Vlack, Addison Wesley Publishing Company, Massachusetts 1980

Engineering Materials an Introduction (T252), The Open University 1982

Engineering, Science Pocket Books, J O Bird, Newnes Technical Books 1983

Introduction to the Selection of Engineering Materials, An, D P Hanley, Van Nostrand Reinhold 1980

Introduction to the Properties of Engineering Materials, An, K J Pascoe, Van Nostrand Reinhold 1978

Materials: A Scientific American Book, W H Freeman 1967

Materials for Building, Lyall Addleson, volumes 1–3, Newnes–Butterworth 1975

Materials Processing (T352) The Open University 1982
UNITS 1 Introduction and Basic Concepts of Processing
15 Finishing Processes

Modern Surface Coatings, P Nylen, John Wiley 1965

The New Science of Strong Materials or Why you don't fall through the floor. J E Gordon, Pelican 1979

Properties of Building Materials, Geoff Taylor, second

Properties of Concrete, A M Neville, Pitman 1981

Polymer Materials, Christopher Hall, Macmillan 1981

Textbook of Polymer Science, Bill Meyer

Science and Engineering of Materials, The, Donald R Askeland, Prindale Weber and Schmidt, Boston 1984

Stone Decay and Conservation, G G Amoroso and V Fassinia, Materials Science Monographs 11, Elsevier 1983

Structure and Properties of Materials, The
Volume 1, *Structure*: William G Moffat, George W Pearsall, John Wulff
Volume 2 *Thermodynamics of Structure*: Jere H Brophy, Robert M Rose, John Wulff
Volume 3 *Mechanical Behaviour*: H W Hauden, W G Moffat, John Wulff, John Wiley 1964

Understanding the Earth, edited by I G Gass, Peter J Smith and R C L Wilson, The Open University 1971

INDEX